CAVING PRACTICE AND EQUIPMENT

CAVING PRACTICE
AND EQUIPMENT

Edited by
DAVID JUDSON

DAVID & CHARLES
Newton Abbot   London   North Pomfret (Vt)

(*Opposite title page*) The Cloud Chamber, Dan Yr Ogof.
Three flashes were used to achieve the desired effect.
(*J. J. Rowland, FRPS*)

British Library Cataloguing in Publication Data

Caving practice and equipment.
  1. Caving – Amateurs' manuals
  I. Judson, David
  796.5′25   GV200.62

  ISBN 0-7153-8155-5

© Text: British Cave Research Association
         and David Judson 1984
© Line illustrations: BCRA 1984

First published 1984
Second impression 1988

Typeset by Typesetters (Birmingham) Ltd,
Smethwick, West Midlands
and printed in Great Britain
by Butler & Tanner Limited, Frome and London
for David & Charles Publishers plc
Brunel House Newton Abbot Devon

Published in the United States of America
by David & Charles Inc
North Pomfret Vermont 05053 USA

Contents

1 Clothing and Personal Equipment

DAVID JUDSON

The Cave Environment

Caves within the British Isles are usually regarded as possessing an environment hostile to the human being. They are cold, with air temperatures of 5°C to 12°C and water temperatures of 3°C to 10°C. Once beyond the daylight zone of the entrance portal or shaft, they are completely dark. They are also frequently severely constricted. The caver may be forced to crawl flat-out over a wet muddy floor strewn with sharp pebbles, scale a slippery mud slope or contort himself between the interstices of a huge boulder ruckle which would be totally intimidating in broad daylight!

Thus there are two items of personal equipment fundamental to caving: (1) a suitable outfit of protective clothing; (2) a durable and reliable lighting system. Requirements for the outfit of protective clothing may vary for every caving trip. Whilst most caving within the British Isles will involve getting wet, the clothing requirements for a photographic or surveying trip into the upper parts of the Lancaster/Easegill System will be different from those for a similar trip into Dan-yr-Ogof (where 1.2m deep wading occurs at the end of the public 'show cave' section) or for a trip down most of the active Yorkshire potholes in anything other than a drought.

Quite different environmental conditions are likely on caving trips in other parts of the world. In certain high areas of the Alps there are ice caves, and air and water temperatures will be considerably lower than at home. In the tropics, Borneo, New Guinea, South America, the high temperatures and humidities may call for shorts and teeshirts.

Lighting is a more constant requirement. Only the needs of foreign caving expeditions are likely to dictate the choice of carbide lamps over the more usual rechargeable battery lamps,

and extreme size of passages may influence the type of lamps used. All caving trips require every caver to carry a good light, but the likely duration of the trip will affect the reserve of power and thus the type of lamp required.

Clothing

Throughout this book, when dealing with equipment, we first examine the working conditions and/or user requirements with a view to arriving at performance requirements or a specification, rather than placing emphasis on the merits or otherwise of any one proprietary make. In this way our findings should not become dated when new and possibly better products come on the market.

In the case of protective clothing for cavers, because of the variety of conditions encountered, some of the user requirements are in conflict with one another. The need for an abrasive-resistant material conflicts directly with the need to maintain lightness of weight and flexibility of all the joints. The need for exclusion of cold water in parts of some caves conflicts with the need to be well ventilated and cool through the drier sections of the cave.

Since the body core temperature must be maintained within very fine tolerance limits at 37°C, and average cave air temperatures in Britain fall within the 5°C to 12°C range, there is *prima facie* a serious need for body insulation. This is most needed when the body is at rest – or most nearly so. It is a problem which is normally met with only during such activities as cave photography. The problem really shows itself after an accident when the body is forced into a completely passive role – a situation not usually planned for. Only where large quantities of cold water are met with does the problem become serious. Often this may not occur as planned for either! The problem is partly that the water will usually be cooler than the neighbouring air, but more because of the instant heat-loss characteristics of the solid/liquid interface. Some of the newer materials produced from man-made fibres now being used for protective clothing are considerably better than those made from traditional natural fibres. The solution is to ensure that a layer of insulating air is trapped close to the skin.

The Drysuit

The first-developed method of ensuring that air is maintained close to the skin was through the use of the drysuit. These thin rubber or imitation-rubber suits were originally for use in cold-water diving. They had elaborate seals at wrists, ankles and neck. Normal woollen clothing was worn beneath and usually some sort of protective garment over the top. These suits were fine for open-water diving and for a limited number of cave dives, but had a limited use in general caving. The ex-army exposure suit or 'goon suit' was a development of this principle for deep-water wading rather than diving. It had a draw-cord around the neck, but no watertight seal as such. This was an improvement for caving use since a degree of ventilation could be gained around the chest whilst traversing drier sections of cave. But they still had inherent in their make-up the tendency to 'cook' the wearer in all but the wettest of caves. They could never be made sufficiently robust to stand up to the constant wear and tear of the cave environment if worn as a regular item of clothing. Fine for specialist use, such as for surveying a particularly wet section of cave passage where considerable and continuous immersion was the general rule, but not otherwise. In the mid-1960s the caving drysuit reached its ultimate development in the 'Berger Suit'. This was designed by Dr Ken Pearce and others primarily for long working trips into the Gouffre Berger. The Berger Suit was a one-piece garment of neoprene-coated nylon fabric with a gatherable chest pouch of thinner material. It came complete with feet and fine rubber wrist seals. It could be packed away into a very compact pouch when not being worn. This was excellent for special uses, but hardly robust enough for regular caving.

The Wetsuit

During the late 1950s and early 1960s an entirely different approach came to the caving scene with the introduction, again from open-water divers, of the neoprene wetsuit. Although, somewhat surprisingly, it took almost a whole decade to become fully accepted in the Northern Pennines, it did provide an answer to most of the problems that cavers had been attempting to combat for many years. Although water penetrates at ankles, wrists and neck, a thin layer of air trapped next to the skin forms the basis of a high degree of protection from the cold water. For the perfectionist a patching session is usually necessary after every trip, but routine maintenance is not vital to the overall efficiency of the suit. A lump taken out of one elbow will not impair the efficiency of the rest of the suit. This less critical nature of the wetsuit has undoubtedly been a major factor in its widespread acceptance.

The cushioning effect of the air trapped within the wetsuit also has a spin-off for cavers in that it affords protection against bumps and abrasion. It is worthwhile to build up additional protection particularly at knees and elbows with extra layers of neoprene.

Wetsuits can either be purchased off-the-peg, made to measure, or bought as a kit-of-parts. For those with normal proportions the off-the-peg suit is to be recommended. Minor modifications can be made later if necessary. For ultimate economy the kit-of-parts cannot be beaten, but it is a false economy to purchase one unless you are in possession of the skills required to put the kit together. An assistant is needed for careful 'taking-off' of measurements. These should be taken with the aid of lines drawn around the body in the horizontal plane 50mm apart. The shape of certain parts of the anatomy when drawn out flat often takes a lot of believing, and the tendency to make 'ad-hoc' cut-offs should always be avoided!

A number of different types of material, 4mm and 6mm thick, with or without a nylon lining, are usually available. Whilst 4mm is satisfactory for most caving purposes when new, it is fragile and has a greatly reduced working life compared with 6mm material. The 6mm nylon-lined material of British manufacture is now made to a high standard and is certainly better than most of the foreign material available. Although the nylon lining does add some 15 per cent to the cost of the suit it represents an investment in terms of extra strength when the garment is being put on and taken off, as well as extra comfort. Non-lined neoprene is now almost a thing of the past. Neoprene can also be obtained either as 'Smoothskin' or as 'Sharkskin'. This latter finish is supposed to have a better resistance to tearing and to give improved friction characteristics. Many cavers make – or purchase off-the-peg – wet-socks, for wearing inside the boots. Their extra thickness should be taken into account when boots are being purchased.

The wetsuit hood has become another common accessory, particularly for use in the very wet pothole systems of the Northern Pennines.

Semi-dry Outfits
For caving trips that are not likely to involve more than limited immersion in water (no wading more than two/three feet deep, and no waterfall climbing), a semi-dry outfit will be the most suitable. Since even in the driest of caves there will be a certain amount of moisture met with, the ordinary cotton boiler suit has now been largely replaced by one made from some form of damp-proof material. This can be one of a number of patent lightweight plastic-coated, woven-fibre materials.

The important criteria here are lightness of weight and resistance to abrasion and tearing. The Ghar Parau Suit as manufactured by Ladysmith Busywear Ltd of Leeds was one of the first in this field. The Mark I version was made for the 1972 Ghar Parau Expedition; it had all-internal pockets, elasticated wrists and ankles, a belt, and a hood with draw cord. The Mark II version has external pockets which tend to give extra protection to the front of the suit. 'Endurosuits', 'Daleswear Suits' and Petzl PVC Suits are now available on the market and like all other items of clothing the materials can be bought and a suit made to measure as a cheaper alternative to the off-the-peg article.

Beneath the outer protective layer, an ordinary set of woollen or man-made fibre clothes is usually worn. An improvement on the traditional swimming trunks, trousers, tee-shirt and sweater outfit, is the one-piece fibre-pile suit. These garments give good overall insulation and are therefore particularly good for long-duration working trips such as are often necessary with cave photography and cave surveying. Being one-piece there are no heat leaks at the waist and there is no trouble from rucking-up in tight crawls. Also with man-made fibre materials it is not quite so tragic if the wearer does suffer an unplanned immersion – they do not tend to have a high long-term water retention and the insulation is not totally destroyed when wet.

Clothing in General
For the casual caver who will not be involved in more than four or five caving trips each year the wetsuit provides the best all-purpose answer.

For the more active caver who is likely to be caving regularly in different types of cave, there is no single perfect answer. Although some cavers appear to be quite happy to wear a wetsuit for each and every trip regardless of moisture or temperature, most prefer something else for the drier trips. He will be best advised to acquire, with time, a number of outfits suitable for the differing requirements. A wetsuit is the logical start, with a semi-dry outfit for the longer drier type of trip, and possibly a drysuit for the special project where a good deal of chest-deep wading is involved.

Footwear
Caving footwear is required to tramp cave floors – slippery mud, liquid mud, pools, pebbles, dry rock, wet rock – adhere to thin aluminium ladder rungs and possibly grip greasy rock faces. It will need to give support to feet and ankles as well as a good degree of adhesion to whatever the surface. A good mountain-walking type of rubber sole is the best all-rounder. Vibram or Itshide and their better imitators are the ones to choose. It is a personal choice whether the upper should take the form of a traditional leather boot, on the pattern of the mountain-walking boot, or whether it should be of the wellington-boot variety. The leather boot is usually better in low temperatures since it has better insulation; it is also thought to be better for rock-climbing. The wellington boot has the advantage of being more easily put on and taken off – which can be handy in alternating wet and dry sections of cave passages. The fact that this form of footwear is often issued free to employees in the building industry and to those in a good many other outdoor occupations is

perhaps the greatest factor in favour of wellingtons! However, there are two important details which should over-ride the main choice: climbing boots must not be fitted with hook-fasteners, since they are easily damaged, become useless in the caving environment and are lethal on ladders; wellingtons or boots must have a good sole with a deep-pattern tread giving a firm grip.

Fig 1 Caving boots with deep-tread soles and either eye-holes, or 'D' ring lace fixings (as shown here), but NOT with open-clip fixings

The 'Whernside Welly' is a specially made product for cavers; it embodies the best points of boot and welly – a welly upper welded to a climbing-boot sole. It is also available in lace-up rubber-boot form and now comes with internal steel toe-protectors in accordance with Health and Safety Executive requirements.

Within the boot one good thick pair of wool/nylon socks is recommended. Some people prefer two thin pairs, others prefer a pair of wetsuit socks. The latter have a tendency to give an excessive amount of movement within the boot and should be questioned where rock-climbing might be involved.

If you are going to wear a drysuit with feet, make special allowance for this when purchasing footwear. Usually the footwear will need to be one whole size larger than otherwise. This will create a problem when you are not wearing the drysuit – an extra pair of socks will help here.

Lighting

After clothing, lighting is the most important item of caving equipment. Since caving is an activity which necessitates the use of arms and hands, it is not surprising that at an early date the light source came to be fixed to the head.

The first cave explorers in Britain used tallow-dip candles secured to the brims of their felt hats with either a piece of string or wire or a small lump of clay. This was an idea picked up from the early metal miners – the lead miners of Yorkshire and Derbyshire, the copper miners of North Wales and the Lake District and the tin miners of Cornwall.

Cavers' lighting systems have always closely followed those of miners in Britain. After the demise of the candle in the 1920s and 1930s, the carbide lamp became the common form of lighting. The Daylight and the Premier cap-lamps provided a compact unit which could be worn on the helmet and the papier-mâché helmets of the time came specially prepared with holes for their wire fixings. Although the larger and heavier handlamps have often been used by cavers for special activities such as underground digs and survey trips, they have never been suitable for regular caving.

The Premier caplamp is still available but is now much less commonly used by cavers than during the 1950s and 1960s. Many factors have contributed to this; the start of the trend was the availability of the various surplus (following mine closures) types of electric rechargeable miners' caplamps. A well-maintained miner's caplamp should require no attention in use, whereas even the best-maintained carbide lamp will need regular attention underground; the water needs to be topped up every two hours or so, the carbide supply approximately every four hours, and towards the end of a fill of carbide the jet may become blocked or the filter-pad choked up. Furthermore, stringent cave-conservation measures in some of our larger cave systems, Dan-yr-Ogof, Ogof Ffynnon Ddu and Agen Allwedd, have ruled out the use of carbide lamps altogether because of the many unsightly dumps of spent carbide that were appearing. Ironically the largely wet pothole systems of the Northern Pennines where carbide can be lost in the stream are precisely the places where carbide lamps are at their most impractical – even with a spray deflector they will not cope with a climb or descent of a waterfall pitch.

The Carbide Caplamp

This unit is the most compact form of the carbide generator lamp principle, first developed for domestic use during the nineteenth century. The use of carbide for lighting probably reached its peak in the early 1920s when it became the norm for cars and motorcycles. Here a central generator unit with pipes to the various lamps at the front and rear was the most common. The caplamp followed from the various models of handlamp used by metal miners and railway companies.

The Premier lamp is the only model in common use today. A similar model is manufactured in the USA and these are seen in Britain from time to time. The market is now almost completely restricted to cavers and part-time metal miners.

There are essentially two elements: the water reservoir with jet and reflector assembly at the top; the carbide container beneath. The top unit is screwed onto the base unit trapping a heavy rubber sealing-washer between. A control lever on the top allows water to drip from the reservoir into the generator through a variable taper nozzle which projects into the centre of the generator chamber. A felt filter pad in a brass holder screws into the base of the reservoir beneath the gas supply pipe. The reflector assembly houses the gas jet as well as a flint-striker unit. Premier also manufacture 100mm and 150mm reflectors which can be useful in larger cave passages.

There are important rules to bear in mind when using these lamps underground.

1 Before filling make sure that the lamp is clean, especially jet, gas supply pipe and filter pad.

Two small carbide lamps for helmet mounting

2 Use only clean, dust-free carbide and never fill the chamber more than two-thirds full (there must be space for expansion).
3 Check regularly that the reservoir is well stocked with water and top up with *clean* water whenever the opportunity presents itself.
4 Always carry a set of prickers securely attached to the lamp and always have a working flint unit (thus no need to carry matches).
5 Always carry a sufficient supply of spare carbide as well as a suitable container in which to carry the spent carbide from the cave.

Although many cavers carry a water container this is rarely necessary in British caves.

Belt Generator Carbide Lamps
It has long been the practice in Europe to use a carbide generator on a waist-belt, with a strong flexible pipe supplying gas to a lightweight helmet-mounted burner. These helmet units have become sophisticated, with flint, hot-wire or even piezo-electric striking devices built into the reflector/spray-deflector unit.

This system utilises the best features of the carbide lamp, with a lightweight helmet unit and a long-duration generator set (up to ten or twelve hours from one filling) and is very good for walking and for dry vertical caving. However, when flat-out crawling is necessary there arises the dual problem of retaining the water supply in the reservoir and preventing gas escaping back through the water nozzle, and of preventing spent carbide from clogging the filter pad and gas supply pipe. Also, all the commercially manufactured models to date have for reasons of strength and simplicity been cylindrical in form. Thus they tend to be more of a physical nuisance, in both crawls and tight fissures, than a battery pack. The gas supply pipe must be non-crushable and non-inflammable, whilst still remaining highly flexible. In practice this can probably never be as neat and flexible as the best of the electric cables.

Belt generator lamps should be seriously considered for overseas expeditions, particularly if re-charging elecric cells is likely to present a problem, and more so where the caves are likely to be large and dry. The caves of Mulu in Sarawak, Borneo, provide a first-class example of where this type of lighting unit is ideal. The

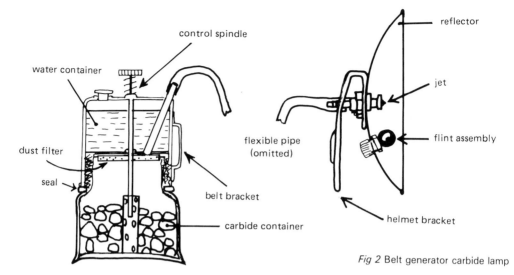

Fig 2 Belt generator carbide lamp

passages of the Mulu caves are often so large that the increased light output obtained from a large generator coupled with a large-size reflector can give a distinct advantage over any other form of lighting – at the same time the bulk of both generator and reflector causes few problems in these spacious surroundings.

Disposable-battery Electric Lights
These are fine for novice cavers who are involved only in the occasional short caving trip, and for use as a back-up emergency system. Unless constructed to at least the same high standard as the miner's caplamp they cannot be regarded as a suitable light-source for regular strenuous caving. Apart from the generally fragile nature of most, if not all, of the commercially-manufactured products, they are impractical due to the high cost of suitable disposable batteries.

Rechargeable-battery Lamps and Miners' Caplamps
Firstly, miners' caplamps, which set the standard of construction that should be aimed at in home-made units: there are two basic types commonly available and in general use in British caving – both were originally designed and built for the large coal-mining market. As a result they are constructed to a high standard of robustness and durability and are also designed to be spark free. Certain elements, such as the sealed fusable-link, are built to a specification not required by cavers.

The two types are:

1 The lead-acid (Oldham/Exide) types running at a nominal 2×2 volt = 4 volt rate.
2 The nickel/iron or nickel/cadium (Nife/Ceag/Eddison) types running at a nominal 3×1.2 volt = 3.6 volt rate.

The differences in construction, design, and electro-chemical characteristics between the two types stem from the two different types of cell involved.

Miners' Caplamps – Acid Cells
There are two manufacturers of this type of unit, Oldham and Exide, although other firms have produced them in the past and old head-lamps and cell tops may be found bearing the names Patterson, Ceag, etc.

Characteristics of the acid-cell types are that they have a nominal voltage of 2 volts and therefore use two cells to achieve a working 4 volts. When new they have a capacity of ten to twelve hours on main beam (approximately twenty-four to thirty-six hours on side beam). They give best results if used regularly, and never fully discharged or left in a low condition for any prolonged period. If not in use for more than two or three weeks they must be left fully charged, preferably topped up with a small additional charge every few weeks. They always have a plastic outer case, due to the highly corrosive nature of their acid electrolyte. Although this tends to make for a rather lighter unit than the stainless-steel cases of the alkali cells, it does

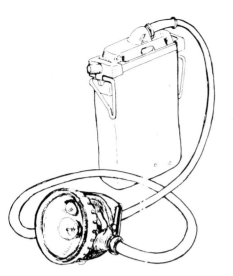

Fig 3 A typical lead-acid rechargeable electric lamp or 'miner's caplamp' with waist-belt holder and auxiliary lamp

Eddison and Ceag. As the trade name Nife suggests, the original models were of nickel-iron construction. Most cells are now of the improved nickel-cadmium construction.

Characteristics of the alkali-cell types are that they have a nominal voltage of 1.2 volts and therefore use three cells to achieve a working 3.6 volts. When new they have a capacity of twelve to fourteen hours on main beam (up to forty hours on side beam). The cell is much more robust in use than the acid cell. In contrast with the acid cell, if out of use for any length of time, the alkali cell is better left fully discharged. So long as they are kept well maintained with suitable-strength electrolyte and filled to the correct manufacturer's level, their life should be almost infinite. They are considerably more expensive than acid-cell units. Again a guarantee of proven capacity is the only certainty of a good unit. A visual inspection should indicate if the cell is much newer than the rest of the unit.

Minimum accessories are merely the necessary tools for gaining access to the headset and the cell-top. A special filler or charging plug is not usually required.

have the disadvantage that with regular use the corners can become so abraded that they leak.

If you are buying second hand, a guarantee of the hours of light being given by the unit when on main beam should be sufficient. Eight hours should be the minimum acceptable unless the price is very low. A generally good physical appearance (including no corner wear) is no indication that the cell is a good one. A cell which has never been used but has been left on the shelf for twelve months or so in a discharged condition is likely to be useless.

Shape and surface texture of the reflector are factors worth considering before purchase. Some of the earlier types of headpiece had a deep-set parabolic reflector. These give an excellent pencil beam but poor all-round visibility as well. The various types of matt-surfaced reflectors are worth experimenting with.

Minimum accessories for this type of lighting unit are a satisfactory means of topping up the electrolyte; special filler-plug, or pipette with thin rubber tube extension, and the necessary tools to gain access to the battery top and the headset. The bayonet plug for charging via the headset is also useful.

Miners' Caplamps – Alkali Cells

There are several manufacturers of this type of unit; the most commonly available are Nife,

Alkali or Acid Battery?

Since the National Coal Board has recently changed over from alkali to acid batteries the choice has been influenced in favour of the acid unit. The two probable main factors influencing the Coal Board were the cheaper purchase price of the acid units together with the reduced risk of burning from the electrolyte. Since the Coal Board change there have been more second-hand acid cells on the market and it has also become easier to obtain acid as opposed to alkali-unit spare parts.

A comparison of the pros and cons of the two types of unit is shown below:

Characteristics	Acid	Alkali
Robustness	***	*****
Ease of charging	***	*****
Left uncharged	*	*****
Left charged	***	***
Life expectancy	***	*****
Cost to purchase	**	*
Weight	**	*
Danger from electrolyte spillage	**	*

*poor, **fair, ***good, ****very good, *****excellent

Acid Battery Lamps: Types Available
Oldham types W, Y, YR and R have been extensively used by cavers. They are all similar in external appearance, their cases being moulded from a hard black rubber compound. The type R is the main one from this group in use by cavers today; it is also the only one still being manufactured. A special filler-funnel is required for topping up and this screws into the front in place of the removable plug.

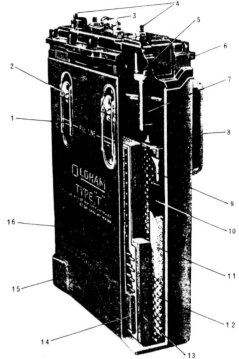

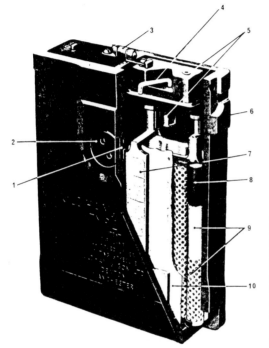

Fig 4 Sectional view of the Oldham type 'R' battery: (1) Rubber seal; (2) Removable plug for topping up; (3) Fuse; (4) Gas vent link; (5) Rubber lid with non-spill device; (6) Toughened hard rubber container; (7) Negative pasted plate; (8) Positive active material; (9) Porous sleeves; (10) Separator

Fig 5 Sectional view of the Oldham type 'T' battery: (1) Visible electrolyte level; (2) Venting and topping up aperture; (3) Fuse; (4) Battery terminals; (5) Post seal; (6) One-piece polycarbonate lid; (7) Anti-spill device; (8) Integrally moulded belt loop; (9) Antimonial lead spine; (10) Positive active material; (11) Woven glass-fibre inner sleeve; (12) Perforated outer sleeve; (13) Absorbent separator; (14) Negative plate; (15) Toughened corner; (16) Polycarbonate container

The Oldham type T is a development of the type R with most of the weaknesses designed out of it. The case is of polycarbonate in one piece with lid, and it has integrally moulded belt loops. It is usually bright red in colour. There is a transparent window in the front face of each cell which shows the electrolyte levels at a glance, and these incorporate dual-function apertures for topping up and venting. Whilst greatly reducing maintenance time, these vents do bring the problem of the cells sucking in water if totally immersed during caving. A minor modification such as tapping the holes and inserting a couple of small screws will easily solve this problem. (NB The screws/plugs must be removed before charging!)

Exide Triclad and Ceag CgL2 are both similar in construction to the Oldham type R battery unit. They are both fully interchangeable with the Oldham battery top and caplamp and also with the Youle units.

Caplamp Units
Although the complete alkali battery unit and caplamp is no longer available, used second-hand units are likely to be on the market for a long time, and the caplamp units from them for even longer.

For ease of charging go for a unit which has the bayonet plug-in charging facility in the lamp unit. In this way mistakes over polarity will be eliminated and there will be no need to open up the battery top other than for periodic cleaning. Earlier types such as Ceag and Nife do not have this facility, but some of them have a much deeper hyperbolic reflector – essential if a really powerful focused spot-beam is required, a great asset in the exploration of large and high cave passages.

So long as you have correct-voltage bulbs for the type of battery you use, most other factors concerning choice of caplamp are a matter of personal choice. These factors can be summarised thus:

Feature	Weakness	Advantages
Type of reflector:		
Parabolic	Poor all-round light	Good pencil beam
Spherical	Poor pencil beam	Good all-round light
Diffused	Poor on distance	Good all-round light
Twin bulbs	More complicated	Safety factor and good as an economy measure
Single bulbs	No safety factor	Lightness of weight

Although the recommended bulb voltages are 3.6 for alkali and 4.0 for acid (based on three-cell and two-cell units respectively), 3.5-volt and 3.8-volt bulbs can be used and will give an increased light output in the region of 10–12 per cent. They will also give reduced bulb life in the order of 60–70 per cent of normal life expectancy.

Bulbs for underground lighting should be in accordance with BS 535:1973. These are krypton filled (as opposed to the more usual argon-filled types) and thus give about 17 per cent more light output for a given wattage.

For more light 1.25 amp instead of the usual 1.0 amp should be used (if obtainable). For more duration a 0.75-amp bulb might be used. This would give thirteen hours of light from a battery normally giving only ten hours with a 1.0-amp bulb. Pilot bulb specifications are less important, but krypton-filled types are available in sizes from 0.25 amps up to 0.48 or 0.5 amps.

Care of Battery Lamps – Charging Requirements

With the acid battery, perhaps the most important factor is correct charging: not just quantity of charge, but also rate of charge. Of all the different charging methods, the 'modified constant potential method' is the best on balance, and the most accepted. This involves a charge of 5 volts being applied through a ballast resistor of 0.33 ohms 3 watts. If the starting current is 1.8 amps, by the time the battery has become fully charged (about twelve hours for a healthy recently discharged battery) the current will have dropped to approximately 0.1 amps. Thus even if the battery is accidentally left on charge for two or three days there will be negligible damage done. The resistor also has the advantage that if the battery is left connected to the charger after switching off there will be little loss of charge back through the charger. This system of charging is now built into most commercially available acid-battery-charging units. The single or multiple units made by or for Oldham, Exide or Ceag are of this type.

With other types of battery charger it is much easier to accidentally overcharge acid-cell units. Repeated overcharging will seriously shorten the battery's life. Undercharging is not so serious, but reduced capacity may lead to problems in the cave. For more detailed information on construction and care of lead-acid cap lamps see Cowlishaw (1974).

Helmets

A protective helmet should always be worn, no matter how short in duration or simple in character the cave is. In the first recorded fatality in British caving, a small stone thrown casually down Alum Pot by a passer-by fractured the skull of a caver wearing only a soft hat. Had that caver been wearing a suitable hard helmet, as worn by all cavers today, injury would have been unlikely.

In lieu of a special British Standard on caving helmets, BS 5240:1975 (General Purpose Industrial Safety Helmets [amended 1976]) is the most appropriate for general guidance. This does not include the necessary extras of adjustable chinstrap, lamp bracket and cable clip, but does cover the polypropylene shell design and its strength, as well as design and strength of the internal support cradle. These cradles are adjustable, so that all heads can be accommodated by the one model. Although these polypropylene helmets are considered by some cavers to be less comfortable than the older papier-mâché ones, they give a higher level of protection, particularly from falls and from falling rocks.

Increased protection can be gained by using a climber's helmet (to BS 4423:1969), but this is practical only for dangerous underground activities such as rock-face or high aven climbing. The extra skull-coverage given by this type of helmet becomes a serious hindrance to movement and tends to restrict hearing. These helmets have no front brim and are generally regarded as too warm and clumsy for general caving.

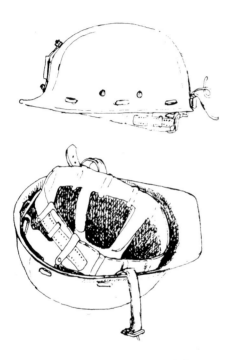

Fig 6 Caving helmet with adjustable cradle/head band, chin strap, lamp-bracket and string for securing the light cable at the back

Most caving supply shops now stock helmets of the BS 5240 type fully adapted to caving use, with chinstrap, lamp bracket and cable clip. It is important to check that the helmet can be adjusted internally to give a firm fit. Sometimes, when a heavy lighting unit such as a carbide caplamp is fitted on the front bracket, you will need some form of counter-balance at the rear; otherwise the helmet will slip down over the eyes at regular intervals! When carbide is being used as the main form of lighting, the counter-balance can be made up from a bell-battery and small auxiliary electric unit. As

little as possible should be put on the head, and this is a major reason for not recommending the use of carbide as the primary light.

A helmet 'borrowed' from a construction site, provided that it is of the BS 5240 type (and not the lighter BS 4033:1966 type), can be converted satisfactorily into a safe caving helmet with the provision of the three home-made extras. Lamp brackets are best kept as simple and lightweight as possible consistent with strength. They can be made from sheet brass or sheet steel; take care that the lamp unit points downwards a few degrees below the line of the helmet brim. Chinstraps can be conventional leather or canvas with a small buckle at the side, or for bearded cavers a length of cycle inner-tube (complete with the pressure valve at the side) can be suitably arranged to form a luxury pneumatic version! Again the cable clip can be either a small metal clip bolted or riveted to the rear of the helmet, or a piece of string or wire – so long as it is permanently affixed to the helmet and then tied around the cable separately.

Minor Accessories

Watch, gloves, whistle, waist-line and karabiner, ammunition box – these items may or may not be a good thing to have with you. On a short duration trip into a simple horizontal cave none of these items may be necessary. On a longer trip with vertical climbs and pitches, such as Giants Hole (Derbyshire), Longwood–August Hole (Somerset) or the farther reaches of Dan yr Ogof or Ogof Ffynnon Ddu (South Wales), it will be helpful to have most of these items with each party.

Watch
Although the Omega Speedmaster and other expensive high-quality diving watches have been loaned to overseas caving expeditions from time to time, none has proved really reliable against the extreme rigours of everyday caving. Money is better spent on a £5 to £10 waterproof or 'water-resistant' model of the diver's type and then taking a little care of it when underground. The best idea is to carry it, together with food, surveying gear and so on, inside the ammunition box, perhaps wrapped in a handkerchief or clean rag. It is only during cave-diving exploits that there is any real need for an absolutely

waterproof watch or for it to be instantly available on the wrist.

Gloves
Many cavers never wear gloves; a few will not venture underground without them! There are three types of circumstance where they are likely to be essential:

1 For the expedition or professional caver, where the amount of wear and tear on the skin during the course of a week is greater than the growth of fresh skin tissue.
2 Where an excessive amount of lifelining or other ropework is required, or for activities such as bolt-hole drilling.
3 For caving where water or cave earth is known to be polluted.

Leather gloves will not withstand constant wet conditions. Perhaps the most versatile are the PVC industrial gloves with knitted wrists. They are lightweight, hard-wearing and cheap.

Whistles
Although a whistle is essential only for vertical systems, especially wet ones, it is a good idea to make a habit of carrying one around the neck on all trips. It can be useful for attracting attention in almost any emergency: surprisingly often there is more water present than expected, and it can be impossible to communicate reliably by voice on a pitch as short as 20m when there is a large volume of water falling down it. The old-fashioned railway whistle, metal or plastic, with a retained 'pea', is the most reliable type. Many of the more modern-looking plastic whistles make only a very weak or high-pitched sound, of little use in a wet cave! The signal code for lifeline work should be known to all who venture down vertical caves: S-U-D; one blast 'Stop'; two 'Up'; three 'Down'.

Waist-line and Karabiner
Although some consider it an outdated habit, the practice of wearing a 4 or 5m length of nylon line together with a screw-gate snap-link around the waist is still a good one. Five metres is about the best length to have; any shorter and it is not much use for general assistance to members of the party, or as a handline across exposed or difficult traverses; any longer and it becomes a serious obstacle in negotiating squeezes etc. Choose 9mm nylon or other rope

of this weight. The type or rope for your use depends on the type of lamp you will be carrying. Nylon is destroyed by dilute acids, and terylene by alkalis. Thus with a lead/acid cell anything other than nylon should be used. Terylene-fibre rope is the strongest weight-for-weight and also has the highest melting point. On the other hand, if a Nife cell is to be used, nylon is undoubtedly the best choice.

Ammunition Box
The ex-army ammunition box has proved to be a universal hold-all for the caver. Of the three sizes – all with similar end-hinged lid and neoprene seals – the smallest, 75mm wide × 170mm high × 255mm long, is sufficient to take simple surveying gear and some food. The middle size, 90 × 185 × 255mm (only slightly larger), is the most popular; whilst the largest one, 145 × 185 × 280mm, is particularly useful for the cave photographer. With an internal capacity of approximately 6.6 litres this more or less equates to the maximum size of rigid container that you can carry down most caves. All these ammunition boxes, apart from being robust and waterproof, have a good carrying handle on the top and a further wire handle on the opening end. They can be conveniently carried along walking passages by fixing a carrying strap or sling through both of the handles. This arrangement is also reliable for pitch-hauling, but take the precaution of modifying the closing catch first.

Because of their solid design and waterproof seals, ammunition boxes make useful containers for delicate electronic devices, ie radio-location transmitters and receivers (see Chapter 12).

Other items of personal equipment, such as sit and chest-harnesses, are dealt with in Chapter 3.

Emergency Equipment

Every member of the caving team must consider what he should take with him in respect of emergency equipment.

Since the most vital part of a caver's equipment is his lamp, this should be the first item considered. So long as a carbide lamp has a working flint striker, and sufficient spare carbide is carried, then a set of prickers and a jet will suffice for spare parts. It is important that the carbide is carried in a suitable container, at least a polythene jar with an airtight screw-top lid. If this is also inside an ammunition box it will be even safer. Remember, though, that in an increasing number of caves the use of carbide is banned on conservation grounds (see Chapter 15).

With the miners' caplamp, rather than carry spares it is better if members of the party carry a spare alternative form of lighting. This could be a compact dry-cell unit (similar to a miner's lamp or a torch), a compact rechargeable cell unit, one of the disposable chemical light-sticks or a complete spare carbide lamp. The latter item must be complete, with at least one filling of carbide and either matches or, better, a flint unit that works. If a hand-torch is chosen, one using three or more U2 cells should be regarded as the minimum standard.

Next in importance is food, covered more fully in Chapter 14. A little 'instant energy' food – chocolate, fudge, glucose, raisins and dates – can make a great deal of difference to a party in difficulty or unexpectedly delayed by high water levels, flooding, boulder falls, an unexpectedly weak member of the party, illness or a minor injury.

In the more complex cave systems, eg Ogof Ffynnon Ddu and Lancaster/Easegill, it can be useful to carry a photocopy of the cave survey or, perhaps better, a set of notes listing the critical junctions and turnings. Cave surveys (see Chapter 11) are often either inaccurate or difficult to follow, especially where there are many passages at different levels. It has been known for the carrying of such a survey to be the direct cause of a party becoming hopelessly lost! Usually a member with experience of the particular cave is more valuable than copies of the cave survey.

All the above items should fit easily into one or two of the smallest-size ammunition boxes. If the amount of emergency equipment is beginning to exceed this quantity, then a serious reappraisal should be carried out. Caving parties have had accidents for no better reason than because they were carrying too much emergency or contingency equipment!

2 Ladders and Lifelines

DAVID ELLIOT

The two most commonly used vertical techniques employed by British and American cavers are single-rope techniques (SRT) and the more traditional use of flexible wire ladders and travelling lifelines. European cavers, however, choosing to use ladders for one reason or another, have adopted a different lining method, known as self-lining. With this technique the lifeline is fixed in the pitch alongside the ladder. The rope is used for abseiling during the descent and to safeguard the ascent by trailing a jammer on the rope alongside the climber.

The increase in the popularity of SRT in recent years has greatly reduced the use of ladders, to such an extent that minor pitches are often seen rigged with rope alone when a ladder and lifeline might be more to the point.

Single rope and ladder techniques should be regarded as complementary tools for negotiating the vertical bits of caves – each with a valid role. In future it is unlikely that the deeper, more inaccessible systems will ever be entirely laddered again in the traditional manner, whereas ladder techniques are sometimes preferable on short, tight, or awkward pitches and for use with novice groups.

LADDERS
Safety – Traditional Approach

At its simplest the conventional use of ladder and lifeline involves climbing a flexible wire ladder while protected against a fall by a travelling lifeline secured from above or via a pulley from below. The lifeline is operated by another member of the team, firmly secured to prevent him being dragged from his position should the ladder climber fall. This system naturally works best when all the members of a team are fully competent; it also allows experienced cavers to safeguard the less experienced. Paradoxically it is this function of traditional laddering which is the basis of both its strength and weakness as a technique. Whereas SRT demands a high degree of personal competence from each individual, laddering – or at least lifelining – is a joint effort, and security on a ladder is gained only by delegating responsibility to the lifeliner. Although perhaps less critical with laddering than with SRT, the choice of anchor points and correct rigging is vital to a caver's safety. Resourcefulness and ingenuity are often called for and only adequate experience and a thorough knowledge of the principles involved ensure competent rigging. Laddering is not easy.

Generally two or three independent anchors are required at each pitch, one each for the ladder and lifeline and if necessary an additional one for a pulley.

Rigging

Provided there is no risk of falling down the pitch while doing so, it is often convenient to attach the ladder before the lifeline and lower it down the pitch out of the way. Where there is any risk of falling, a lifeline should be arranged before approaching the pitch lip. Ladders may be anchored either by a wire tether or by a spreader and karabiner used directly to a bolt hanger or in conjunction with rope or tape slings (Fig 7). Wire tethers are perhaps best employed on jagged flakes where sharp edges might cut a tape, also for long belays where rope or tape would stretch unduly, although in this case extra ladder can often be run back to the anchor instead. Most established ladderers use wire tethers, though there are few occasions when a tether presents any advantage over the stronger and more versatile alternative of rope or tape slings. On the other hand, wire does not abrade easily and is less affected by battery acid.

To ensure that the ladders are not dropped down the hole, attach one end to the anchor point before linking the lengths together and lowering them down the pitch. Throwing ladders down a pitch is about the best way of tangling them and, with resin-bonded ladders, smashing the resin out of the rung ends.

Cavers use ladders to negotiate pitches. There are no 'ethics' of any sort involved in their use; the easier the ladder is to climb the better, and careful rigging may take much of the hazard out of an awkward situation. Some of the main points to consider are:

1 Avoid as far as possible objective hazards such as water and stone-fall.
2 Rig the ladder within easy reach and make sure there are sufficient rungs above the pitch lip to facilitate getting on and off – the most dangerous part of a pitch is at the top.
3 Avoid running the ladder over sharp edges or flat against rock where the rungs are difficult to grasp.
4 Where possible avoid dangling the ladder into tight crevices or constrictions that make it difficult to climb. Just hanging the ladder anywhere is rarely good enough – select the best hang possible in the circumstances.
5 Spare ladder at the foot of the pitch should be coiled and fastened so that it hangs a few centimetres above the floor. Otherwise it will suffer from being trampled underfoot.

The application of wire tethers or spreaders is largely governed by the type of anchor available. In general, wire tethers are used when a ladder is belayed directly to a natural anchor (Fig 7) and a spreader used when the ladder is fastened via a karabiner to a tape sling or bolt hanger (Figs 8 and 9). Perhaps the simplest situation is where a wire tether utilises a straightforward thread or spike belay close to the pitch head. Here it is often useful to wrap the tether around the anchor where there is a tendency for it to seesaw in use, and this technique may also be used to shorten an unduly long tether (Figs 10 and 11).

Too short a tether will result in overstressing both the tether and the end tails of the ladder. The angle assumed by a wire tether should be such that the end wires of the ladder are not bent enough to damage them (Fig 12). Ladders should never be supported by a rung, as these

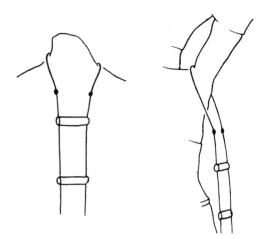

Fig 7 A wire tether can be used around natural anchors

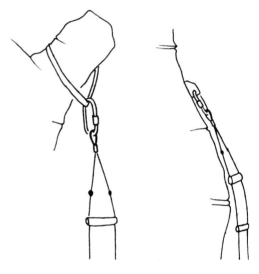

Figs 8 – 9 A spreader should be used when the ladder is hung from a tape sling and krab (*left*) or from a bolt hanger (*right*)

are weak (Fig 13). The wire tether itself will be permanently kinked and weakened if bent over too small a radius (Figs 14 and 15). Similarly, wire tethers should not be threaded around tape slings (Fig 16) as this weakens the tape considerably. Whenever a knob, spike or flake-anchor is used it must be secure in the direction of applied load, without any tendency to slip off when the load is released (Fig 16). Try to arrange the two sides of a tether or tape sling to be as nearly parallel as possible so that any load

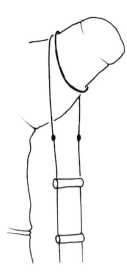

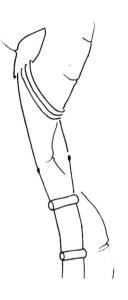

Figs 10 – 11 Looping the tether around the anchor can increase friction and so stop the ladder 'see-sawing' (*far left*) or it can be used to shorten a lengthy tether (*left*)

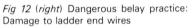

Fig 12 (*right*) Dangerous belay practice: Damage to ladder end wires

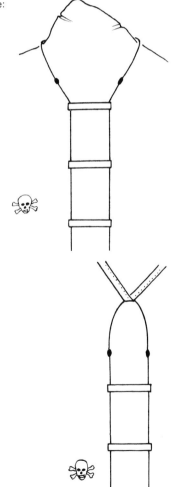

Figs 13 – 15 Dangerous belay practice: (*above*) supporting the ladder on a rung; (*right*) pulling the tether over a sharp anchor; (*far right*) weakening a tape sling by attaching directly to the wire tether (cf Fig 10)

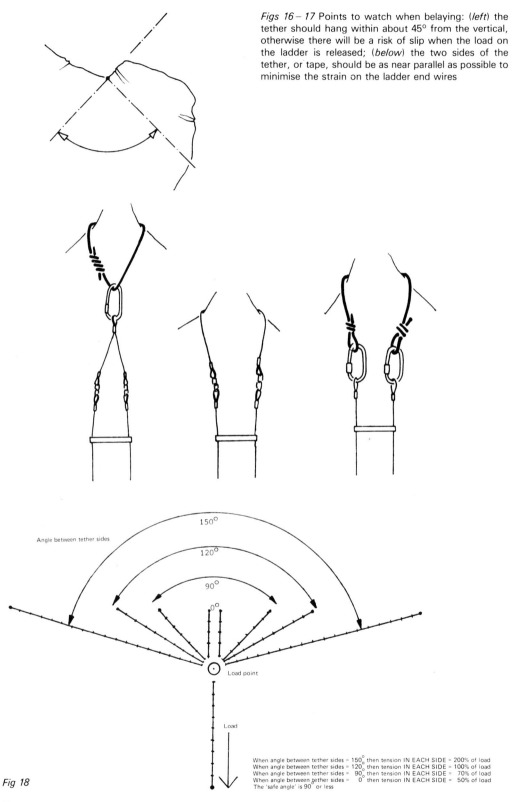

Figs 16 – 17 Points to watch when belaying: (*left*) the tether should hang within about 45° from the vertical, otherwise there will be a risk of slip when the load on the ladder is released; (*below*) the two sides of the tether, or tape, should be as near parallel as possible to minimise the strain on the ladder end wires

Angle between tether sides

150°

120°

90°

0°

Load point

Load

When angle between tether sides = 150° then tension IN EACH SIDE = 200% of load
When angle between tether sides = 120° then tension IN EACH SIDE = 100% of load
When angle between tether sides = 90° then tension IN EACH SIDE = 70% of load
When angle between tether sides =   0° then tension IN EACH SIDE = 50% of load
The 'safe angle' is 90° or less

Fig 18

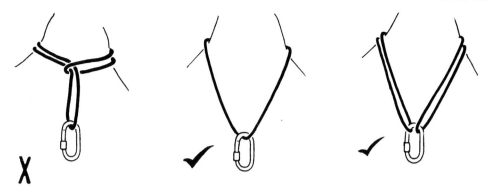

Figs 19 – 21 Points to watch when belaying: a 'Lark's Foot' produces a large angle between the tape sides (*left*). The problem can be solved by using a single loop with krab (*centre*) or doubling the tape (*right*)

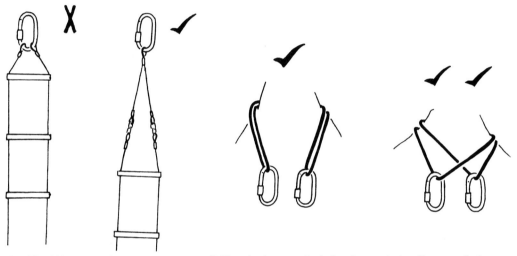

Figs 22 – 4 Wire spreaders and alternatives: (*left*) end wires attached directly to a krab will eventually become weakened. Less bending will occur at the point where the wire leaves the rung if a spreader is used. The ladder is now likely to twist. A better alternative is a double sling with two krabs, or (*centre*) a krab through each eyesplice, attached to two separate short slings

applied is taken equally between the two (Fig 17). This is important, because as the angle between the two sides increases they begin to pull against each other and, for example, when this angle reaches 120° the tension in *each* side equals the total applied. Above this the tension increases alarmingly (Fig 18), and in practice the safe angle is 90° or less when each side supports around 70 per cent of the total load.

If a tape sling is attached to an anchor by threading through itself in a 'lark's foot' then the angle in the loop is inevitably large, and also exerts a tearing action on the tape (Fig 19). One solution is to use the tape as a single loop (Fig 20) or, better, doubled with both ends of the loop brought down to the karabiner (Fig 21).

The function of a spreader in attaching a ladder is to lessen the angle the end tails assume when fastened into a karabiner (Fig 22). The short sections of wire rope where they leave the top rung are the most vulnerable points of a ladder, because repeated acute bending prematurely weakens it.

A ladder hanging free from a spreader attachment will tend to twist and entangle the lifeline. It is generally better to clip a suitable karabiner through both end tails, even though some stressing of the wire is inevitable.

An alternative method uses two karabiners clipped directly into the eyesplices, one for each side of the ladder, and fastened to a doubled sling (Fig 23) or to two separate shorter slings (Fig 24). The latter is about the strongest way there is of belaying a ladder.

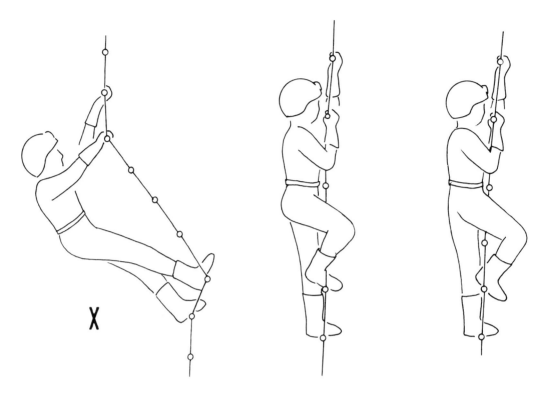

Figs 25 – 7 Ladder climbing: free hanging pitch. (*Left*) with the hands gripping the ladder rungs from the front, a large amount of the body weight is taken on the arms; (*centre*) the powerful leg muscles are allowed to take the load by keeping the ladder close in to the chest. Both feet may be in front of the ladder, or (*right*) one may be put in from the back

Climbing

Ladder-climbing is always hard work, and expertise is a matter of commonsense and practice. Some guidelines may help avoid the more obvious pitfalls. Perhaps the most common mistake for people unused to climbing flexible ladders is to climb them from the front like a rigid builder's ladder. This way the lower part of the ladder swings away and places a great deal of strain on the arms (Fig 25); body weight is efficiently lifted only by the powerful leg muscles, arm strength being used mainly for balance. The most straightforward method of climbing uses the arms wrapped around the ladder, with the hands gripping the rungs at about head height and hugging the ladder in towards the chest. Feet are placed from the front of the ladder, with the rung located beneath the instep, and the legs bent slightly outwards so that the ladder passes between the knees (Fig 26). It is a matter of balance; keeping the ladder close into the body ensures an up-right position and directs most of the weight onto the thigh muscles. Climb steadily, a rung at a time, by moving one foot and the opposite hand together, keeping the trunk as near vertical as possible and resisting the temptation to reach up for rungs above head height. You can vary the leg movements by climbing with one or both legs wrapped around the ladder and placing the feet onto the rungs heel-first. This method holds the ladder close, but is slower and only of use on free-hanging pitches (Fig 27).

Where the ladder rests against a wall, keeping the rungs under the instep is effective in bracing the ladder away from the rock with sufficient clearance for hands and feet. It is often better in this situation to grasp the rungs from the front rather than behind and also to lean back to pull each rung away from the wall and afford a better grip on the rung above (Fig 28). Another useful technique where the ladder rests against sloping rock is to twist yourself and the ladder sideways through 90°, so that

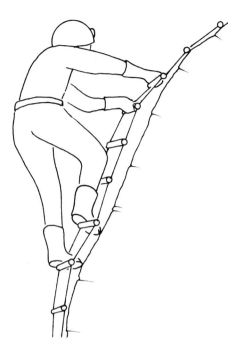

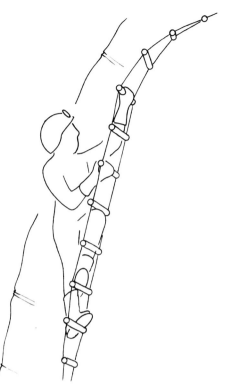

Figs 28 – 9 Ladder climbing: against a wall. (*Left*) either method gives clearance for the hands - fending off with the feet and pulling with the hands, or (*right*) twisting the ladder through 90°

Figs 30 – 2 Resting: (*above*) attachment krab should pass around the side wire as well as the rung; (*right*) a 'runghook' with cow's-tail is a more comfortable arrangement; (*far right*) although far less satisfactory than a sit-harness, a little rest can be gained by attaching a krab to a load-bearing waist belt. However, the legs are still supporting most of the weight

the rungs are at right angles to the rock surface and you climb with one shoulder against the rock (Fig 29).

Resting

You can rest on a ladder by attaching a karabiner fastened to a sit-harness or load-bearing belt, which allows you to let go and rest your arms. Ladder rungs are very weak and this is safe only if the karabiner encloses one of the side wires (Fig 30). This may result in an awkward rest position and on a long pitch the combination of 'rung-hook' and short cow's-tail is perhaps better (Fig 31). Resting in a sit-harness is the safest and most comfortable method; on a ladder much of the body weight can be supported by the legs (Fig 32), and a load-bearing waist-belt is often considered (just about) adequate.

Minor Difficulties

Occasionally the dubious technique of lowering the lifeline alongside a ladder will cause it to become threaded between the rungs, which creates a problem for the climber on his way up. He then has to clip onto the ladder, unfasten his lifeline, disentangle it from the ladder and fasten it back on again. If he has not taken the precaution of wearing a suitable harness and karabiner, he must either go back down and try again, or do it all one-handed while clinging onto the ladder. This is avoided in the first place by loosely coiling the lifeline and throwing it down the pitch out away from the ladder, or by using a 'pullback technique' (see page 34).

On awkward pitches the lifeline may become twisted around the ladder, which necessitates clambering round the ladder to release it. This is often easier further down the pitch where the ladder is more likely to be hanging free, rather than tight against the rock.

Derigging

Derigging a ladder from a pitch of any length is unlikely to be a matter of just hauling it up. If there is any possibility of the ladder snagging a projection or jamming irretrievably in a crack then it will! Sometimes just jiggling the ladder about from the top will free it, but often you have to descend the pitch for some distance and partly dismantle the train of ladders. On a badly

Fig 33 When detackling certain pitches it may be necessary for the last man to free the ladder as it is hauled from above

broken pitch where difficulties can be anticipated, the last man to ascend might stop at a ledge now and then and pull the ladder up in stages. Alternatives (often combined) are lowering a second rope with the object of hauling the ladder up from the bottom, or attaching the lower end of the ladder to the climber, who can guide it past obstacles as he climbs (Fig 33).

It is essential, while hauling a ladder from any exposed position, to be safely belayed and also to avoid hauling too energetically. If the ladder snags, it will very likely be torn from your grasp and disappear down the pitch. This is a good reason for not disconnecting the ladder from its belay until it is completely withdrawn from the pitch. There have been tragic instances of unbelayed cavers caught off balance by a snagged ladder pulling themselves over the lip of the pitch and falling to their death.

Ladder Construction

When introduced into British caving as a successor to natural-fibre/wooden-runged ladders, lightweight metal (or electron) ladders underwent development during which practically every conceivable type of material and method of construction was tried and evaluated. Eventually the most practical ladders, in terms of use and construction methods, were singled out and adopted by caving clubs and manufacturers. As a result only two standard types of ladder construction are now generally used by cavers in Britain; the 'pin-and-resin' method and a crimping method generally known as 'pressure-bonded'. They differ only in the method of rung fixing.

Lightweight metal ladders consist of two strong, steel cables forming the supports, with rungs of light alloy tube. The ladders are made up in convenient lengths (usually 8–10m) with a fitting at either end to enable separate lengths to be linked together.

Commercially available ladders are usually expensive, but savings can be made by constructing ladders privately. Access to basic workshop facilities and a certain amount of expertise are required, neither beyond the reach of most active caving groups.

Pressure-bonded

Pressure-bonded rung fixing involves the use of a press and dies and is thus suited to large-scale production. An alloy plug is inserted into the end of each rung which is then drilled and threaded onto the wires, before being squeezed in a press between suitable dies to form a crimp around the wire. This method is neat and strong, as strong as the wire if correctly applied, but the crimping equipment is specialised, and resin methods are better suited to the home workshop. The crimping process often leaves sharp burrs at the rung ends which may damage unprotected wrists and forearms if not removed.

Pin-and-resin

The pin-and-resin method consists of drilling and treading suitably bunged rungs onto the wires, which are then fixed into position by driving a steel pin or galvanised 'clout' nail through the wire inside the rung. The joint is strengthened and sealed by pouring an epoxy or

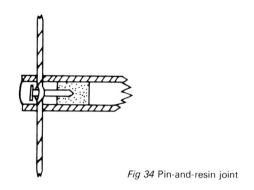

Fig 34 Pin-and-resin joint

polyester resin compound into the rung ends (Fig 34).

Wire Rope

The wire rope normally used in ladders is galvanised steel rope of 7×19 construction (seven strands containing nineteen wires each) with a wire core (as opposed to hemp or fibre). Commonly used wire ropes are either 3mm or 4mm in diameter with breaking loads of 725kg and 1000kg respectively.

Rungs

The rungs are made from round-section duralumin alloy tubing of 12–15mm outside diameter, with a wall thickness of 16SWG. For the technically minded, HE30TF is a suitable alloy.

End Assemblies

The end assemblies (Fig 35) are designed for linking separate ladders as well as for belay purposes, and consist of an eyesplice at the end of each wire rope containing a C-link or some other means of linking the ladders together (karabiners, *Maillon Rapides*, etc). The eyesplices are formed by wrapping the end of the wire rope around a suitable thimble and securing it with a 'Talurit' splice or similar fastening. Talurit splices are ferrules of work-hardening aluminium alloy which are crimped onto the rope using a hydraulic press and accurate dies. This forms a very strong joint.

Thimbles can be of stainless or galvanised steel, or even of nylon or other suitable plastic materials. They should be sizeable enough to avoid weakening the rope by bending it over too small a radius, and also permit the use of standard (10mm diameter) karabiners for attaching the ladder.

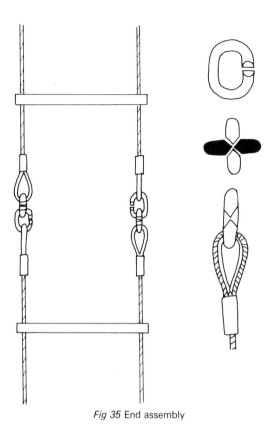

Fig 35 End assembly

C-Links
C-links are an ingenious device of split chain links used to join separate ladders. They are made from a length of 8mm high-tensile chain with two 45° saw cuts at right angles to each other through the weld of each link (Fig 35). C-links are the weak point in a ladder system; they should be carefully made and samples tested for strength.

Resin Materials
Two types of resin are used in ladder construction: epoxy resins such as Araldite, and polyester resins of the Cataloy type. Both comprise a two-part mixture of resin and a catalyst hardener mixed together immediately before use. Epoxy resins are by far the stronger of the two, but are also much more expensive; polyester resins are adequate.

Rung Spacing
The distance between rungs is partly a matter of preference, but experience shows the optimum spacing between rung centres to lie between 25cm and 30cm. It is best to standardise on a particular spacing: differently spaced ladders on a long pitch cause breaks in climbing rhythm.

Identification
Ladders can be identified and marked with their date of manufacture, length, etc, by stamping with metal die-stamps on the two end rungs. A less satisfactory method is fitting identity tags to the end assemblies, but these tend not to last very long. Resined ladders can be colour-coded by adding a suitable dye to the resin during construction (glassfibre materials suppliers stock suitable dyes). One caving group have their alloy rungs anodised in different colours before construction.

Maintenance
Lightweight metal ladders need little maintenance other than washing and drying after use and a regular inspection for damage and signs of wear and corrosion. A periodic treatment which helps to preserve the wire ropes is to dip the ladders into a solution of lanoline dissolved in white spirit (1kg to 10 litres), drain off the surplus liquid and hang them up to dry. Coating ladders with grease makes them unpleasant to handle and unless ladders are to be used or stored in wet conditions for extended periods this precaution is probably unnecessary.

Coiling Ladders
Wire ladders may be coiled using any method which is neat, simple, does not stress the wires over too sharp an angle and does not require more than one person to do it. An effective method is to take one end of the ladder and link the C-links around the ladder, forming a small loop with the first rung lying adjacent to the third rung. Coil the ladder by rolling it up, placing the side wires within the coil and the successive rungs alongside each other. The coiled ladder is secured by undoing the inner set of C-links and fastening them outside the coil, then fastening the outer set of links at the centre of the coil. Slightly longer end wires help with this and the result should be a coil which cannot come undone accidentally and is easily carried. However, repeated acute flexing of the end wire at the point where it leaves the rung results in weakening and premature failure. It is far better if the ladder is simply coiled and

stuffed into a tackle-sack without fastening the end wires. Again, ladders are best stored simply rolled into loose coils with the ends left unfastened.

Ladder Accessories

Tethers
Tethers are lengths of wire rope with an eye-splice and C-link at each end which may be used to attach a ladder to an anchor point. Generally wire rope tethers are subject to rougher treatment below ground than the ladder ropes and consequently are often made from heavier wire, usually 4mm diameter, 1000kg breaking load, although, as with ladders, the connecting C-links are by far the weakest part of the system, often failing below 250kg.

Warning: while adequate for attaching the ladder which normally is subject to little more than body weight, wire tethers (or rather C-links) must never find their way into the life-line system, where they are potentially lethal.

Tethers may be made up to any required length, but anything over about 4m becomes unmanageable and lengths below 1m are largely obviated by the use of 'spreaders'. When not in use tethers may be wound into coils of about 15cm diameter, with the free end wrapped around the coil a few times and the C-links joined together. While wire rope tethers are widely used for ladder attachment at present, they are rapidly being superseded by more versatile spreaders and rope or tape slings.

Spreaders
Spreaders are short wire tethers with an additional fixed eye at the centre. They are used only to anchor ladders, in order to reduce the angle the ladder and ropes assume when attached by a karabiner directly to a bolt hanger or other point belay. Spreaders are made from the same wire rope as tethers, with equal legs about 20cm long fitted with an eyesplice/C-link assembly and the wire crimped around a thimble to form a central eye. In use the C-links are attached to the ladder and connected to the anchor by a screw-gate karabiner fastened through the central eye. An alternative version with a central chain-link or *Maillon Rapide* can be used as a spreader or a very short tether.

LIFELINES

The sole function of a lifeline system is to safe-guard the ladder climber; to do this effectively the lifeliner must be securely anchored and able to brake and control the rope should the climber fall. Most cavers are only too familiar with the 'experienced' lifeliner who considers attaching himself to the rock superfluous, being more than strong enough to hold a 'small' fall unaided. Avoid this bloke altogether, he is stupid! Even a metre or so of slack rope in the system can result in a fall producing forces of 200 or 300kg, and his chances of holding this are nil. He will either let go of the rope to save himself, or be pulled over the edge and land on someone's head; in neither case is he of any use to the falling climber.

Because lifelines are effectively used in a 'top-roping' situation where only relatively minor falls are possible, the low-stretch ropes used in SRT are perfectly suitable. More extensible climbing ropes may be preferred for 'traditional' lifelining techniques, but are less suitable for abseiling and therefore proscribed for self-lining use.

One very important related point: in any situation where the climber may be left dangling from the end of the rope, a waist-tie is an unsatisfactory means of attachment. Compression of the diaphragm and rib cage may lead to unconsciousness and death in a matter of minutes. A sit-harness is *essential* in order to direct the load onto the thigh and buttock region where it is most safely and comfortably supported.

Traditional Rigging

There are many methods of attachment used according to circumstance, and only practised familiarity with a range of different methods will provide the necessary versatility. Amongst the most useful methods are those using the rope alone:

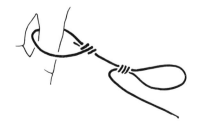

Fig 36

1 With a 'thread' belay, the end of the rope is tied directly to the anchor with a bowline or reversed figure-eight knot. A figure-eight knot is tied at the appropriate distance, stepped into and adjusted around the waist.

2 In the case of a 'spike' or 'flake' belay, the end of the rope is tied around the waist with a bowline, then a figure-eight loop tied in the standing rope at the correct distance and dropped over the anchor.

Fig 37

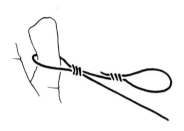

3 An 'adjustable' method is possible for both spike and thread belays by first tying the end of the rope around the waist with a bowline. A bight of the standing rope is passed around the anchor, adjusted for length and then secured to the waist-loop with a figure-eight knot tied as shown.

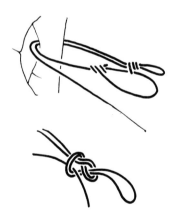

Fig 38

The same technique may be used for attachment to two anchor points, tying both off into the waist-loop with separate figure-eight knots (Fig 39). In the case of 'thread' belays, the rope must be threaded through the anchors before tying onto the end.

Most belays are simplified by the use of a harness and screwgate karabiner. The remainder of the methods described assume

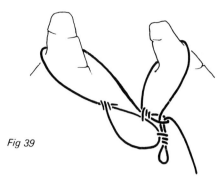

Fig 39

that these are worn.

4 If the anchor is located suitably close by the pitch, the simplest method is to thread a sling around it and clip this directly into the harness karabiner.

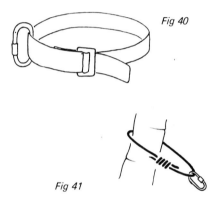

Fig 40

Fig 41

5 The end of the rope is tied directly around the anchor, with a figure-eight loop tied at the appropriate distance in the standing rope and clipped into the harness karabiner. This method uses the least amount of rope of all.

Fig 42

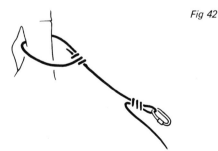

6 Where a sling and karabiner are used around an anchor, the rope may be secured midway with a figure-eight loop and a second figure-eight loop in the end of the rope attached to the harness karabiner.

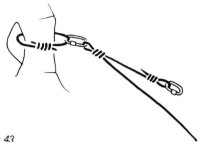

Fig 43

Fig 46

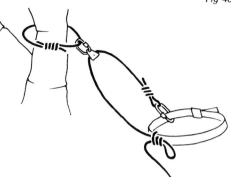

7 An adjustable method can be arranged with a figure-eight loop in the end of the rope attached to the harness karabiner and a bight of standing rope running either directly around the anchor or through a krab and sling. After adjustment for length the rope is secured by a second figure-eight loop clipped into the harness karabiner (Fig 44) or tied directly around the harness (Fig 45).

This last method of attachment, via the pulley, is the most widely used technique where a double rope is to be arranged for the return. It has the advantage that the lifeliner need untie only one knot before he is ready to descend and at no time need be unprotected or disconnected from the rope (Fig 47).

Fig 44

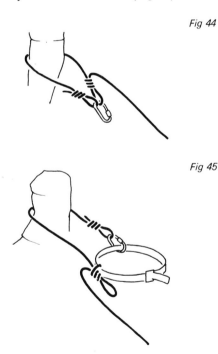

Fig 45

Fig 47 Lifeliner attachment: the most convenient method of attachment

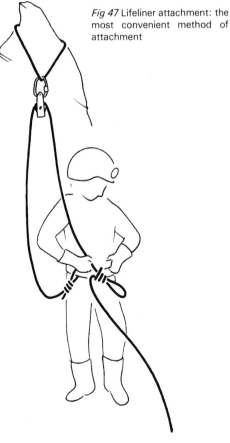

8 Where the double-rope pulley is located in a suitable position for lifelining from the top of the pitch, it is possible to tie directly into it using the previous method (Fig 46). Fixed side pulleys require the rope end threading through them, whereas swing-cheek or strap pulleys may be attached anywhere along the rope.

Lifelining Techniques

Once the lifeliner is securely belayed, the ladder climber fastens onto the other end of the rope. The rope then passes through the lifeliner's guiding hand, around the small of his back and a twist taken around the arm before it is held in the braking hand (Fig 48). The basic principle utilises the friction of the rope wrapped around the lifeliner's body to help control the rope in a fall, which entails tightly gripping the rope and bringing the braking arm across in front of the chest to maximise the friction (Fig 49). The strain on the lifeliner is often severe and the braking hand should be gloved to lessen the chances of his instinctively letting go as the rope cuts into his hand. To ensure that undue strains are not placed upon him while controlling a fall, the lifeliner's belay system must have no slack in it at all, and be arranged in as direct a line as possible to the anticipated load, so that any force is transmitted directly to the anchor (Fig 50). The lifeliner should be far enough back from the pitch lip to obviate any possibility of being dragged over the edge, and in a

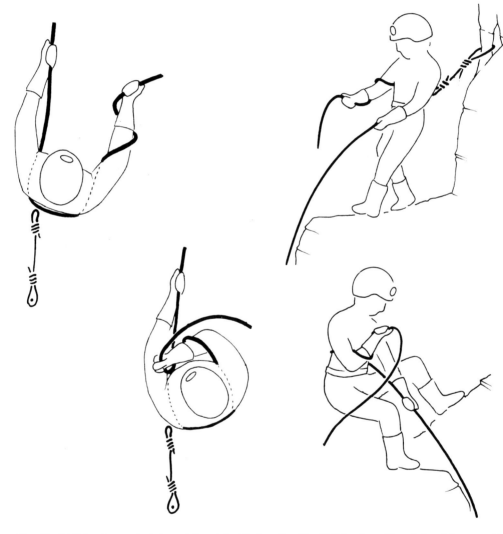

Figs 48 – 9 Lifeliner's rope technique: (*above*) the 'live' end of the rope passes through the lifeliner's left hand and is wrapped around the right arm to act as a brake (or vice versa); (*below*) if the climber slips or falls, the braking arm is whipped across the chest

Figs 50 – 1 Lifeliner's position: (*above*) there must be no slack in the belay sling. The sling and the live rope should be in a direct line; (*below*) a stable stance must be assumed — sitting, or perhaps standing with feet against projections (lifeliner's belay omitted for clarity)

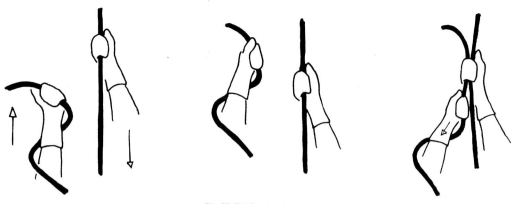

Fig 52 Taking in the rope

stable position sitting down and/or securely braced against any projections (Fig 51).

Top-roping

The active rope is paid out and taken in with the guiding hand; the braking hand is slid along it so that the rope is never completely released. The sequence is as follows: in the rest position the braking hand is held close to the body with the guiding hand a half-metre or so away. As the rope is taken in, both hands move an equal distance in opposite directions. The guiding hand is then returned to its original position where, still gripping the rope, it also temporarily grasps the dead rope in front of the braking hand, allowing the braking hand to be slid back to its original position close to the body (Fig 52). As a climber descends, the life-liner allows the rope to slip through his grip so that the rope between them is just taut: he must not feed the rope out and allow slack to accumulate. This way any fall that does occur should be no more than a metre or so until the rope becomes tight and the lifeliner arrests it. Subsequently the climber is either allowed to regain the ladder or is gently lowered to the foot of the pitch.

With top-roping each member of the party may be safeguarded apart from the lifeliner, who must be protected on his descent from below with the lifeline running through a pulley at the pitch head.

Double-roping

One of the party at the foot of the pitch belays himself to a suitable anchor, out of danger from stone-fall and secure with an upward pull, then takes in the slack rope ready to lifeline the

climber down. The person at the top of the pitch may now release his attachment from the anchor and he should already be fastened to the other end of the rope and is protected by the rope running over the pulley as he climbs down. Both ends of the rope are now at the foot of the pitch with the middle passing over a pulley at the pitch head (Fig 53).

Wherever a double-rope system is arranged for the return, particularly where the rope hangs in a waterfall, the two ends should be tied together, preferably around the ladder. Otherwise falling water tugging at one end of the double rope may work it gradually through the pulley so that the returning cavers find it piled up uselessly at the foot of the pitch.

The reverse procedure is adopted for the ascent. The lifeliner is first up and is protected by the double-rope system as he climbs. Once up he re-establishes his belay at the pitch head and then lifelines the rest of the party in turn. This is basic double-roping – there are variations to suit different situations, intelligent use of which assists progress through the cave. However, the practice of abseiling down the double-rope in order to speed things up is potentially extremely dangerous and can only be condemned as an unsafe practice.

To ensure the smooth operation of a double-rope system, the pulley should be located reasonably close to the ladder and if possible with a clear run down the pitch. A double rope should never be rigged so far back from the pitch head that it twists beneath the ladder, nor hung so that the pulley is below the pitch head. The anchor selected for a pulley needs to be secure in the direction of applied load and ideally twice as strong as the lifeline rope. If a

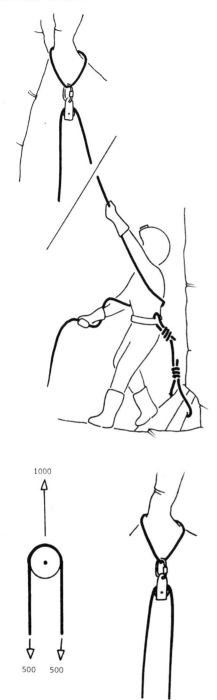

falling climber generates a force of 500kg on his way down, then it requires an equal and opposite force to restrain him! If both these forces are acting in approximately the same direction over a fixed point, in this case a pulley, then the load on the pulley and its anchor is around twice the original force generated, ie 1000kg (Fig 54).

Body Ballast
Many caves exhibit a lack of anchor points at the foot of pitches suitable for lifelining from below, and so far I have yet to see a bolt installed for this purpose (not that I want to!). Where there is no anchor available at the foot of a pitch to provide a belay for a double rope, one or two of the party may simply attach themselves to the lifeliner as additional 'ballast'. Perhaps the most convenient way of doing this is by linking harness karabiners and, provided that the combined lifeliner and 'ballast' are substantially heavier than the ladder climber, the system is functional and safe.

Pullback System
When a team is returning up a pitch by lifelining from above in the conventional manner, the rope has to be returned to the foot of the pitch after each man. If the rope is lowered down there is a chance of it getting snagged up, or threaded through the ladder. It is better to coil the rope loosely and throw it down the pitch out away from the ladder. Should it prove difficult to get the rope down due to the shape of the shaft, then a pullback system may be arranged. The rope needs to be twice the length of the pitch and each climber ties on in the middle of it, generally with a figure-eight loop to the harness karabiner. As each climber reaches the top and unclips, those at the bottom can easily pull the rope back down.

Bottom-lining Assistance
Where the pitch head is awkward or constricted, it may be easier to lifeline all except the last man from below on the double rope. Apart from its protective role the lifeline may also be used to assist the climber on long or difficult pitches by means of a steady pull on the rope. The lifeliner himself should act as 'anchor man' by lifelining in the normal manner, with

Fig 53 – 4 Lining from the base of a pitch: (*above*) the lifeliner must be securely belayed, held by another caver, and/or have a number of people helping with the taking-in; (*below*) with a fall on a double line, the force on the belay (everything above the pulley) will be the sum of those in the two sides of the lifeline — beware!

additional people pulling on the rope in front of him as he takes it in. Double-roping from the foot of a pitch, these helpers may stand and pull hand over hand on the rope like bell-ringers, though at a pitch head they must be belayed or at least well back from the edge. Such a belay is easily arranged using a spare rope with figure-eight loops tied in it at intervals for each person to clip into.

The idea is not to drag somebody forcibly up the pitch, but to provide a steady assisting pull of around 20–25kg. Heaving and jerking on the rope are more of a hindrance than a help.

Direct Belaying

The methods described so far are the traditional British techniques of lifelining, which form the means by which most novices are introduced to caving. However, these techniques are outdated, clumsy and inefficient, and the security they afford is largely illusory. The majority of vertical caving accidents in this country result from mismanagement of these techniques. Consider a few points:

1 The intrinsic safety of the lifeline system depends almost entirely on the lifeline man's handling of the rope; if he is tired, distracted or just incompetent, safety is at risk.
2 What is to be gained by interposing a caver between the lifeline and the belay? This is a weak link in the system. Should a fall occur the lifeliner either lets go or, if he is able to arrest the fall, is then trapped within the lifeline system. He is unable to do anything other than lower the fallen climber, and in certain situations he is powerless.
3 The lifeliner (as well as the climber) is at risk if a fall occurs, and if his belay fails he will also end up at the bottom of the pitch.

Far better if the lifeline is attached directly to the belay by some mechanical device and the lifeliner stands alongside and controls the rope passing through it. The two main advantages here are:

1 Such devices are far stronger than any caver; they do not fail, and any load is transmitted directly to the anchor with no strain on the operator. The lifeline system is therefore much stronger.

2 The operator is not trapped within the system; he can with minimal effort lower the fallen climber or anchor him securely to the belay and then be free to go to his aid.

Descenders/Jammers
Mountaineers have used mechanical belay devices to good effect for years, and there are various gadgets available designed specifically for this purpose (Fig 55).

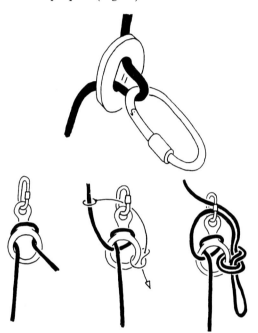

Figs 55 – 6 Lifeline controllers: descenders. (*Above*) a Sticht Plate — often used by mountaineers — rarely used underground; (*below*) if the lifeline is passed through a descender, effective and easy holding of a fallen climber is possible. The rope can be easily locked-off

Certain of these are described under climbing techniques (Chapter 2, page 29), but these are specialised tools, rarely used underground. Much more practical is the use of the conventional descender or karabiner, basic equipment for every caver. Running the rope through a descender anchored to the belay upside down is an effective method of lifelining (Figs 56, 57). A fallen climber is easily held, lowered, or the descender 'locked off', enabling the lifeliner to leave the rope and organise some means of rescue. Some 'self-lock' descenders work particularly well for this technique and may also form the basis of a simple hauling system

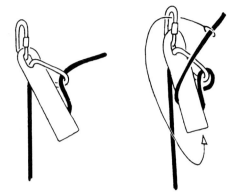

Fig 57 Lifeline controllers: descenders. These devices should only be used on 'straightforward' pitches, since their inherent friction makes it impossible for the lifeliner to assist the climber with a strong pull

Fig 58 Lifeline controllers: arrangements for hauling. (Left) lifelining with auto-lock descender — note different rope path; (right) conversion to simple haul system to assist a tired climber or haul a fallen climber

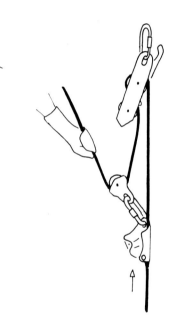

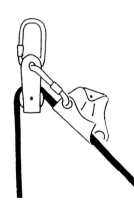

Fig 59 Lifeline controllers: jammers. The main disadvantage of using a jammer in the system is that it may be impossible to lower the person on the other end of the rope!

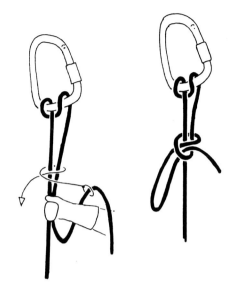

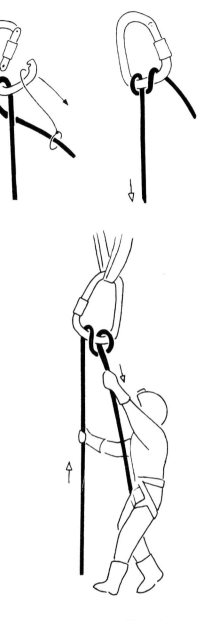

Figs 60–2 Lifeline controllers: friction knots. (*Above left*) the Italian Hitch: an extremely useful knot for lifelining; (*below left*) a simple two-handed operation will take in slack rope as the climber ascends. A sudden fall reverses the knot, and the rope is easily held with one hand; (*above*) the hitch can easily be locked-off, or by feeding rope into it the climber can be lowered to the base of the pitch

extremely well, but is comparatively weak (perhaps 400kg) and, as a jammer operates only in one direction, it will not function as a lowering device. Once it is loaded you must then find some means of lifting the load before the jammer can be released. There are ways and means (see Chapter 4, page 90) but if you are alone at the pitch head when the ladder breaks with neither the strength nor skill to lift the fallen climber, then he is stuck in an unenviable position.

Italian Hitch

The best lifelining method requires no special equipment, and consists of just a simple knot tied around a karabiner. There are many ingenious methods of belaying using various configurations of rope and karabiner to form 'self-locking' knots, which run easily in one direction but not the other. The safest and most adaptable is a versatile 'friction' hitch known in Britain as the 'Italian hitch', easily recognised by its distinctive rope-across-rope friction contact. The easiest method of forming the hitch around a karabiner is that shown in Fig

should it prove necessary (Fig 58).

A disadvantage of descenders is that they are designed to create friction along the path of the rope. This inevitably gives some drag when taking up the slack rope; and direct hauling through the device, perhaps to assist a tired climber, is not possible. .

An alternative method uses a pulley/jammer arrangement, such as might be used for hauling tackle from a long pitch (Fig 59). This works

37

60. The hitch allows the rope to move in only one direction controlled by friction created by tension in the non-loaded rope. With this friction and the 'tightening' effect on the karabiner, you can arrest even a very severe fall with one hand. In addition, while unloaded, the hitch is reversible; by pulling on the non-loaded side it will rotate through 180° around the karabiner and, thus inverted, the rope will slip in the opposite direction. It is a simple matter to take in the slack rope as the climber ascends, using one hand to lift the load rope and the other to pull it through the hitch (Fig 61). Should the climber fall, the knot will automatically reverse itself, and holding the non-loaded rope will then arrest the fall with little effort. Subsequently either the climb can be resumed, the hitch 'locked off' (Fig 62), or by releasing rope into the hitch the climber can be lowered.

Nothing could be simpler or more effective, but bear in mind two points: firstly, the reversing action of the Italian hitch is essential to its operation and the karabiner must be wide enough across its base to allow this – there are karabiners made specifically for the purpose; secondly, ensure that the running rope does not undo the locking sleeve of the karabiner.

Even though these techniques are a great improvement on the traditional method, the basic concept of lifelining from the top of the pitch is suspect in itself. The fact that the rope travels up and down the pitch with each climber creates communication and rope-retrieval problems and the need for at least two people to operate the system. The greatest danger lies in the fact that the rope is not fixed; security for the climber is entirely dependent on the lifeliner, who may or may not be doing the job properly. Apart from the lifeline, the climber is clinging with his bare hands to a ladder system with an overall strength of perhaps 200kg or 300kg. Far better if the rope is fixed in the pitch alongside the ladder and each climber protects himself by trailing a jammer solidly attached to his harness along the rope as he climbs – this is the technique of self-lining.

Self-lining

The rope is fixed in the pitch parallel to the ladder. It is used for abseiling during the descent and to safeguard the ascent by trailing a jammer along the rope attached to the climber's harness. In order to stop, to make some adjustment or to rest, the climber clips himself to the ladder with a short cow's-tail and rests in his sit-harness.

Self-lining has many advantages:

1 The technique is much faster than conventional lifelining and also requires less rope.
2 Manoeuvres with the rope are eliminated and the necessary communications reduced to a minimum.
3 The climber no longer depends on the expertise of the lifeliner; he looks after himself, and because both the ladder and rope are solidly anchored, he is safe.

Should the climber lose his grip or the ladder fail, he will simply hang from the jammer. Here it is essential that the caver wears a sit-harness, carries a descender while climbing and is able to use this to abseil back down to the foot of the pitch. There are various straightforward release techniques which make this possible, but without this option the caver might find himself dangling dangerously in mid-pitch, possibly under a waterfall.

Equipment
Basic self-lining equipment consists of a sit-harness, long and short cow's-tails, descender and jammer, and a few karabiners (Fig 63). A chest-harness is generally not necessary, except with certain types of jammer (Fig 64) where both SRT and ladders are being used in the same cave.

Rigging
The rope is rigged in much the same fashion as for SRT (Fig 65). The main requirements are the use of double belays at each pitch, provision of a traverse-line where necessary, and the use of bolts and intermediate anchors to arrange a safe hang and avoid abrasion.

The ladder is rigged to one of the anchors supporting the pitch rope. Wire tethers and slings are rarely used, the ladder being attached to the same point as the rope.

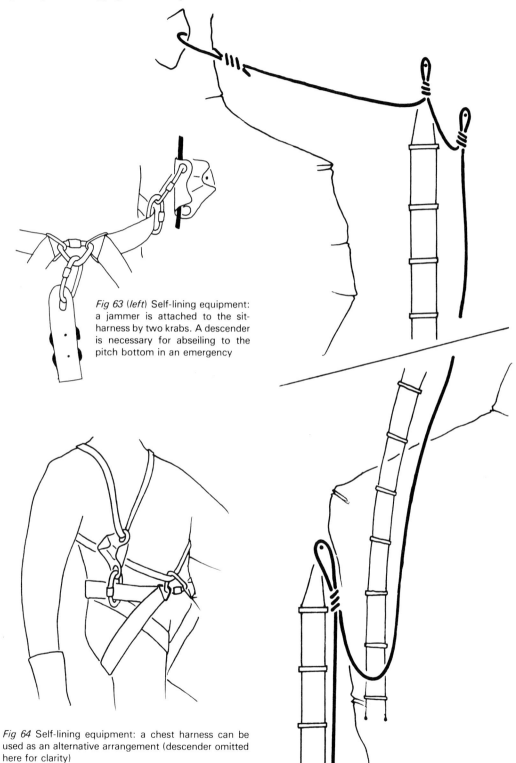

Fig 65 (*right*) Pitch rigging for self-lining

Fig 63 (*left*) Self-lining equipment: a jammer is attached to the sit-harness by two krabs. A descender is necessary for abseiling to the pitch bottom in an emergency

Fig 64 Self-lining equipment: a chest harness can be used as an alternative arrangement (descender omitted here for clarity)

Descent

The pitch is approached with the long cow's-tail clipped into the traverse line for safety, or, where the pitch is very easy of access, into the karabiner holding the rope. The descender is installed on the rope and locked off – the caver then double-checks the equipment in the pitch (bolts tight, krabs screwed up etc) and his own equipment (harness properly fastened, krabs/*Maillon Rapides* screwed up, descender correctly loaded, etc). When satisfied that all is well he unclips the cow's-tail and begins the descent. Intermediate anchors are

passed in the normal manner by hanging from the short cow's-tail while the descender is transferred to the lower rope (Fig 66). Here using the ladder makes releasing the cow's-tail particularly easy.

Tight vertical sections where the descender creates problems by digging into the chest are more simply passed by abseiling with the descender attached to the short cow's-tail. Bear in mind that with the descender at about head height, long hair and unkempt beards are liabilities (Fig 67).

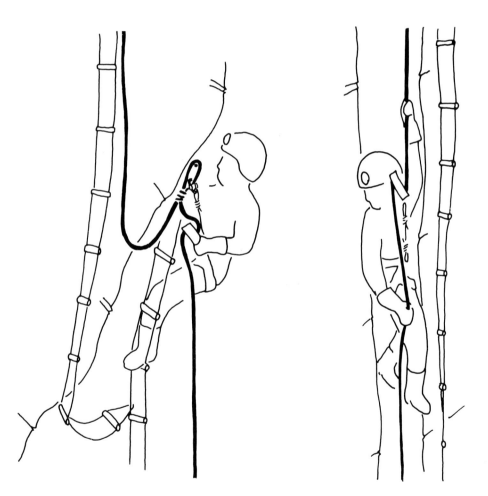

Figs 66 – 7 Self-lining: descent. (*Left*) intermediate anchors are passed by using a short cow's-tail; (*right*) tight sections can be more easily negotiated by having the descender attached to a short cow's-tail

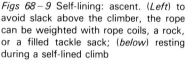

Figs 68 – 9 Self-lining: ascent. (*Left*) to avoid slack above the climber, the rope can be weighted with rope coils, a rock, or a filled tackle sack; (*below*) resting during a self-lined climb

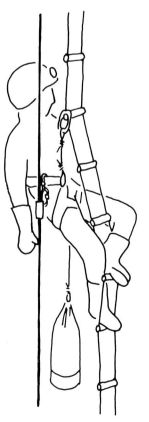

Ascent

The jammer is installed on the rope and attached to the harness, either by a single karabiner and D-ring or by two karabiners (Fig 61). The jammer should not be clipped directly to the harness with a single karabiner, as this causes it to twist on the rope. Trailing the jammer on a sling is also dangerous, since you risk a fall-factor 2 fall (albeit a small one) should you come off the ladder. An ovoid or pear-shaped krab makes clipping in and out of the jammer much easier.

Before climbing check that the jammer is running freely and jamming correctly, and that you have a descender clipped to your harness in case you have to get down again.

With a slack rope it may initially be necessary to stop every few metres and pull the rope through until it runs of its own accord. It is important not to accumulate slack rope as you climb, because of the large shock-load that would result if you fell. You can avoid this by weighting the rope with a tackle-sack, a coil of rope or a suitable rock (Fig 68).

Tackle is carried at the side, clipped to the waist-belt or the harness where it does not catch on the ladder. In tight sections it can be dangled beneath on a hauling cord.

To rest during the climb, clip the short cow's-tail around one of the ladder cables and sit back in your harness, rest your feet on the ladder and let your arms dangle to restore circulation (Fig 69).

At the top of the pitch, attach the long cow's-tail to the belay or the traverse-line before releasing the jammer from the rope. On a steeply sloping traverse-line, attach yourself first to the belay with the short cow's-tail, transfer the jammer to the traverse-line and clip into this with the long cow's-tail. Transfer the short cow's-tail to the traverse-line so that you can self-line yourself along the traverse line by sliding the jammer ahead. Where the traverse line is anchored midway, use both cow's-tails on the rope and transfer one past the anchor before unclipping the other.

Muddy Rope

With muddy ropes there is a danger that a sprung-cam jammer might slip and not grip the rope sufficiently to stop a fall. Cleaning the cam is generally ineffective and under these conditions only certain cam-loaded jammers attached to the harness are safe (Fig 70).

Release Technique

Should the ladder break or the caver fall off it, he will simply dangle from the rope held by the jammer. In a good harness under favourable conditions he can sit there comfortably for a while; can wait for his mates to replace the ladder with another, or have some SRT gear slid down the rope. Under a waterfall, however, survival time may be very limited. To be safe he must be able to redescend to the foot of the pitch without delay. Self-lining without this ability to abseil back down is equivalent to suicide.

The release technique, though simple, needs practice before it will help you in an emergency. Dangling from a rope deep underground is the wrong place to make mistakes. Proceed as follows:

1 While hanging from the jammer, connect the descender to the front of the harness (if not already in place).

2 Improvise a stirrup by wrapping the rope around your boot three or four times on the opposite side to the jammer. Pass the rope behind the calf first and cover the first wraps with the subsequent ones to prevent them slipping. Alternatively complete the wraps with a half-hitch, or tie a clove-hitch around your boot (Fig 71).

3 Lift this boot a little and install the descender on the rope immediately beneath the jammer.

4 Place the free boot on top of the other, stand up and release the cam of the jammer, securing the safety catch (if any) in the open position. Detach the jammer from your harness by unclipping the karabiner from the D-ring (Fig 72).

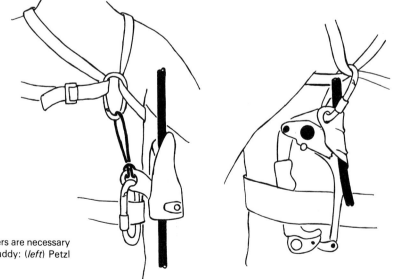

Fig 70 Cam-loaded jammers are necessary when the rope is very muddy: (*left*) Petzl 'shunt'; (*right*) Bonaiti

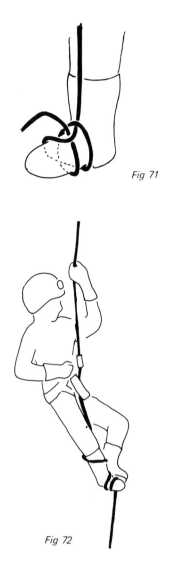

Fig 71

Fig 72

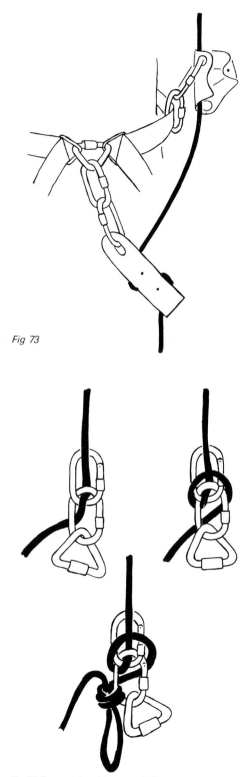

Fig 73

5 Transfer your weight to the descender (a self-lock descender is most suitable), clip the rope into a braking krab if necessary, undo the stirrup and begin the descent. The jammer, which is locked open, is left to slide down the rope on top of the descender.

A few general points: releasing the jammer from the rope is often made easier by attaching the descender with two karabiners instead of one (Fig 73). The same release technique is also possible without a descender using crossed karabiners (Fig 74) or an Italian hitch (Fig 75). From the foot of the pitch, provided there is someone at the top, you can recover the ladders and have them hauled back up on the rope. If

Fig 74 Crossed karabiners technique

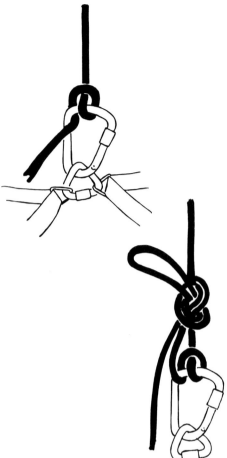

Fig 75 Italian Hitch method

not you will need to improvise an SRT rig and climb out or find somewhere comfortable and wait for help.

Self-rescue

Although much safer than the traditional method of protecting a ladder climber, self-lining techniques are not infallible. When things do go wrong, exactly as in SRT, safety is linked to mastery of self-rescue techniques (See Chapter 4, page 90 et seq).

Self-rescue techniques allow you to recover the helpless victim of an accident from mid-rope where he would certainly die, and also enable somewhat fitter cavers to get out of the cave unaided instead of dying of cold. The value of any such technical exercise depends heavily on having previously practised it safely on the surface. Improperly carried out these

rescue techniques could well kill someone. But a successful escape from one dangerous situation will repay hours of patient practice.

Signals

Clear and concise communications from the top of a pitch to the bottom are a great aid to efficiency and safety, particularly with lifelining where the security of a climber depends on the person holding the rope.

Climbing Calls
Where verbal contact is possible a system of spoken or shouted climbing calls is adequate:

1 'Take-in' (climber) indicates that the climber is fastened onto the rope and waiting for the slack rope to be taken in.
2 'Taking in' (lifeliner) means that the lifeliner is belayed and is taking in the slack rope.
3 'That's me' (climber) indicates that the rope is taut to the climber.
4 'Climb when ready' (lifeliner) signals that the lifeliner is ready for the climber to ascend.
5 'Climbing' (climber) indicates that the climber is ready to ascend.
6 'OK' (lifeliner) verifies that the lifeliner has heard and is taking in.

Additional calls such as 'Slack' may be used by the climber when he wants more rope paid out or 'Take-in' when he wants spare rope pulled in. Do not shout 'Take-in slack', since the life-liner may hear only the last part and let out the rope instead.

Whistle Signals
Where verbal communication is difficult due to the length or shape of a shaft or excessive noise from falling water, whistle signals are more audible. Each member of a team should carry a whistle around his neck in such circumstances.

One blast   = 'Stop'
Two blasts = 'Up'
Three blasts = 'Down'

This system fails to safety in that should all the whistle blasts not be heard, the rope is held or taken in, rather than paid out. The same code could apply to visual signals made by flashing a lamp in the rare event of a line of sight being possible.

The warning call 'Below' is used when anything accidentally falls or before anything is thrown down a pitch.

Self-lining and SRT

With self-lining and SRT, where each climber is largely independent, the only signal likely to be needed is one to indicate when a rope is cleared ready for the next abseiler or climber. The call is 'Rope-free' or four whistle blasts.

Emergency Call

Probably the best (and the most likely) emergency call is 'Help'. Where this cannot be heard all the way to the cave rescue organisation depot, the international emergency call is six short whistle blasts repeated at one-minute intervals, or alternatively a longish continuous signal repeated at intervals.

3 SRT Equipment

DAVID ELLIOT

As a natural development of traditional ladder and travelling lifeline techniques, through self-lining systems employing a fixed lifeline, further techniques were evolved where both the ladder and reliance on other cavers could be dispensed with.

Single-rope techniques (SRT) describe the passage of vertical pitches by means of a single fixed rope, using specialised equipment and the associated techniques of abseiling and prusiking. The advantages of SRT are far reaching, especially in that the tackle requirements are greatly reduced, making exploration possible for very small teams of cavers, which in turn implies greater freedom and speed of movement. The radical advancement of these techniques during the last decade has meant that currently SRT in one form or another is used almost exclusively for the exploration of deep cave systems throughout the world. Ladders and lifelines are reserved for occasional short or awkward pitches and for use by novices.

There has been a complete change of emphasis in terms of safety between the two techniques. Unlike the ladder/travelling lifeline system where each caver is dependent on a remotely operated lifeline, protected and partly assisted by his team-mates, in SRT the emphasis is on self-reliance and freedom of movement. Every caver must therefore be competent in the necessary skills and in all other respects capable of looking after himself. Single-rope-techniques, very much single-person-techniques, foster a healthier attitude with regard to training and safety than ladders and lifelines ever did.

It is beyond the scope of this and the next chapter to encompass all the skills and background knowledge fundamental to SRT, or the relative merits of the different techniques and associated hardware. However, some of the equipment, certain of the most commonly used climbing techniques and the methods of rigging pitches for SRT are outlined. Further skills require background reading, training and a deeper understanding of the factors involved: anyone not prepared to make this sort of commitment to personal safety should consider some other form of recreation. This chapter describes the basic SRT equipment and outlines its capabilities, some understanding of which is essential to safety. Caving equipment is subject to harsh use under far from ideal conditions, but is designed to require only the minimum of maintenance. All that any of this equipment needs to keep it in working order is washing and drying; this should never be neglected.

Harnesses

A caver's harness is his means of suspension from the rope. It must allow sufficient freedom over the range of movements involved in his style of climbing and not hinder general moving around between pitches. It needs to be strong and secure enough to sustain the shock-loads developed in a fall (potentially up to 12kn) without serious failure or damage to the caver. It must also be durable enough to withstand hard use in caves and still remain safe.

Sit-harness

SRT dictates the use of a sit-harness as the basic means of support in order to direct the caver's weight onto the thigh and buttock region where it is most safely and comfortably taken. Straps under the crotch are generally not a good idea and 'leg-loop' type harnesses are perhaps the best designs (Fig 76). A further refinement is a retaining strap which will prevent the loops slipping down the legs while crawling (Fig 77).

Fig 77 A retaining strap prevents the leg-loops from slipping whilst crawling

Chest-harness

The function of a chest-harness varies with different systems, but in general they are required to either tow a body-mounted jammer (Fig 78), or hold the climber upright on the rope (Fig 79). Designs also vary, but whatever the system and whatever the chest-harness, it must be used only in conjunction with a sit-harness and the two linked so that any load is transmitted directly to the sit-harness (Fig 78). Hanging from a chest-harness alone is extremely dangerous; compression of the rib-cage may lead to unconsciousness and death within minutes.

Another important safety factor is that the main point of attachment at the front of any harness should not consist solely of a karabiner, which in this position is often subject to a three-way loading. This is almost certain to stress the gate section of the karabiner, which is its weakest point and may fail at very low loads, perhaps as little as 300kg. Far better to link the harness with a screw-sleeved *Maillon Rapide* (M/R) of 9mm or 10mm diameter, which is not only far stronger but may be loaded in any direction without significant loss of strength (Fig 80). One further precaution is to arrange the opening sleeve of the M/R at the bottom (Fig 81) so that the result is not disastrous should the sleeve work loose. It makes sense to cultivate the habit of checking this now and then.

Harnesses are invariably made from nylon or polyester webbing. Nylon is generally considered the best harness material, except where there may be chemical contamination from battery acid. In these circumstances a polyester (acid-resistant) harness might be

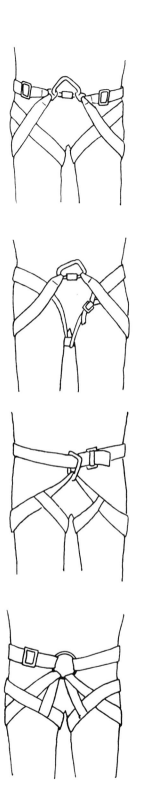

Fig 76 Leg-loop-type sit-harnesses

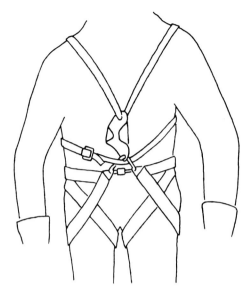

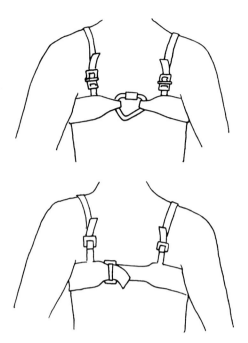

Fig 78 Chest harness used to tow a body-mounted jammer. Note that the chest-harness is linked to the sit-harness to ensure that the load is transmitted to the latter

Fig 79 Chest harness for keeping the climber upright

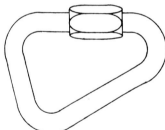

Figs 80–1 Main attachment point: (above) a *Maillon Rapide* should be used as the main point of harness/descender attachment; (right) if the *Maillon Rapide* sleeve becomes unscrewed, then this arrangement (with the gate at the bottom) should not prove disastrous

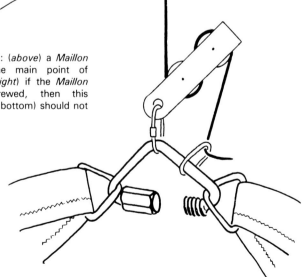

considered desirable, and the converse applies in the case of strong alkalies such as Ni-Cad electrolytes – although in either case the only safe solution is to avoid absolutely any such contamination.

Descenders

Abseiling is the skill of sliding down a fixed rope under full control, and a descender is the brake or friction device that converts kinetic (movement) energy to heat and makes this possible. The rope is threaded around the descender attached to the sit-harness and the device then provides almost all the friction needed to control the descent, only light hand pressure being required in addition. The braking power of a device is a function of the friction created between itself and the rope and is affected by the caver gripping the rope and the weight of the rope beneath.

Simple Descenders

There are three descenders in general use amongst British cavers, the Figure-8, the Rack and the Petzl (Fig 82). The well-known Figure-8 device is a rock-climber's tool generally unsuited to SRT, while both the Rack and Petzl were specifically developed for single-rope techniques and function a great deal better as a result. The Petzl is probably superior to the Rack on almost all counts apart from ease of control on extremely long free-hanging pitches, over 150m. As pitches are usually split into sections no longer than about 50m, we can probably discount the Rack as having anything special to offer.

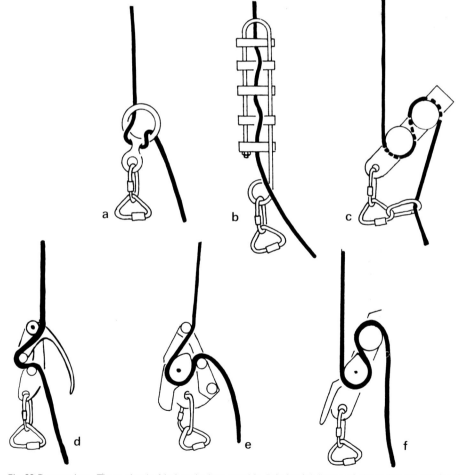

Fig 82 Descenders. Three simple friction devices used in Britain: (a) figure-of-eight; (b) 'Rack'; (c) 'Petzl'. *Fig 83* Descenders. Three self-locking devices — releasing the handle stops the descent: (d) Lewis 'Self Lock'; (e) 'Multiscender'; (f) Petzl 'Stop'

Auto-lock Descenders

Apart from these conventional descenders, there are many self-locking descenders designed specifically for caving. The three main designs are shown (Fig 83). Each has an integral handle which allows the device to function more or less as a conventional descender; releasing the handle, however, causes an eccentric cam to lock onto the rope and halt the descent. This feature obviates the need to lock off the descender manually during manoeuvres and also acts as a fail-safe in an emergency. Such descenders doubtless indicate the shape of things to come, although they have yet to gain widespread acceptance and certain designs are dubious. One possible disadvantage of existing designs arises from the need to release the handle for the device to lock onto the rope, whereas a thoughtless or panicking caver might instinctively grip the handle tighter and worsen the situation.

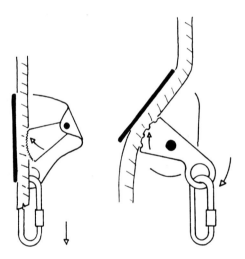

Figs 84 – 5 Ascending devices: method of working (*left*) sprung-cam ascender; (*right*) cam-loaded ascender

Jammers

Fundamental to any rope-climbing system are jamming devices which will slide up the rope then lock and not slide back down it. All jammers work on the same basic principle: a cam traps the rope against the body of the device when a directional load is applied. These devices are of two main types: (1) those in which the load is taken on the body of the device and the cam is initially operated by a spring – sprung-cam devices (Figs 84, 86) and

(2) those where the load is applied directly to the pivoted cam by a lever action – cam-loaded devices (Figs 85, 87).

All these jammers are by and large interchangeable and a few trials will determine what works best with a particular climbing rig. Sprung-cam jammers, while much easier and quicker to put on the rope, rely on a toothed cam to grip the rope initially and may slip on muddy or iced-up ropes, whereas cam-loaded devices do not. However, most cam-loaded devices have a tendency to slide down the rope while not loaded. Typically, sprung-cam jammers fail at around 400kg or 500kg by the action of the cam cutting into the rope; cam-loaded jammers tend to fail at higher levels (apart from the Shunt, which slips at around 250kg) by slipping down the rope without much damage.

Whatever the type of jammer and however carefully used, sooner or later for one reason or another it will fail. In a rig using only two jammers this is a serious matter and there is much to be said for incorporating a third jammer into the rig or at least carrying a spare.

Karabiners

Karabiners ('krabs') are available in both steel and aluminium alloys in a multitude of colours, shapes and sizes. Any screwgate krab with a breaking load of 2000kg or more is suitable for use underground and many uses may be met by a lesser specification. Steel krabs are harder wearing than alloy and withstand cave usage much better. Running a dirty rope over an alloy krab will soon wear and weaken it. Alloy krabs score only where weight is important. All krabs are strongest loaded along the major axis (end to end) and weakest when loaded sideways across the gate (minor axis) (Fig 88). Here the load is transferred to the hinge-pin which is only 2mm or 3mm in diameter and may fail at very low levels. The quoted breaking load of a karabiner represents low tensile loading along the major axis, and certain manufacturers, though not all, also quote a figure for the minor axis (across the gate), with the locking sleeve screwed up in both cases. The strength of a 'pin and slot' type latch (Fig 88) remains the same whether or not the sleeve is screwed up, although its intrinsic security will be lessened. With the somewhat outdated 'cross-type' latch (Fig 89) the krab may

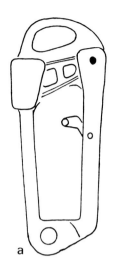
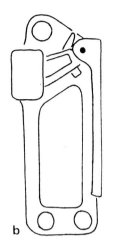

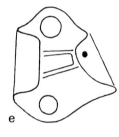

Fig 86 Ascending devices
Available sprung-cam types:
(a) Jumar
(b) CMI
(c) Petzl-handled jammer
(d) Petzl 'Bloquer'
(e) Clog
(f) Petzl 'Croll'

a

b

c

d

e

f

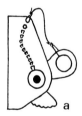
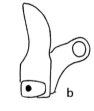
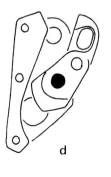

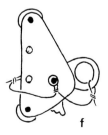

Fig 87 Ascending devices
Available cam-loaded types:
(a) Gibbs
(b) Shunt
(c) Hiebler
(d) Multiscender 2DL
(e) Bonaiti
(f) Lewis 'Roller'

a

b

c

d

e

f

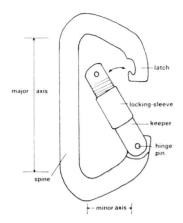
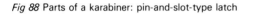

Fig 88 Parts of a karabiner: pin-and-slot-type latch

only reach 50 per cent of its quoted load if the sleeve is not screwed up. Under dirty conditions mud may prevent the latch from closing properly, and both types of karabiner are equally weak if the latch is not engaged and the krab acts simply as a hook, reaching perhaps only 25 per cent of its quoted breaking load. Bear in mind also that these figures apply to new karabiners: none of them get any stronger with wear!

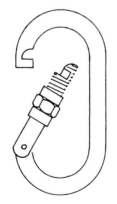

Fig 89 Karabiner with cross-type latch

Damaged or suspect karabiners should be broken and disposed of rather than delegated to non-critical uses such as tackle-hauling. If kept, such krabs invariably find their way dangerously back into the system when gear runs short on a trip.

Maillon Rapides

Maillon Rapides are solid metal links closed by a sturdy screwed sleeve and thus capable of with-

standing a load applied in any direction (Fig 90). They are used wherever a strong, secure fastening is required that need not be opened and closed frequently. *Maillons* are extremely weak when the sleeve is not screwed up; moreover, even slight loading in this condition will distort the body sufficiently to prevent the sleeve from being properly fastened subsequently. Although screwing the sleeve up fingertight is adequate for most purposes, you need to carry a spanner to deal with the occasional stiff one.

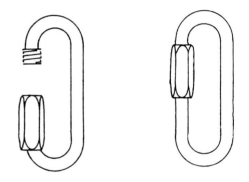

Fig 90 A *Maillon Rapide*. This must only be loaded with the sleeve closed

Bolt-anchors

SRT and the implicit need to avoid rope abrasion demand that strong anchor points are available exactly where they are required. Occasionally natural rock features may prove suitable, or cracks where chocks or pitons might be placed; natural anchors are often useful for traverse lines and back-up belays where the

Fig 91 Self-drilling anchor

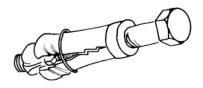

Fig 92 'Rawlbolt' anchor

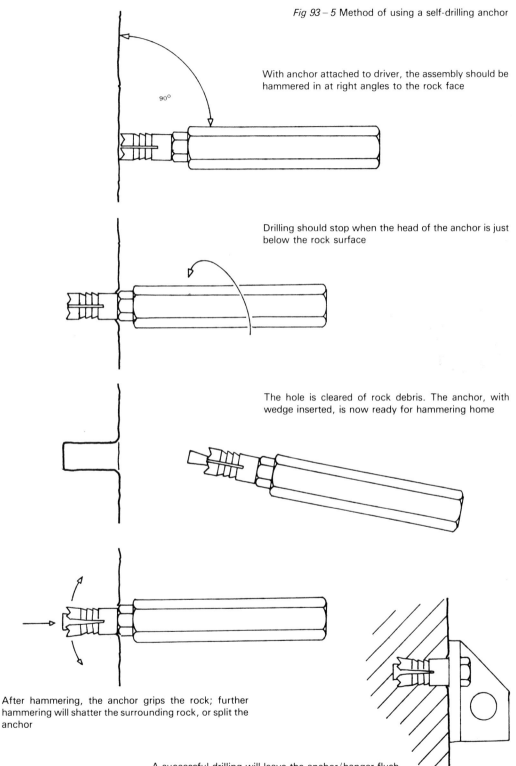

Fig 93 – 5 Method of using a self-drilling anchor

With anchor attached to driver, the assembly should be hammered in at right angles to the rock face

90°

Drilling should stop when the head of the anchor is just below the rock surface

The hole is cleared of rock debris. The anchor, with wedge inserted, is now ready for hammering home

After hammering, the anchor grips the rock; further hammering will shatter the surrounding rock, or split the anchor

A successful drilling will leave the anchor/hanger flush with the rock

exact position is not critical, but it is almost always necessary to rig the rope in the pitch from bolts.

Types of Bolts
All of the many different types of bolts require an accurately sized hole to be drilled in the rock, and all depend on some form of expansion device within the hole for their security. Two types of fastening are commonly used: the fixed 8mm self-drilling anchor (Fig 91), and the Rawlbolt type of removable anchor (Fig 92).

8mm Self-drilling Anchor Self-drilling anchors are made from hardened tubular steel, with cutting teeth at one end and threaded to accept an 8mm diameter bolt at the other (Fig 91). The hole is drilled directly into the rock by fitting the anchor to an adaptor tool (driver) and using this as a percussion drill (Fig 92). By repeated blows with a light hammer while the driver is rotated clockwise, the cutting teeth bite at a different place each time and the hole is deepened. You need to remove the drill from the hole frequently to clear the powdered rock, by tapping it out of the anchor and blowing the hole clear by means of a short length of plastic tubing. It takes between ten and twenty minutes to drill the hole depending on location and the nature of the rock.

Select an area of sound rock free from any fissures or veins of calcite and, with the hammer, clean the immediate area of any weathered surface-rock or irregularities. It is important to drill at right angles to this surface so the hanger will rest correctly against the rock

and not stress the bolt unnecessarily. The first few millimetres of drilling are the most critical; care is needed to keep the cutting teeth in exactly the same position until the hole is deep enough to guide the drill (about 6mm). Continue drilling until the full length of the anchor is just below the surface of sound rock (about 2mm) (Fig 92), then remove and clear both the anchor and the hole completely of any spoil. Lightly press the conical expansion wedge into the end of the anchor (Fig 93) and replace it in the hole; then, this time without rotating the driver, hammer the anchor home (Fig 94). This forces the cone into the anchor, causing it to expand and grip the sides of the hole. Do not overhammer, as once the anchor is properly set excessive hammering is likely to split the anchor or flake off the surrounding rock. Unscrew the driver, check the anchor, insert a little grease (to combat corrosion) and fit a high-tensile bolt and a hanger (Fig 95). A spanner will be needed for tightening.

Do not Overtighten the Bolt A bolt breaks when the total force applied (load plus tightening force) exceeds its breaking load. By overtightening, the load which can be supported is reduced – finger-tight plus half a turn with a spanner is sufficient.

A few general points: it is important that the hole is drilled deep enough so that the anchor does not protrude unsupported from the rock (Fig 96). To be hard enough for drilling, these anchors are extremely brittle and may snap off under such conditions. Equally bad is a cone-shaped hole caused by careless drilling, since

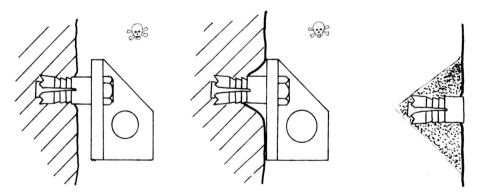

Figs 96 – 8 Dangerous drilling practice: (*left*) the anchor can snap if the hole is of insufficient depth; (*centre*) the anchor is stressed due to careless drilling; (*right*) the shaded area represents stressed rock. There should be no cracks near this area

the anchor is stressed rather than the surrounding rock (Fig 97). Where the rock is soft, for instance flowstone, the expansion cone may be driven into the base of the hole instead of the anchor; also if the hole has been drilled over-large the sheath will not expand sufficiently to grip the sides. The anchor grips by stressing the surrounding rock (Fig 98) and will split it if located too close to cracks or edges or in thinly-bedded rocks.

Hangers

Bolt-hangers permit the rope to be attached to the fixed anchor by means of a high-tensile steel bolt (set-screw). The function of a hanger is to transfer the load via the anchor to the rock without excessively stressing the fixing bolt. This means that the bolt is loaded in 'shear' (ie perpendicular to the bolt) and the hanger design should minimise any leverage or bending action on the bolt. The most common types of hanger consist of a shaped metal plate to which the rope is attached by a karabiner or *Maillon Rapide*. The shape of the hanger and its attachment hole determine the orientation of the krab in relation to the rock surface. There are two main configurations: (1) where the krab

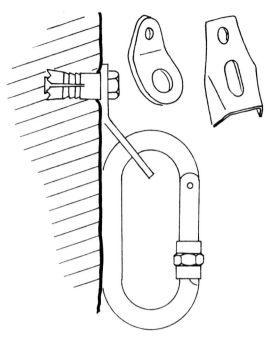

Fig 100 Plate hangers with karabiner perpendicular to the rock

lies parallel to the rock (Fig 99) and (2) where the krab sits against the rock at right-angles (Fig 100).

(1) These are the most common types of general-purpose hanger, used wherever the loading is more or less perpendicular to the bolt. A disadvantage is that, being close to the rock, the knot of the attached rope may sometimes abrade, though often this can be avoided by adding a second krab to extend the attachment and turn the rope through 90° (Fig 101). Use: general purpose.

(2) A more specialised style of hanger primarily designed for use with symmetrical oval karabiners, where the krab rests against the rock at right-angles and serves to hang the rope clear of the surrounding rock. Where this is not the case and the karabiner hangs free, the hanger may be severely stressed (Fig 102). In certain locations this hanger might be used to support loads at an angle of up to 45° away from the rock (Fig 103), but careful thought must be given to the forces involved. There are hangers of this type intended only for use with 7mm diameter *Maillon Rapides*, which are similar but smaller and should not be confused with those intended for oval karabiners. Use:

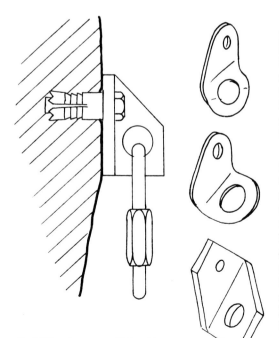

Fig 99 Plate hangers with karabiner parallel to the rock

Hanger problems:

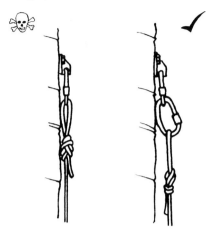

Fig 101 Knot abrasion and a cure

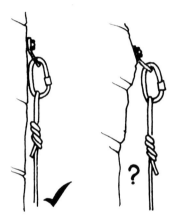

Fig 102 Careful consideration must be given to the forces stressing the hanger

Fig 103 Careful consideration must be given to the forces pulling the hanger and bolt

intermediate anchors; Y-anchors.

(3) There are various types of hanger requiring neither krab nor *Maillon Rapide* where the rope is fixed directly to the hanger. This has certain advantages:

1 Substantial weight-saving – no krabs.
2 Elimination of a potential weak point in the krab gate.
3 Direction of applied load is less critical.
4 Often the strength of the belay is substantially increased.

The most widely known hangers of this type are CAT, Ring-hanger, Bollard hanger, Channel hanger (Fig 104).

Bolts (Set-screws)

All hangers are secured by bolts (set-screws). Take care that these are of high-tensile steel (marked 8.8 on the head of the bolt) and of the correct length to screw fully into the anchor without protruding (11–12mm); different hangers require different length bolts. Most hangers have the bolt held captive by a steel circlip or better still by a rubber or plastic O-ring recessed into the base.

Rawlbolts

A Rawlbolt consists of a split steel shield containing a tapered bolt, which is inserted into a pre-drilled hole and grips by expansion of the shield as the bolt is tightened (Fig 105). There are different types of Rawlbolt (Fig 106), both the 'bolt-projecting' and 'loose-bolt' types require a separate hanger plate, although versions of the loose-bolt type are available with an integral forged or welded eye (Fig 107). In the sizes commonly used by British cavers (10–12mm diameter) such bolts are extremely strong (12mm: 5600kg), often stronger than the hangerplates attached to them, and they also have the advantage over self-drilling anchors of being removable. A disadvantage of eyebolts (as opposed to simple hanger-plates) which weakens them under shear loading results from a bending movement caused by the projecting eye to the threaded section at the neck of the bolt. Certain eyebolts project more than 70mm from the rock.

Rawlbolts in Britain either are intended as more or less permanent belays, in which case they are heavily greased on insertion and left in place in the cave, or suitable holes are drilled

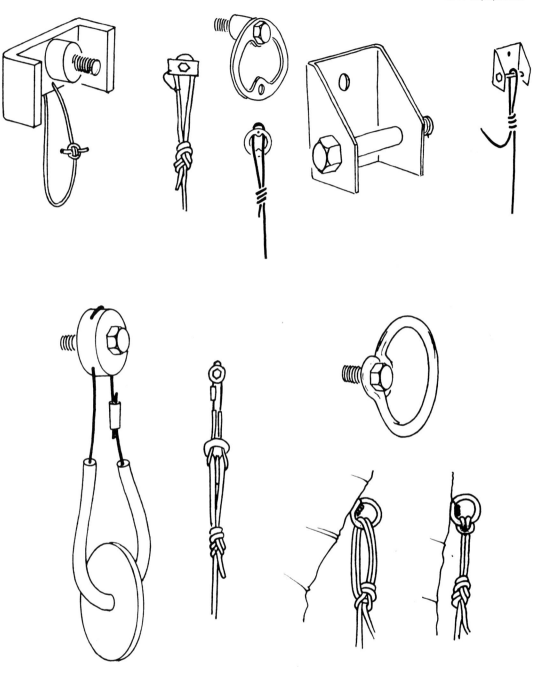

Fig 104 Examples of hangers not requiring a krab: (top left) bollard hanger; (top centre) new bollard hanger; (top right) channel hanger; (bottom left) CAT hanger; (bottom right) ring hanger

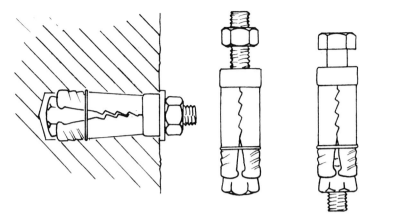

Figs 105 – 7 Rawlbolts: (*left to right*) the outer sleeve grips the rock, after expansion by the inner, tapered bolt; bolt-projecting type; loose-bolt type; eyebolt

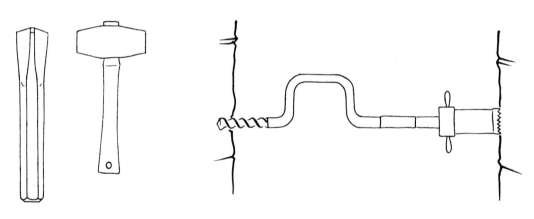

Figs 108 – 9 Rock-drilling methods: (*left*) star drill and lump hammer; (*right*) rock drill. When braced against the opposite wall this can drill a 40mm-deep hole in less than twenty minutes

and left for each team to supply their own bolts and remove them as they leave. In theory this system has certain advantages for main belays, the only major drawback being the difficulty of drilling suitable holes, aggravated by using unnecessarily large bolts. For example, a 12mm diameter Rawlbolt requires a hole of 24mm diameter by about 100mm deep.

Drilling Rawlbolt Holes In the absence of power tools (ie air-drills) a stardrill and lump-hammer (Fig 108) and/or a brace and bit are used to drill the hole. This might take anything from a half-hour to four hours depending on the hardness of the rock and the position of the hole. Hold the stardrill perpendicular to the rock face and pound it with the lump-hammer while you turn the drill to prevent it jamming. Remove the drill frequently, and blow the powdered rock out of the hole using a length of plastic tubing. A much faster and less strenuous method requires a special 'rock-drill' which utilises a carbide-tipped twist-drill jacked out against an opposing wall to provide the necessary pressure (Fig 109). Properly adjusted, the cutting rate is far better, perhaps 100mm in fifteen to twenty minutes.

'Ethics'

Traditionalists have expressed concern that modern bolting techniques result in caves being littered with unsightly bolt holes and rusty anchors. Perhaps so, but in caving safety is the overriding consideration, and the placement of artificial anchors not yet fraught with the ego-ethical problems that currently beset rock-climbers. It is far more important to stay alive than to rig a cave aesthetically using only natural rock features. If there does not happen to be a suitable natural anchor, then an artificial one must be placed. Do not under any circumstances be tempted to jeopardise your life for anybody's 'ethics' but your own.

The Rope

The rope is the single most important element in the SRT system; your life will hang from it, so the selection and care of ropes is vital.

The best modern caving ropes are meticulously designed pieces of textile engineering possessing remarkable properties. However, the situation is complicated by different ropes having varying properties designed into them, which might make them ideal for one purpose but potentially lethal for another – high or low stretch for example. · It is necessary to understand the properties and capabilities of a rope to be able to use it effectively.

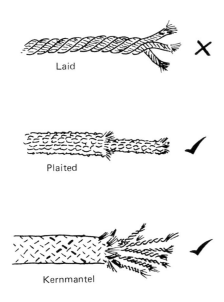

Fig 110 Rope construction

Rope Fibres

For caving, the advantages of synthetic over natural-fibre ropes are not in dispute; natural-fibre ropes have no place at all underground. Neither have ropes of the traditional laid or twisted construction, which have been entirely superseded by 'kernmantle' types (Fig 110). At present there are only two common fibres suitable for making SRT ropes: polyamide (Nylon) and polyester (Terylene). A possible third fibre, a polyaramide (Kevlar), is still at the experimental stage so far as caving is concerned. Polyamide and polyester fibres are roughly equivalent in terms of tensile strength. Polyamide is an inherently stretchy fibre used to great advantage in very extensible climbing ropes which are required to absorb immense shock-loads. Polyester fibres have less inherent stretch, which simplifies the construction of a low-stretch rope but also lessens its capacity to absorb a shock or 'dynamic' load. It is possible to construct a low-stretch rope from either Nylon or Terylene – the relative importance of this factor is considered later. Polyaramide (Kevlar) is an amazing fibre, weight for weight stronger than steel, but with very little stretch and so prone to damage from abrasion that it must be sheathed in another more resistant fibre before it can be used in a rope at all.

Construction

'Kernmantle' rope consists of a core of more or less parallel bunches of fibres accounting for perhaps 60–70 per cent of the mass of the rope. These are contained in a tightly woven protective sheath.

The core is the main load-bearing part of the rope, determining both its breaking load and its stretch. In SRT the caver effectively climbs up the sheath, so this must be strong (at least 30 per cent of the overall breaking load) and constructed not to slide down the core should the sheath be severed. In practice this seems to occur only with a new rope; after a little use the sheath tightens and beds into the core preventing any appreciable slippage.

There is no such thing as the ideal rope for underground use, and probably never will be. Various fundamental properties might be considered, and from these we can learn the limitations of existing ropes and work within them until something better is developed.

Rope Size
The thinnest ropes of any real use are about 9mm diameter, largely because with current technology it is impractical to build sufficient strength and energy absorption into a thinner rope. Ropes of around 12mm diameter probably represent the practical maximum, both for reasons of weight and because jammers and descenders are not designed to work on thicker rope. Optimum size seems to be 10–11mm if only on grounds of mass. A thin rope, although perhaps of adequate breaking load, has a proportionally greater surface area than a thicker rope, so is more vulnerable to weakening from general deterioration or to significant abrasion damage due to severed fibres. If 9mm rope is considered adequate in this respect, then 11mm rope of the same construction will provide a greater margin of safety, but with the disadvantage of increased weight and bulk.

Rope Strength
The strength of a rope comprises two main elements: its 'ultimate tensile strength' (UTS or breaking load) and its 'energy absorption capacity' or ability to absorb a shock-load. It is far more important that a rope be capable of absorbing the dynamic loads resulting from a fall than have a very high breaking load. Consider first the tensile strength, the figure quoted on a reel of rope; here current opinion indicates a breaking load of about 2.4 tonnes as reasonable for a new rope. This might appear excessively strong, but tests have shown that the breaking load of a rope may be halved after only moderate use underground; knotting the rope, which is necessary to be able to use it, can halve it again. Thus the effective breaking load of a used rope (not badly worn or damaged) might be rather different to the manufacturer's quoted figure.

Energy Absorption
Any rope's capacity to absorb a suddenly applied load depends on the amount of stretch built into it. The lower the rope's stretch, the higher the dynamic loading or 'peak impact force': the force developed in the rope when

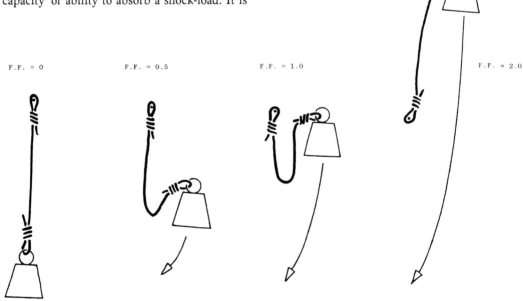

F.F. = 0   F.F. = 0.5   F.F. = 1.0   F.F. = 2.0

Fig 111 Fall factors: the fall-factor is a term used to describe the relationship between the length of a fall and the length of rope available to intercept it. The energy of a falling body is proportional to the distance fallen. The capacity of the rope to absorb this energy is proportional to its length. By dividing one by the other H/L we arrive at a fall-factor which varies between 0 and 2. It is the relationship between these two factors which is important not their value. For example, in the case of a fall-factor 1 fall (ie where the fall and length of rope are equal) a 2m fall onto 2m of rope produces the same shock-load (peak-impact force) as a 10m fall onto 10m of rope

arresting the fall, transmitted along the rope to the caver at one end and the belay at the other. The more the rope stretches, so the impact force decreases as energy is absorbed by the rope. Consequently it is vital to have a rope with a certain amount of stretch.

The current recommendation for SRT use is a rope with the capacity to accommodate a load of 80kg at a fall-factor of 1 with the peak impact force generated in the rope not exceeding 1200kg (12kn). Fall factors are explained in Fig 111 and the figure of 12kn, although very high, is the force that a human body (in a suitable harness) might withstand under favourable conditions without sustaining major injury.

Static Stretch
An ideal SRT rope would be inelastic when loaded up to 200kg or so (a typical value for an energetic climb) and increasingly elastic at higher loads, thereby avoiding bouncy ascents and the possibility of dangerous reciprocation against rock, but retaining the shock-absorbency needed to arrest a fall safely. A static stretch of 2 or 3 per cent under a load of 80kg (subject to test conditions) is acceptable. Recent development has produced rope of composite construction (static/dynamic rope) with an inner core of some low-stretch material, and the bulk of the rope of more elastic construction. The low-stretch core determines the low-load elongation of the rope which might be as little as 1 per cent, but the core is designed to break when a substantial load is applied, say 600kg. This allows the more elastic main body of the rope to absorb the remaining energy without reaching a prohibitively high peak impact force. Subsequently the section containing the broken core is cut out of the undamaged part of the rope. Such ropes exist today; there are versions manufactured both from Terylene and from Nylon with a Kevlar core. These ropes are at the forefront of caving technology and only time and research will tell if the concept of a static/dynamic rope is a realistic one.

Abrasion Resistance
Abrasion resistance is an important factor in a caving rope; it probably determines its useful life. No rope is adequately abrasion resistant and there are no guidelines on the relative resistance of various types of rope. Limestone is

harder than rope and any rope rubbing over rock will abrade. The only safe solution is to avoid abrasion altogether by meticulous rigging. Apart from surface abrasion which is more or less obvious, a rope will abrade internally owing to particles of grit trapped between the fibres, which is why thorough washing is so important.

Heat Resistance
Both the rope materials considered (Nylon and Terylene) suffer a decrease in strength with an increase in temperature, weakening above about 140°C or 150°C and melting at around 250°C or 260°C. Since all descenders employ friction they all become hot. Fortunately temperatures high enough to damage rope are beyond the bounds of normal safe technique. Considering that metal devices become too hot to hold at around 70°C and that, in Britain at least, ropes are more often wet than not (and might be wet deliberately) this is a minor factor.

Chemical Resistance
Although polyamide, polyester and Kevlar are extremely stable polymers affected by very few common chemicals, polyamide (Nylon) is severely affected by the quite dilute electrolyte acids of a lead-acid caving lamp, and polyester (Terylene) by strong alkalis. In both cases the corrosive damage takes place within minutes, so subsequent washing is no answer. The only solution, as has already been pointed out, is to avoid contamination altogether.

Even polyester (Terylene), commonly (mistakenly) regarded as acid-proof, is affected by strong acids. While battery acid as such is relatively dilute, if left to dry on equipment it will increase in concentration as its water content evaporates until it reaches a harmful level. Chemical damage to ropes is as dangerous as it is insidious – unlike abrasive damage it has little visible effect; the first (and last) indication of a contaminated rope is likely to be when it breaks. It would be very useful to dye ropes with some type of reactive indicator-dye which would give a distinct visual warning of dangerous contamination.

Sunlight
Rope materials are degraded by sunlight, more particularly by ultraviolet light. This effect on a particular rope over a given period is impos-

sible to quantify, but a rope in regular use underground and stored in a cellar will be least affected. Only the surface fibres of a rope, which contribute little to its strength and serve to protect the fibres beneath, are susceptible, so any weakening should be marginal. In the absence of precise figures, it makes sense to dry and store ropes in the shade.

Rope Care

It is just as important to use and care for ropes properly as to select a suitable rope in the first place.

New Ropes

A new rope should be washed before use. Washing removes lubricants used in the manufacturing process and also shrinks the rope; this compacts the sheath and tightens it onto the core, improving its wearing properties. Soak the rope overnight (in the bath?) in clean water with an occasional brief agitation, drain and then remove the surplus water by pulling the rope through an anchored descender. Repeat the process, then hang it up to dry. This will help prevent sheath slippage during the initial few trips to counteract any before the sheath is properly bedded. All ropes, particularly Nylon ones, shrink by varying amounts up to about 10 per cent. Washing serves to roughly determine this amount before cutting and marking ropes for length, so that after a while the rope is really as long as it is supposed to be and does not leave you dangling a few metres from the floor.

Identification

As an absolute minimum, ropes should be marked to indicate length, type (static or dynamic) and age. There are many ways of doing this, the main criteria being durability and legibility. An easy method is to paint the ends of the rope according to a simple colour code, but this works only if everyone concerned knows what the code means. One system uses a particular colour specifying general rope type (eg red – SRT; blue – lifeline) in a number of bands around the rope to indicate length, say one for every 10m. A rope with three red bands would be a 30m SRT rope.

Information is generally better written than coded, and this can be done simply. First melt-weld the end of the rope to prevent it unravelling and then bind it tightly about 5cm from the end with a couple of turns of ordinary white plastic adhesive tape. The information can be written on this with waterproof (ball-point pen) ink and then protected by a couple of coats of clear plastic glue or varnish. Type of rope might be indicated by a simple colour code (explained by a further abbreviated heading) with the length and the date written, for example (on red tape) 'SRT – 30m (5/82)', which is a 30m SRT rope dating from May 1982. The actual colours are obviously not important, although it would be good if a standard colour code could be adopted amongst cavers. This method of marking, though crude, remains legible for a considerable time and can be easily renewed.

A more sophisticated method is to bind the end of the rope with coloured adhesive tape and then mark it with printed figures such as those used by electricians for marking cables, held in place by clear PVC heat-shrink sleeving. Never bind the end of a rope in such a way that increases its diameter significantly, nor makes more than 2cm or so rigid – you are just asking to get it snagged-up somewhere.

Carrying Ropes

Cavers are often remiss in their attitude to rope care. A rock-climber seen carelessly treading his rope into the ground or dragging it through grit and mud would be considered quite daft; many cavers seem to take it as a matter of course that equipment is treated in this manner.

Ropes should *always* be carried below ground in a tackle-sack, which if properly designed is far easier to handle than coiled rope, and will protect the rope from damage. The same sack lined with a polythene bag closed with a rubber band will also exclude water, mud and grit. If a rope gets dirty on the way to a pitch, the dirt and grit are ground in during use, damaging metal gadgets and rope alike and making it subsequently impossible to remove all the grit from the rope. Apart from physical damage and silt, ropes carried in sacks are also to some extent protected from chemical contamination from leaking lamps.

Packing

Ropes can be coiled and stuffed into the sack (in the order they will be used in the cave) or

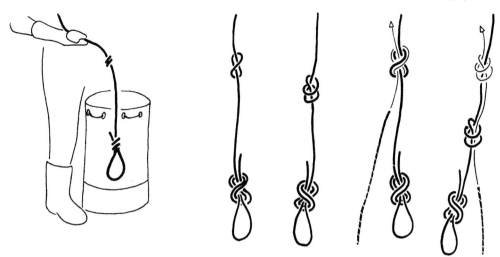

Figs 112 – 13 Safety-first when packing ropes: (*left*) a stopper knot is essential before packing into the rope bag; (*right*) two knots are best — the lower for standing in whilst another rope is fed through the upper knot and tied off

Fig 115 Spare rope should stay in the tackle bag after the descent and the bag attached to the rope by its hauling loops

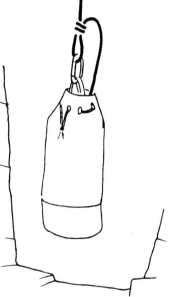

Fig 114 The rope should be fed into the bag with no twists or small coils

packed loose in such a way that they can be drawn out as required without tangling. The first method is convenient for several short ropes of differing lengths, which are more easily sorted out in separate coils. The second is better for long ropes and on pitches where there may be a danger of loose rocks. In this case the sack is carried attached to the caver's harness and he feeds the rope out as he descends. Should he

reach a ledge with loose rocks, he can kick them down the pitch without fear of damaging any gear below.

There are certain precautions before packing the rope into the sack. It is imperative that a stopper knot is tied in the lower end (Fig 112). This prevents inadvertent abseiling off the end should the rope prove too short. With the arrangement shown (Fig 113) the descender stops against the first knot (a), and the second loop-knot (b) can be used if necessary to stand up in. Subsequently a further length of rope can be added as shown.

The rope is fed into the sack avoiding making small coils which put twists into it and can cause it to tangle during the descent (Fig 114). At the foot of the pitch spare rope is left in the sack, which is suspended a short distance above the floor by its hauling loops (Fig 115). This protects the excess rope from being trodden on and from damage by falling rocks, and also serves as a weight, making climbing easier on the return. Hauling the rope up from the pitch head, it is far less likely to snag with a fairly streamlined tackle-sack at its end rather than a coil of rope.

Coiling
Ropes are coiled for storage, and certain very stiff ropes which are not easily packed into sacks might be coiled for carrying around the shoulders and used on surface pitches. If you cannot get it into a tackle-sack, do not take it underground. Fig 116 shows two methods of coiling. For storage it is necessary only to coil the rope loosely and secure it with a loop of cord.

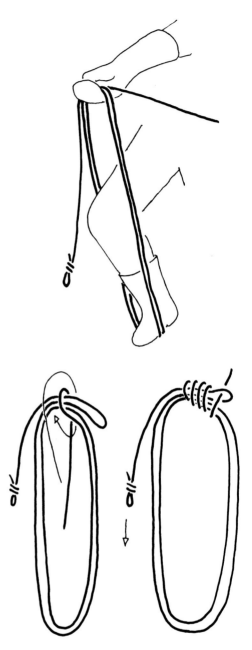

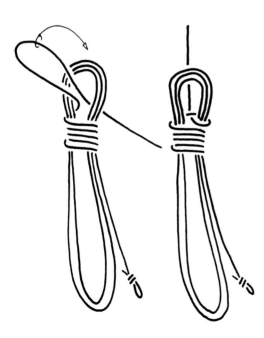

Fig 116 Methods of coiling ropes: SRT rope should never be taken into a cave unless in a tackle sack. Coiling, as shown here, should only be necessary for storing ropes, and for carrying them to and from surface pitches. (*Above*) method 1; (*left*) method 2

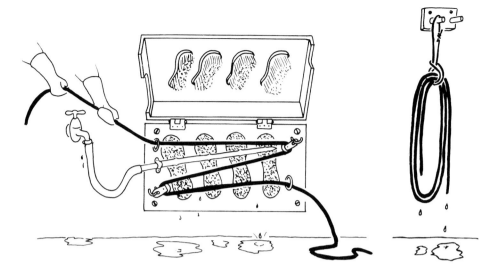

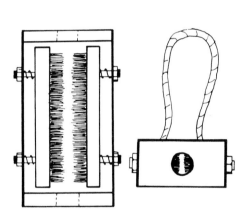

Fig 117 Rope washers: (*above*) fixed rope washer. A permanently mounted device enables long ropes to be washed quickly and easily (*left*). The rope is loosely coiled and hung from a loop of cord (*right*)

(*left*) A portable rope washer. Two scrubbing brushes will soon pay for themselves!

Washing and Inspection

Wash and inspect ropes for wear or damage after each use. Thorough washing removes the fine silt particles which abrade the subsurface fibres and weaken the rope as well as making it stiff. Superficial mud can be removed by sloshing the rope around in running water until it runs clear (a stream by the cave). However, this is rarely sufficient, and more stubborn dirt might call for soaking and then pulling a few times through a pair of opposed scrubbing brushes or a descender anchored under water, until the rope is clean. A rope-washing machine is a useful labour-saver which will pay for itself many times over the years, allowing long lengths of rope to be washed in a few minutes

(Fig 117). For the fastidious, ropes may be washed in a domestic washing machine in warm water (40°C) only. Ropes are best plaited before machine-washing to avoid undue tangling (Fig 118).

After washing, carefully inspect ropes for damage and signs of excessive wear. Run the rope through the hands a few centimetres at a time, flexing it and feeling for soft spots or regions of reduced diameter as well as for the more obvious flaws. If necessary cut the rope at the damaged section and remark it before returning it to the store. There is no merit in drying ropes before storing them; provided that they are kept properly, ropes will take no harm if left to dry slowly until the next trip. Ropes

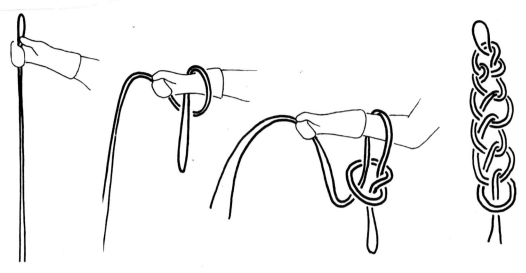

Fig 118 Rope plaiting: by this method tangling is eliminated during machine washing

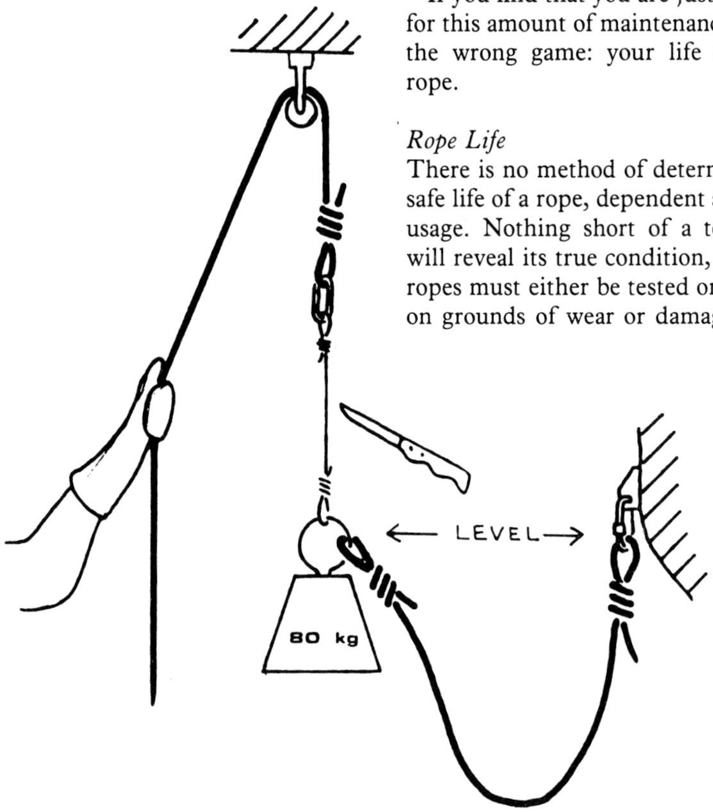

are best stored in a cool, dark, well-ventilated place, hung on untreated wooden pegs or rope loops. Never hang ropes on rusty nails or throw them into a corner.

If you find that you are just too busy (or lazy) for this amount of maintenance, then you are in the wrong game: your life depends on your rope.

Rope Life
There is no method of determining exactly the safe life of a rope, dependent as it is on care and usage. Nothing short of a test to destruction will reveal its true condition, and consequently ropes must either be tested or discarded largely on grounds of wear or damage. A new rope is

←— LEVEL —→

80 kg

Fig 119 A simple drop-test rig

best reserved for the longest pitches; later it can be cut (perhaps at a damaged section) into shorter lengths. A sheathed rope, unless damaged or of the type where the sheath comprises a very large percentage (40 per cent plus) of the overall strength, can probably be used safely until the sheath is almost worn through. When the sheath no longer protects the core, chuck it out. The decision to retire a rope should err on the side of survival.

Fig 119 shows a simple drop-test rig, such as might be built and used jointly by several clubs. The rig is used to apply two consecutive shock-loads resulting from a fall-factor 1 fall with an 80kg mass – if a rope can withstand this, it is OK. The tests are made on 2.5m samples cut from the test rope, a figure-eight knot is tied in each end to provide a test piece 1m long and the sample soaked in water overnight. If the rope supports only one shock and breaks on the second one, then the test must be repeated with a further sample from the same rope. If it again supports a single shock, the rope is OK.

Apply this test annually to all ropes over about four years old and, regardless of age, to any rope about which there is doubt.

New ropes are expensive: this is a good reason for carefully avoiding damage but no reason at all for continuing to use a suspect rope.

4 SRT Techniques

DAVID ELLIOT

This chapter describes the basic skills necessary to negotiate vertical sections of cave safely. The techniques are simple enough, but their value is, initially, in direct ratio to practice on the surface and then to subsequent experience underground. There is no substitute for experience.

Rope-climbing Systems

Books have been written on the subject of climbing a fixed rope and millions of man-hours devoted to studying the 'ergonomics' involved in gaining the fastest ascent for the minimum effort. There are perhaps fifteen sensible methods of climbing a rope safely, and they can be divided into two groups according to the type of leg movement involved: namely, those with an alternate 'stepping' action, and those requiring a sit/stand type of motion.

Each system has good and bad points, and although they all work, their overall efficiency depends on personal expertise and fitness. After working with one particular system for a while and becoming expert at it, it is then difficult to evaluate fairly a method you are unfamiliar with. As a result there are probably many sworn disciples of a particular system who have never tried anything else.

Of the two categories, one system from each

Fig 120 (below and opposite page) Prusiking techniques: step systems

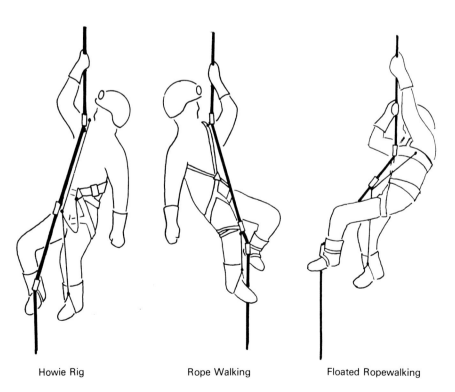

Howie Rig   Rope Walking   Floated Ropewalking

Jumar System

Gossett Rig

Mitchell System

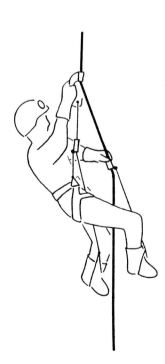

Third Phase System

Pigmy System

A.P.S. (Another Prusiking System)

Fig 121 Prusiking techniques: sit/stand systems

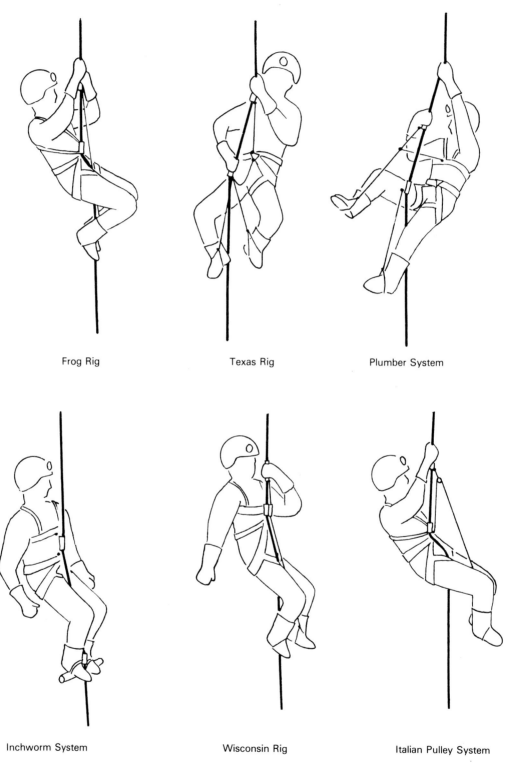

Frog Rig　　　　　　　Texas Rig　　　　　　　Plumber System

Inchworm System　　　　　Wisconsin Rig　　　　　Italian Pulley System

is superior in almost all respects to the others: the 'Howie rig' (Fig 120a) and the 'Frog rig' (Fig 121a). Both systems have their champions amongst the leading cavers of the world.

Howie Rig (Fig 122)

Equipment for the Howie rig consists of a sit-harness, an adjustable shoulder strap, jammers, a combined roller-jammer, plus the necessary footloops, safety-cords and shock-cord. The system uses three jammers; one strapped directly to the foot, one 'floating' at about knee

height attached to the other foot, with a third roller-jammer mounted at shoulder level. To climb you take alternate short steps while pulling on the rope at about head height. The 'floating' jammer is suspended from a length of elastic shock-cord which automatically pulls it up the rope as each step is taken. The upper roller-jammer keeps you upright against the rope and is used to hang from while resting and during manoeuvres. There are safety straps fastened around the ankles and a safety connection between the sit-harness and the floating jammer. Such 'ropewalking' systems use a natural and efficient leg movement well suited to climbing long free-hanging pitches or clocking up the very fast times reached in the surface 'prusik races' popular in America. They are little use for anything else, as we shall see later.

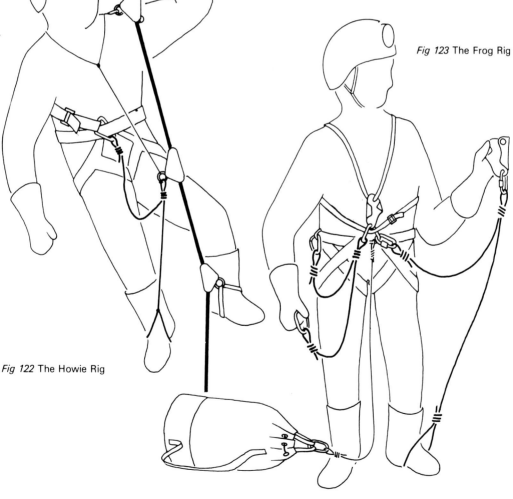

Fig 123 The Frog Rig

Fig 122 The Howie Rig

Frog Rig (Fig 123)

The most widely used prusiking systems in the world are simple sit/stand systems such as the Frog rig. Equipment consists of sit and chest-harnesses, two jammers, twin cow's-tails and a single footloop. The method generally uses only two jammers, one mounted between the sit and chest-harness; the second, higher up the rope, carries a footloop and a safety-link connecting this jammer to the sit-harness. Climbing is largely a matter of standing up and sitting down, using your arms to lift the upper jammer and help you stay upright; attached to the sit-harness are two rope cow's-tails, used as safeguards at pitch heads and during mid-rope manoeuvres.

Both of these systems are subject to many minor variations, and before going any further obvious points must be made; there are no effortless prusiking systems (apart from motor-driven ones), and simple rope-clamps are by no means anti-gravity devices (one reason the term 'ascender' may be misleading). To raise 70kg or 80kg up a rope requires work, and all we can do is direct the necessary effort in more or less the right direction. As the goal is usually up, maximum effort should be directed straight down – and energy expended in any other direction, ie sideways, is less effective. This is particularly relevant to sit/stand systems where the general tendency is to lie back and enjoy it (Fig 124a). Here it is necessary to develop a style of tucking the legs underneath and pulling into the rope with the arms in order to stay upright while climbing (Fig 124b).

Direct point-for-point comparisons of the Frog method and the Howie would be tedious and counter-productive. Either system is suitable for climbing a straightforward pitch.

The differences in performance become apparent when mid-rope manoeuvres are necessary, when emergency situations arise and when the safety aspects are examined. The choice of system then depends on the value you place on these considerations. The system best suited to British caves is without doubt a straightforward Frog rig (Fig 123), with good qualities of safety and versatility. Almost any other system can be evaluated by comparison during some common manoeuvres. You may find that with rope-

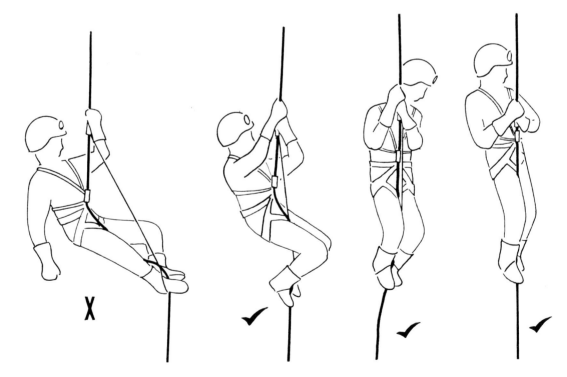

Fig 124 Sit/stand systems: user techniques. (a) lying back is wasteful of energy; (b) leg push should be vertical to minimise effort

walking systems fastening things to the feet makes simple manoeuvres, such as passing a rebelay point, difficult, and using only one leg at a time transforms tackle carrying and self-rescue into epic trials of strength and ingenuity.

Fundamental to the Frog system is a comfort-able leg-loop type sit-harness allowing free and independent movement of the legs while suspended. The harness is linked at the front by a strong (10mm) *Maillon Rapide*, which unlike a krab may be loaded in any direction without significant loss of strength. The 'body-mounted' jammer is either fastened directly into the M/R or attached by a 7mm M/R and supported by a figure-eight type chest-harness. This is just a 3m length of tape with a quick-adjustment buckle at one end, wound around the upper body and threaded through the jammer and the M/R. This harness serves mainly to tow the jammer, and consequently it need be neither load-bearing nor restrictive; by locating the buckle somewhere handy, you can easily adjust the harness while climbing and loosen it between pitches. The 7mm M/R allows you to remove the body-jammer or replace it without undoing the sit-harness. The upper jammer carries a foot-loop and is also linked to the sit-harness so that, should the body-jammer slip or fail, you hang safely from the upper jammer. The foot-loop/safety-cord is tied from a single length of low-stretch cord.

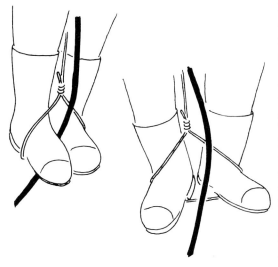

Fig 125 Trapping the rope with the feet makes it unnecessary for anyone to hold the rope at the start of the climb

A large single loop takes either one or both feet, dependent on whether against a wall or free-hanging, and also allows you to trap the rope between the feet while climbing the initial few metres so that no one is needed to hold it (Fig 125). The foot-loop is attached to its jammer by a screwgate karabiner and its length is adjusted so that the two jammers almost touch when the legs are fully straightened. The safety cord linking jammer and sit-harness should be long enough to permit the maximum gain with each climbing cycle, but not so long that the jammer is out of reach while hanging from it. Also attached to the main M/R are two cow's-tails tied from sturdy 10mm climbing rope, one short (45cm) and the other longer (70cm), each with a karabiner at its end. These are necessary for safety attachment at anchor points or traverse lines, such as while gaining the rope at a pitch head, or passing intermediate anchors further down. Because cow's-tail krabs are rarely attached for very long, they may not always be screwed up; for this reason, use asymmetric-form krabs with a 'pin-and-slot' type latch.

On the pitch tackle-sacks are carried on a length of cord reaching from the main M/R to just below the feet. The weight of the sack is transferred directly to the chest-jammer for much of the climbing cycle with no pull on the climber. Using both feet in the loop allows a powerful lifting action and the additional weight beneath helps maintain you vertical to the rope. The same principle with minor modi-fications can also be used to rescue an injured caver from mid-rope.

When carrying a heavy sack, it is possible to adjust the foot-loop cord to run over (rather than be clipped into) its attachment krab (or a small pulley carried for this purpose) and there-by arrange a mechanical advantage (Fig 126). Each step will now gain half the distance, but with less effort. Here you need to clip a long cow's-tail to the upper jammer for safety or ensure that the knot in the foot-loop cord will not pass through the pulley (Fig 127).

Generally there is no need to remove the Frog rig between pitches: clip the foot-loop to the harness and unclip it when you want to climb. Total weight of the whole outfit is around 2kg. Total time for a 20m pitch with one intermediate belay (including removing and replacing jammers) is around three minutes.

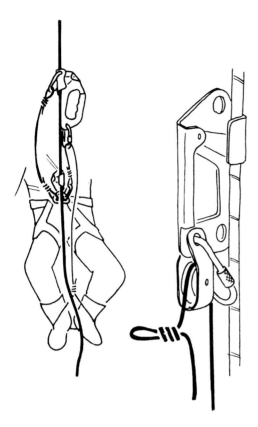

Figs 126 – 7 Methods of reducing leg thrust: (*left*) footloop through a krab or (*right*) through a pulley

Knots

Competence with the basic rigging knots and their application is a fundamental part of caving technique. The strongest rope and soundest belay are of little value if attached by inadequate knots.

Knots weaken the rope by varying amounts according to type. The effective strength of a knotted rope is generally expressed as a percentage of the rope's breaking load without knotting. This reduction in strength varies between about 20 and 50 per cent with the knots commonly used by cavers, though this effect is not cumulative – a chain is as strong as its weakest link.

Although knot strength plays a significant part in determining the load-bearing capacity of a rope on a pitch, there are other considerations. The main features of a good knot are:

1 Strength and security.
2 Versatility.

3 Ease of tying and untying.
4 Readily apparent if not correctly tied.

There are as yet no knots specifically designed for use in caves, and from the many which might be used few are in fact necessary. A knowledge of the characteristics of a few common knots is the most basic rigging skill. The fact that certain knots are traditionally used in particular situations does not rule out the possibility of a better knot for that purpose; tradition (as a substitute for thinking) is no reason for doing anything.

We can divide the common knots into two categories according to their use underground; that is, those used to form a loop for attachment, and those for joining one rope to another.

Attachment Knots
Overhand Loop (Fig 128) The overhand knot is the most basic knot possible, simply a loop of rope with the end threaded through it. The overhand loop is exactly the same only tied in a doubled section of rope; a simple foolproof knot, but fairly weak and difficult to untie after being loaded.

Use: general; loops in footloop cords, tape slings; shock-absorption knot.

Figure-eight Loop (Fig 129) In effect an overhand loop with an additional half-turn within

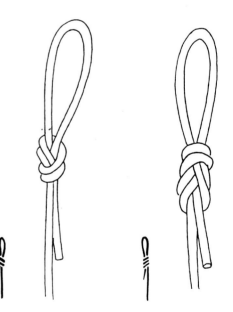

Fig 128 Overhand Loop   Fig 129 Figure-eight Loop

the knot. The figure-eight is the universal caver's knot – simple, strong and extremely versatile, it lends itself to almost every purpose underground. This is the knot against which other knots are measured. The figure-eight loop may be tied either at the end or along the length of the rope, and is easier to untie after loading than the overhand loop.

Figure-eight (reversed) The same knot is tied in a different fashion using the end of the rope for attachment to a thread belay. A single figure-eight knot is tied in the rope, with the end of the rope then taken around the belay and threaded back through the knot following the path of the rope in the reverse direction, forming in effect a second figure-eight knot within the first.

Use: multi-purpose; rigging, general ropework.

Figure-nine Loop (Fig 130) Similar to the figure-eight, but with an additional half-turn within the knot. Stronger than the figure-eight, but bulkier and less easy to untie after loading.

Use: rigging; particularly lightweight rope (9mm) where retention of maximum strength is essential.

Bowline (Fig 131) A safe, simple knot used mainly for attaching the end of a rope to a thread belay. The bowline has a tendency to work loose when tied in stiff or resilient ropes and should always be secured with a back-up knot tied on the same side as the rope end. Even so the bowline is secure only if loaded along its major axis; heavy sideways loading may distort it into a slip knot. Less strong than the figure-eight, the bowline has two advantages: the loop formed is easily adjusted and the knot is easily untied even after very heavy loading.

Use: multi-purpose; general ropework; traverse line attachment.

Double Bowline (Fig 132) The same knot tied in a doubled section of rope, generally for attachment in mid-rope.

Use: rigging; thread belays in mid-rope; rescue, improvised harness.

Bowline on Bight (Fig 133) A variation of the bowline tied in a doubled rope (a bight) with the end loop passed back over the half-completed knot. The result is a bowline with two loops, each adjustable to the other.

Use: rigging; mid-rope attachment, ring hanger attachment, Y-anchors.

Fig 130 Figure-nine Loop   *Fig 131* Bowline

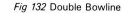

Fig 132 Double Bowline   *Fig 133* Bowline on a Bight

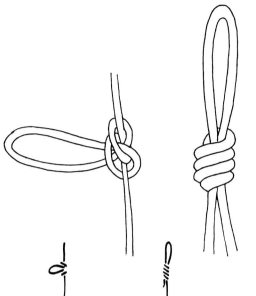

Fig 134 Butterfly Knot   Fig 135 Capuchin Knot   Fig 136 Swami Knot   Fig 137 Figure-8 Bend

Butterfly Knot (Fig 134)   A mid-rope loop knot which may be loaded from the loop or along the standing rope in either direction without distortion. Easily adjustable and readily untied after loading.

Use: rigging; mid-rope attachment (traverse lines).

Capuchin Knot (Fig 135)   A very secure loop knot, in effect half of a double fisherman's knot but tied in a doubled rope. This knot is bulky and prone to jamming under load.

Use: 'blocking' knot with 'cord technique'.

Swami Knot (Fig 136)   A combination of an overhand knot and half of a double fisherman's knot, arranged to form a secure loop in the end of a rope which will not work loose even with resilient sheathed ropes. Prone to jamming under load and may have to be cut from the rope after severe loading.

Use: climber's tie-on to harness.

Junction Knots
Figure-eight Bend (Fig 137)   A variation of the (reversed) figure-eight knot used to join the ends of two ropes of roughly equal diameter very securely.

Use: joining ropes.

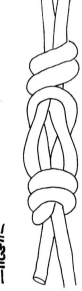

Fig 138 Double
Fisherman's Knot

Fig 139 Reef and Double
Fisherman's Knot

Double-fisherman's Knot (Fig 138)   Consists essentially of two 'stopper' knots tied in opposition to each other in the ends of separate ropes. They are designed to slide together, forming the knot proper. This is a very secure knot, used to join separate ropes or both ends of

76

the same rope to form a sling. It is prone to jamming under load and may in the worst case have to be cut from the end of the rope after particularly heavy loading. This tendency to jam, however, is a good point with a sling.

Use: joining ropes, making rope slings.

Reef and Double-fisherman's Knot (Fig 139) One method of joining ropes and retaining the security of a double fisherman's knot without it jamming under load is to tie a reef knot between the two halves. The reef knot is virtually useless on its own (used only to fasten tackle-sacks), but it does not jam readily even under very heavy load. If each end of the rope is then secured by a double fisherman's knot the result is a combination which, although bulky, is both secure and easily untied.

Use: joining ropes, rescue – hauling.

Safety Loop (Fig 140) With SRT wherever two ropes are joined in mid-pitch a safety loop must always be provided at the joining knot. This is for the caver to attach himself to for protection while passing the knot. Here the tail of the rope from above is left deliberately long and a loop knot (figure-eight) tied in this to provide the necessary attachment point.

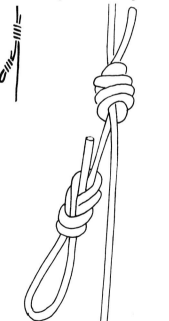

Fig 140 Safety Loop. This must be included when two ropes are joined, so that the knot can be passed in safety

Whatever knots you use underground, you need to practise them until you can tie them correctly, and recognise that this is so, under all circumstances; bearing in mind those times you may be tired, cold or under stress and most likely to make serious mistakes. Habitually check and tighten all knots before use, and secure any knot in the end of a rope by an additional back-up knot such as an overhead or half a double fisherman's knot – half-hitches are insufficient.

Rigging

Rigging pitches for SRT involves some of the most crucial decisions a caver must make. You must be able to arrange a belay which will:

1 Be strong and secure enough to withstand a shock-load (ie as strong as the rope).
2 Provide a free hang to eliminate abrasion.
3 Facilitate easy and safe access at the pitch head.
4 Avoid objective hazards such as water and stone-fall.

Anchors
Rarely will a single anchor of any type fulfil all these requirements and judgement is called for – if this belay fails, you have had it. The first rule is: at least two separate anchors at the top of each pitch. Natural rock belays are one possibility, but either they exist or they do not – generally they do not, or at least not in the right place.

The rope should be anchored high enough to allow easy access and in order to avoid abrasion; it is essential to be able to hang the rope exactly where you want it. This means using artificial anchors, which usually means bolts, specifically the 8mm self-drilling rock-anchor.

Traverse Lines
Where reaching the main rope requires climbing out over the pitch, a traverse line must be installed for safety (Fig 141). This should be fixed at about head height, linking a safe (back-up) belay well back from the pitch (often a natural rock feature) to the main belay. This provides a back-up for the main belay and a safeguard for getting on and off the rope. The first caver rigs the traverse line by attaching the rope to the back-up belay and uses this to

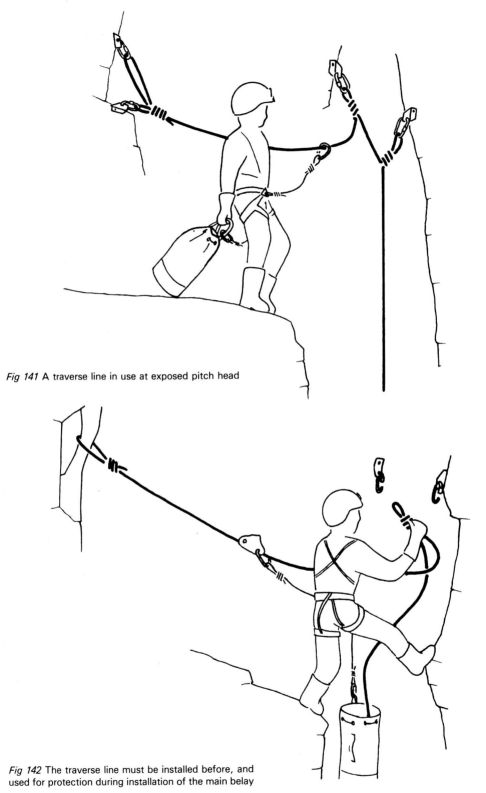

Fig 141 A traverse line in use at exposed pitch head

Fig 142 The traverse line must be installed before, and used for protection during installation of the main belay

protect himself while he installs the main belay (Fig 142). He can do this by using his descender either locked off, or with a knot beneath (Fig 143) by clipping on a jammer, or by attaching his cow's-tail to a loop tied in the rope.

Once fixed, the rest of the team clip into the traverse line with cow's-tails. The back-up belay must be strong enough to support the rope should the worst happen and the main belay fail. However, the main belay is just that, and as such must not fail. Here unless a really good anchor can be found, two separate belays are used; the chance of both these failing simultaneously is far lower.

Main Belay

Commonly two anchors are placed one above the other, and the connecting rope tied with as little slack as possible (Fig 144a). The upper anchor will take a small shock-load should the lower loaded anchor fail. However, there is little point in having two anchor points available and loading only one. Better to use two loaded anchors to form the main belay (Fig 144b), where each takes less than the full load, therefore is less likely to fail and will not cause a shock-load onto the remaining anchor, even if one should fail. Best of all is a Y-anchor (Fig 144c, d) where both anchors are loaded about equally and may even be located on opposing walls, leaving the hang-point in space, exactly where you want it. This technique is particularly useful in many British caves with narrow twisting stream canyons cutting down into the pitch, where it is often impossible to obtain a free hang from either wall. However,

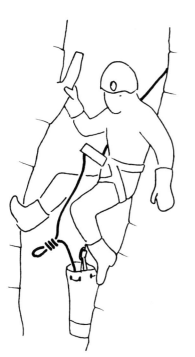

Fig 143 Traverse line protection by a knot beyond the descender

Fig 144 The main belay: (a) there is little point in having two anchor points and loading only one! (b) both anchors should be loaded and it is best if both are equally loaded (c & d)

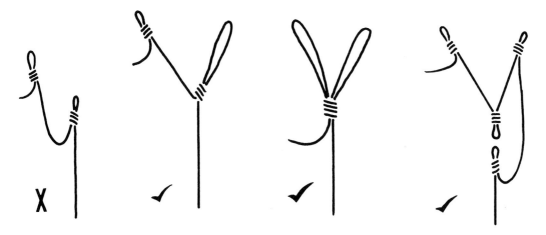

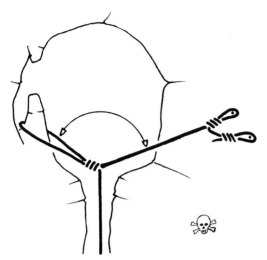

Fig 145 The angle between the upper arms in a Y-belay should never exceed 120°

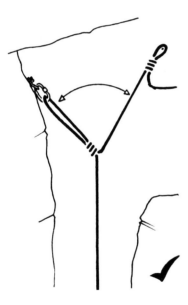

Fig 146 An angle of 90° or less means that each arm has about 70 per cent of the load

each arm of the belay should be under no more stress than the main rope and thus the angle between the two must *never* exceed 120° (Fig 145). Moreover as bolt-hangers are not designed to work at more than 45° from the vertical, an angle of 90° between the two arms is the working rule (Fig 146). Each arm of the belay is then subject to about 70 per cent of the load on the main rope.

Intermediate Anchors

Having installed the main belay the caver descends, and at each point where the rope touches rock he installs an intermediate anchor (or re-belay) at or immediately below the rub point, so that the rope again hangs free below it (Fig 147). The caver must also eliminate abrasion; no amount of abrasion, however slight, is acceptable. A single anchor is normally sufficient, as the re-belay is backed up by the anchor above. Here it is necessary to leave a loop of slack to allow the descender to be locked off while passing the re-belay (Fig 148). The length of this loop is important, for should the intermediate anchor fail a shock-load will be transmitted to the belay above. Normally about one metre is sufficient, but the elasticity of the rope above must be taken into account or the loop may disappear under the weight of a lighter

Figs 147–9 Abrasion elimination: by re-belaying

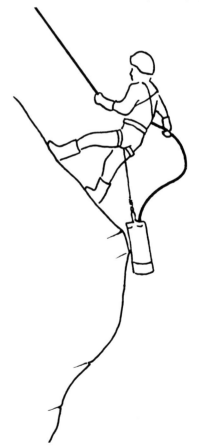

Fig 147 If the rope touches the rock it should be re-belayed at, or just below, the rub-point

person. This technique of re-belaying at abrasion points is continued to the foot of the pitch, whether the rope is simply rubbing against protruding rock or if there are a succession of pitches close together. With a large ledge or perhaps a traverse between two sections of the pitch, requiring more than the minimum amount of slack to be left in the rope, the continuing pitch must be rigged with a double 'main' belay, to obviate the large shock-load which would result from the failure of a single anchor (Fig 149). The caver must also minimise any possible shock-loads.

This intermediate anchor technique where the rope is fixed at intervals in the pitch has

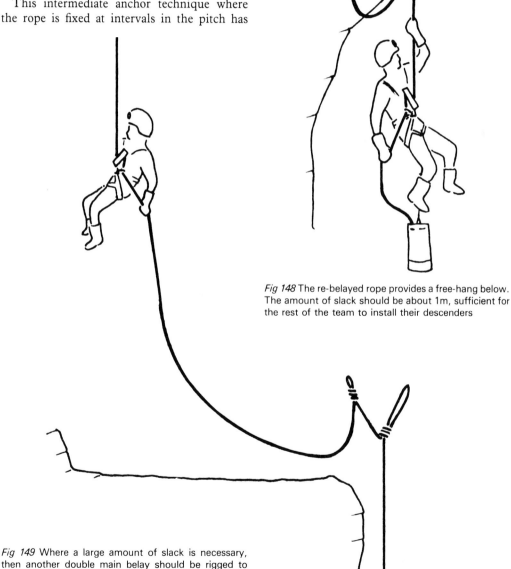

Fig 148 The re-belayed rope provides a free-hang below. The amount of slack should be about 1m, sufficient for the rest of the team to install their descenders

Fig 149 Where a large amount of slack is necessary, then another double main belay should be rigged to avoid any possible shock loads

other advantages apart from avoiding abrasion, eg avoidance of waterfalls. Splitting a pitch into sections reduces any spin or bounce in the rope, and because the rope is attached to multiple belays the safety of the system is increased. Several members of the team can descend or climb at the same time provided that each is hanging from a separate anchor.

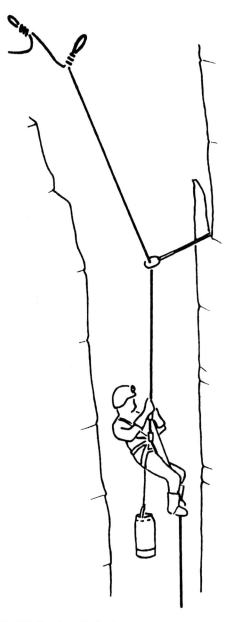

Fig 150 Abrasion elimination: by deviation. Abrasion points can often be effectively avoided by using a sling and a krab on the opposite wall

Deviation

An alternative method of redirecting the rope to avoid abrasion is the technique of 'deviation' (Fig 150). An adjacent anchor (perhaps on the opposite wall) is used to pull the rope away from the rub point by means of a sling or length of cord and a karabiner clipped around the rope. Each caver removes and replaces this karabiner to pass. The force on this belay is not very great as the rope is not fixed to it and would not result in a shock-load should it fail. Many belays are suitable for this technique which would be extremely dangerous if used as an intermediate anchor, for instance a single piton, a stalagmite or a partly-inserted bolt. This makes deviation particularly useful for prospecting, where it may be that the shaft is blocked at the bottom and will not require bolting fully.

Rope Pads

A less satisfactory technique is that of protecting or padding the rope at abrasion points with a mat or a tough sheath fastened around it (Fig 151).

Passing rope protectors is fairly straight-forward, but each caver must take care to replace the mat or sheath in exactly the correct place when he has passed it. Failure to do so could kill the next caver to climb. Padding is acceptable only directly beneath an anchor point; an empty tackle-sack can be used for this purpose.

Shock-loading

The techniques outlined above will serve for most caves, but sometimes more ingenuity is called for. This is fine but, because the rope is a 'static' (ie low-stretch) one, it must *never* be subject to the shock-load arising from a fall-factor of any significance. Apart from the likeli-hood of damage to the caver or the belay, many used caving ropes would break under a fall-factor of only 1 (see Chapter 3, page 60).

Once aware of this absolute limitation, there is scope for improvisation. Generally it is pos-sible to avoid dangerous situations by ensuring that *the main belay is located well below the back-up belay*. This way a fall-factor of 1 is impos-sible, and in most instances no more than a pendulum swing will result with little shock-load. Some thought must be given to the side-ways movement across the rock of the heavily

the level of the previous anchor, reducing the fall-factor to next to nothing (Fig 154).

Shock-absorption Knots
In spite of all that can be done to lessen the fall-factor, a considerable shock will sometimes still be placed on the rope should the main belay fail (Fig 155).

We can take steps to minimise this resultant shock-load by the use of 'shock-absorbing' knots (Fig 156). These are loop knots tied in the unloaded section of the rope which, if loaded, will slip a little and so absorb a certain amount of energy and also release additional rope to help minimise the shock (Fig 157). Such knots are more effective in new rope than old, mainly because they slip more, but even in old stiff rope are better than nothing. Figure-eight and nine knots are no use for this purpose because they do not slip; a bowline on a bight or a simple overhead knot is far more effective. There is little point in placing a shock-absorbing knot in the loaded section of the rope where it will be tightened as the rope is climbed; to be most effective it should be located in the normally lightly- (or non-) loaded section of rope between the main and back-up belays.

The basis of good pitch rigging is common-sense application of a few simple concepts. It is, however, difficult to reconcile this with the

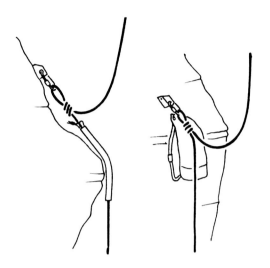

Fig 151 Abrasion elimination: rope protectors. Rope protection can be by sheath or tackle bag. After passing the protector it must be replaced in the correct position

loaded rope (Fig 152). Even this rule is not inviolate; look at the situation in Fig 153, where in order to obtain a free hang the anchor is placed well above the preceding one. This is dangerous since, should the upper belay fail, a fall-factor of almost 2 would result. This would break the rope. Here we can make things safe by tying the belay loop knot at a point below

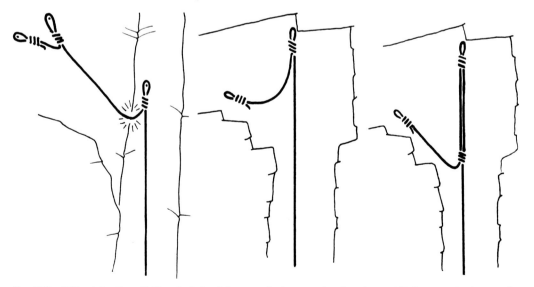

Figs 152–4 Shock loading: (*left*) main belay failure results in rope abrasion; (*centre*) if the caver is close to the belay, main belay failure will certainly break the rope — fall factor is almost 2; (*right*) this situation can be made safe by tying the slack down onto the main rope below back-up belay level. Fall factor is thus reduced almost to zero

Shock absorption knots (*below and right*):

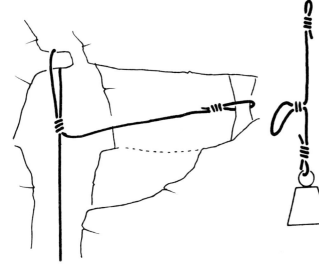

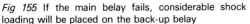

Fig 155 If the main belay fails, considerable shock loading will be placed on the back-up belay

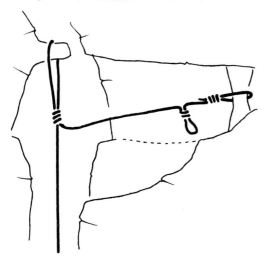

Fig 156 a shock absorption knot will reduce the shock load on the back-up belay

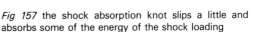

Fig 157 the shock absorption knot slips a little and absorbs some of the energy of the shock loading

Descending/Ascending Manoeuvres

Abseiling an underground pitch is as hazardous as it is exhilarating. Because the techniques involved are simple and relatively effortless, the inherent dangers are not always appreciated.

While abseiling, the descender is the sole point of contact with the rope, and this a sliding rather than a fixed connection. Any loss of control or failure of the descender or its attachment will be serious. A smooth, fully controlled descent places the least amount of strain on the descender, the rope system and the caver's nervous system. Some surface rock-climbers (and the odd half-wit caver) are given to abseiling in apparently great style, thrusting away from the rock with huge bounds and hurtling down the rope in spectacular curves. Any caver performing this way should be given a wide berth. Once control is lost it is always difficult and may prove impossible to regain it.

In mid-rope the caver is very exposed; vulnerable to anchor failure, rope failure, gear failure, water- and rock-fall, loss of control and other indignities arising from carelessness, such as loose hair or clothing drawn into the descender, knots in the rope or running out of rope before the bottom of the pitch. The most skilful caver

tendency for the standard of rigging to decrease along with the length of the pitch. At a big pitch the rope is quite understandably tied to everything in sight, but while 'it'll be reet-nobbut a little un' might reassure some, there is no reason why a belay at the top of a 15m pitch should be any stronger or less likely to fail than one at the top of a 50m pitch. The same forces are involved and the results of belay failure are virtually identical.

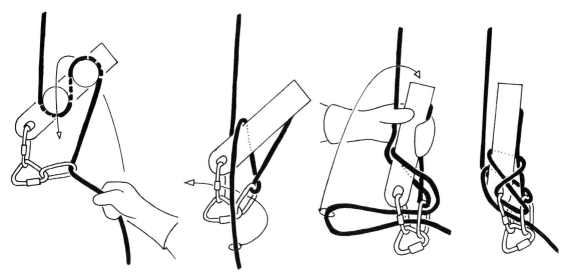

Fig 158 Method of locking the Petzl descender

cannot abseil effectively if knocked unconscious by falling rock, or if his descender falls to bits. To redress the balance towards survival you need to carry prusiking gear on *all* abseils. This enables passing of knots and intermediate anchor points, freeing trapped fingers from the descender, changing ropes and even changing your mind and climbing back up again should the situation prove too hairy! Abseiling down a pitch without the facility for stopping and climbing back is only for the extremely stupid.

Basic top manoeuvres are few and simple but none the less essential:

1 Stop and securely lock off the descender at any point during the descent.
2 Pass intermediate anchor points.
3 Change from abseil to prusik and vice versa.
4 Pass knots in mid-rope.

Descender Lock

The sequence in Fig 158 shows a method of locking the Petzl descender safely. Certain other descenders may present problems with this manoeuvre, either with the amount of rope involved or a tendency to come undone when the descender is not loaded. 'Self-lock' descenders may not need to be tied off, but should be if you do not completely trust them.

Passing Intermediate Anchors (descent)

Descend until level with the intermediate anchor and if necessary lock off the descender, clip the *short* cow's-tail into the krab, *Maillon*

Rapide, or knot loop of the anchor (Fig 159a), then continue abseiling until your weight is taken entirely by the cow's-tail (Fig 159b). Now the descender can be transferred to the rope immediately below the anchor and locked off securely. In order to disconnect the cow's-tail the weight must be removed from it. Often in a pitch there is a ledge or foothold you can stand on momentarily but, if not, place a knee or foot into the loop of rope coming from above and stand up in this (Fig 159c). If all else fails, you could wrap the lower rope around your foot a few times as a foothold, or clip your prusiking footloop into the anchor. Then lower yourself onto the locked descender and check that all is well before unlocking the descender and resuming the descent.

Passing Intermediate Anchors (ascent)

Climbing past an intermediate anchor is simple with the Frog rig; stop a few centimetres short of the belay knot and attach the long cow's-tail to the anchor as a precaution (Fig 160a). Transfer the body-jammer to the upper rope (Fig 160b) followed by the footloop jammer (Fig 160c) and once everything is working well unclip the cow's-tail and continue up.

Climbing past a belay, it is better to transfer the body-jammer first, otherwise the elasticity of the rope above will make unloading this more difficult.

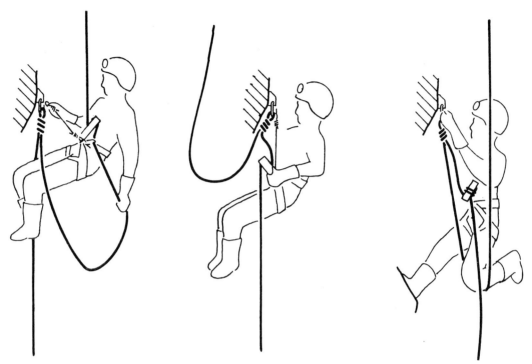

Fig 159 Method of passing an intermediate anchor on descent: (*left*) abseil until level with bolt and attach short cow's-tail; (*centre*) descend further until weight is on cow's-tail, transfer descender to lower section of rope and lock off; (*right*) remove cow's-tail by standing up in rope loop and continue descent

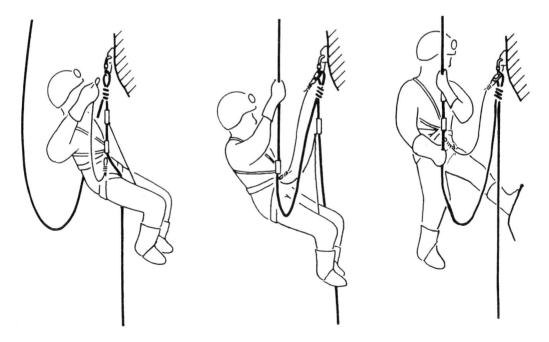

Fig 160 Passing an intermediate anchor on ascent: (*left*) prusik up to the knot and attach long cow's-tail; (*centre*) transfer body jammer to upper rope; (*right*) transfer footloop jammer, unclip cow's-tail and continue to prusik

Descent-ascent/Ascent-descent Changeover
First stop and lock off the descender, then install the footloop jammer on the rope above. Stand up in this and, with one arm crooked around the rope for balance, install the body-jammer. Now disconnect the descender from the rope and prusik up. Changing from prusik to abseil is the reverse; install the descender on the rope just below the body-jammer and lock it off, then stand up in the footloop, disconnect the body-jammer and lower your weight onto the descender. Remove the remaining jammer, unlock the descender and abseil down.

Passing a Knot (descent)
Wherever possible ropes should be joined at intermediate anchors, linking the knots together as shown (Fig 161a) so that failure of the belay krab is not critical. Spare rope should be coiled and hung from the anchor to prevent anybody inadvertently abseiling down the wrong rope (Fig 161b). Where this is not possible and the ropes are joined in mid-pitch, an extra safety loop should be provided at the joining knot – for the caver to attach himself to for extra security during the manoeuvre (see Fig 140). This is not strictly necessary during the descent as sufficient points of contact are main-tained, but it will do no harm to attach a cow's-tail. Abseil until the joining knot stops up against the descender, then install both jammers on the rope above, in effect changing to prusik. Now transfer the descender to just below the knot and lock it off. Here you must prusik down the metre or so of slack rope to immediately above the knot, before changing back from prusik to abseil in the normal manner and resuming the descent (Fig 162).

Passing a Knot (ascent)
To pass a knot in mid-rope you need to transfer the footloop jammer first. Climb up to just below the knot and clip a cow's-tail into the loop provided (Fig 163). Transfer the footloop and then the body-jammer above the knot (it is impossible to do otherwise), disconnect the cow's-tail and continue up.

Use of Cow's-tails
The principle underlying these various manoeuvres is that of maintaining a strong and secure connection (two points of contact) with the rope at all times. Hanging from a single jammer alone has too low a safety margin. By always bearing this in mind and attaching one or other of the cow's-tails whenever a

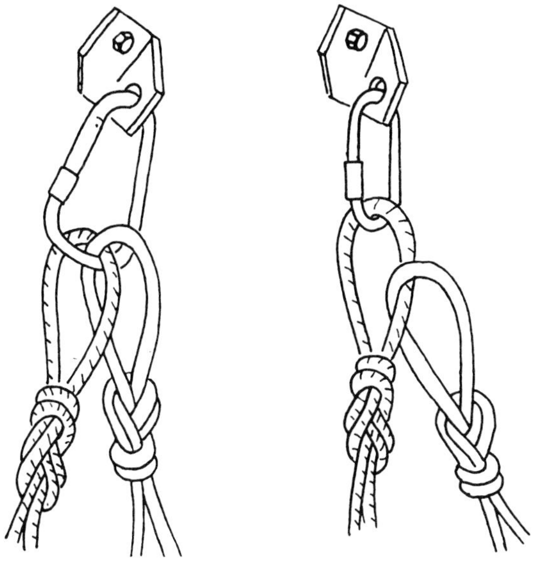

Fig 161 Rope joining: where possible, ropes should be joined at intermediate anchors and the excess rope coiled to prevent an abseil down the wrong rope!

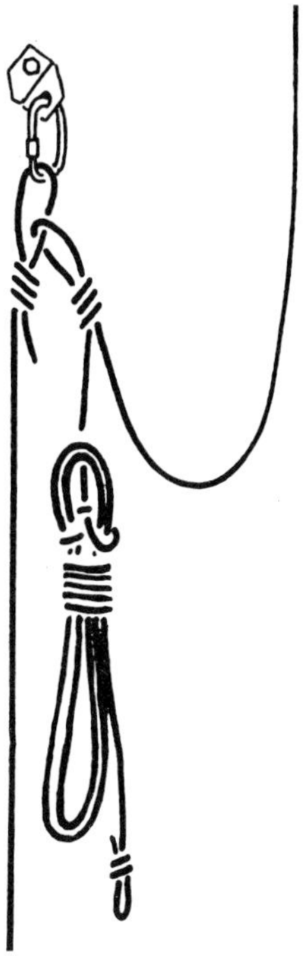

Fig 162 Passing a knot on descent:

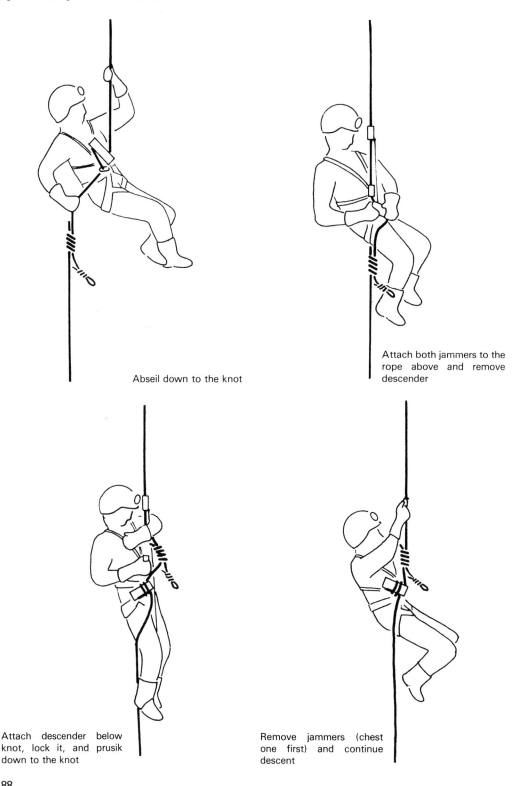

Abseil down to the knot

Attach both jammers to the rope above and remove descender

Attach descender below knot, lock it, and prusik down to the knot

Remove jammers (chest one first) and continue descent

Fig 163 Passing a knot on ascent:

Prusik up to the knot and clip cow's-tail into safety loop. First transfer the foot-loop jammer to above the knot . . .

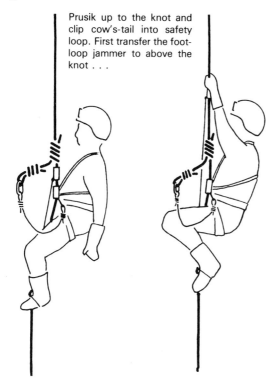

. . . and then the body jammer. Disconnect the cow's-tail and continue the ascent

manoeuvre is required, the result should never prove disastrous even if you make a mistake. Again at a pitch head, the cow's-tail is clipped either into the traverse line or the main belay, while the descender is installed on the rope and locked off. You then hang from this and, when satisfied that all is well, disconnect the cow's-tail, unlock the descender and begin the descent. A similar procedure is followed on the ascent; as the top of the pitch is reached, a cow's-tail is attached to the traverse line/main belay before any jammers are disconnected from the rope. Passing a tie-off point, one cow's-tail is clipped onto the further side before the nearside one is removed (Fig 164). In short, the first action approaching an obstacle is to clip in a cow's-tail, and the last thing to do before moving off is to unclip it.

Signals

With the independence of movement that is a characteristic of SRT, not much communication between the team members is necessary. The call 'Rope free' (or a whistle signal of four

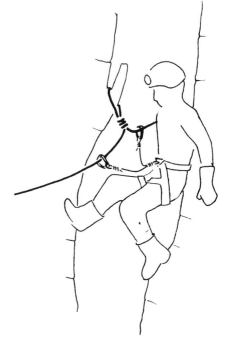

Fig 164 Passing a tie-off point, use both cow's-tails; one is attached on the further side before the other is released

blasts) is used to indicate when an intermediate belay is passed so that the next caver can begin to climb the rope below; similarly while abseiling. To save time, many cavers might climb a long pitch rigged with a number of re-belays at the same time, provided that at all times they are each hanging from a separate belay.

Efficiency

With vertical caving, speed is often synonymous with safety. The time taken to climb the pitches is one aspect, but whether a particular pitch takes ten or fifteen minutes to climb is relatively unimportant and, given reasonable rigs and average ability, most cavers climb at about the same rate. More important is the organisation and competence of the team moving through the cave, so that no time is wasted waiting for each other or for equipment to arrive at the pitch. On the return there is no reason to wait at the top of each pitch until the whole team is up. This results in a long jam and an unnecessary delay at the next pitch. Better if each caver moves more or less independently, provided he carries his share of the equipment. Thus it is more efficient to carry gear up pitches while climbing, than involve another operation hauling it up from the top. Hauling is necessary only on particularly long pitches or where individual loads are too heavy to climb with. Where hauling is unavoidable, a separate, lighter line is used (8mm polypropylene) which saves wear and tear on valuable SRT rope and leaves the main rope undisturbed.

Derigging

The pitch is detackled by the last caver to ascend, but as soon as his tackle-sack is full he should then pass this equipment on, or leapfrog the rest of the team and head out of the cave, leaving the tackle on subsequent pitches to someone else. This is a loose system with many variations, but it is better to avoid the old habit of leaving vast amounts of detackling to the unlucky cavers at the rear. During derigging, all knots, krabs and hangers are left on the rope, which is simply stuffed into the tackle-sack and sorted out later when the rope is washed and returned to the store. Nothing is gained by messing about with this job underground.

Rescue

With SRT as each caver moves independently through the cave, he carries his personal gear and share of the rigging equipment and is entirely responsible for his own safety. However, accidents happen from time to time and injury may make any caver dependent on help from his colleagues; perhaps simply to regain the surface with minimal assistance or, in the worst case, to survive until full-scale rescue. It is easy to assume that your mates (being sound blokes) will naturally attempt to rescue you if necessary – but can they? Could you? Prior training is essential; willingness is no indication of the skill, strength and stamina necessary. The position may be complicated by having only the minimum gear available, perhaps limited to the normal soloing gear of a single caver. It is vital that vertical cavers operating in small groups are *all* capable of helping each other effectively. If this is not the case, you are caving with the wrong people!

Essential first-aid and emergency procedures are discussed in Chapter 17. This section deals only with the straightforward technical skills necessary to carry out an emergency rescue singlehanded.

Take, for example, the situation where a caver is immobilised in mid-rope (say by rockfall) and unable to help himself. Leave him hanging while you rush off for help and he will be either dead or severely distressed when you return. He may easily suffocate or bleed to death and, even if conscious and supported by a good harness, circulation to his legs is severely restricted, which leads to clotting and further complications. Immobile, he is soon prey to hypothermia, particularly in Britain where many pitches are rigged wet. It is vital to get him off the rope without undue delay. There are only two possible courses of action – pull him up or lower him down – and you can do this either from the top of the pitch or level with the casualty in mid-rope. Operating from the top of the pitch has the advantage of freedom of movement and perhaps exposing the rescuer to less risk than working in mid-rope – conceivably what happened to the casualty could happen to you. There are also many disadvantages. Hauling from above is slow and strenuous, and it might prove difficult to get the casualty off the rope at the pitch head.

Lowering is possible only if a spare rope is available and some means can be found of attaching this to the loaded rope. Neither hauling nor lowering is possible from above if the main rope is fixed to intermediate anchors in the pitch. Generally it is better to go down to the casualty, disengage him from the rope, then either ascend or descend with him in tow according to circumstance. Here you can administer essential first-aid, replace any faulty equipment or provide suitable advice. The techniques used are the normal ones of descending and climbing except that there are some tricks that will help, and certain slight modifications are necessary to cope with the extra weight of another person. Remember: a faulty manoeuvre may result in two casualties hanging from the rope or, worse, falling off it.

Basic Mid-rope Rescue
Climb up or reverse-prusik down (it is not possible to abseil on a loaded rope) to a position immediately above the casualty. Attach him to your main triangular M/R with a couple of

Fig 165 Basic mid-rope rescue (*below and right*)

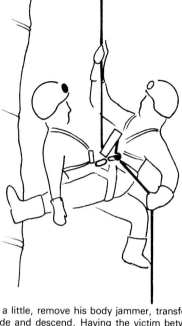

Prusik up a little, remove his body jammer, transfer to abseil mode and descend. Having the victim between your legs fends him off the rock.

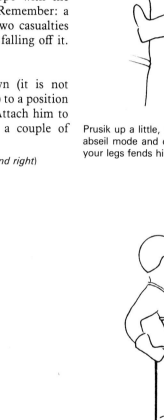

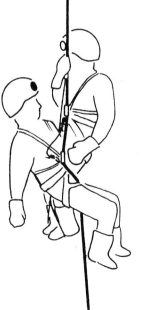

Reverse prusik down to the victim and attach him to your main *Maillon Rapide* with a cow's-tail, or krabs. Remove his footloop jammer.

On a narrow pitch the victim will have to be below the rescuer attached by a cow's-tail krabs or one of *his* cow's-tails (you may need yours to protect yourself; he will not) and remove his upper jammer from the rope (Fig 165a). A straight karabiner attachment is best against a wall, where with the casualty positioned between your legs you can use both feet to fend off the rock (Fig 165b). In a free-hanging or narrow pitch it is better if he hangs below on a cow's-tail (Fig 165c). Using the strength of both legs and taking short steps, ascend a little to take the weight and remove his body-jammer from the rope. The hapless casualty is now dangling from your main triangular M/R like a heavy tackle-sack. From this position you can either climb up (given sufficient strength) or change over and abseil down, using more or less the normal techniques. Generally it is better to abseil down to safety, then subsequently if necessary arrange some more efficient means of getting the casualty up the pitch. Abseiling is easier; intermediate anchors can be undone or passed as normal but using the footloop to help unclip your cow's-tail. Because of the increased weight the descender may provide insufficient friction for a safe descent and should be supplemented by a single turn around the braking karabiner (Fig 166). This is always a sensible precaution – the extra turn may be removed later if it proves unnecessary. Use auto-lock descenders with caution; they may prove impossible to release under the combined weight of two people.

Mid-rope Counterbalance Rescue
An alternative method of disengaging the casualty from the rope demands less effort but is more complicated and requires a jammer, a krab (and pulley?) and a length of cord (foot-loop?), all of which might be taken from the

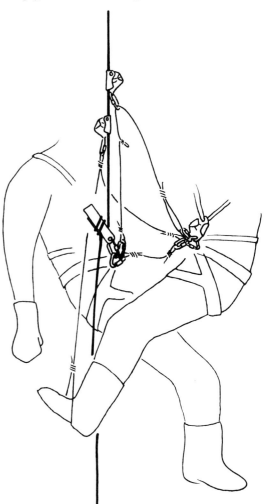

Fig 167 Counter-balance method of mid-rope rescue: after attaching the victim to the rescuer, the victim's upper jammer is transferred to the rope above and the victim attached to the rescuer through this by a foot-loop or cord. When the rescuer's body jammer is released both bodies are counter-balanced thus enabling release of the victim's body jammer. The victim's descender is now attached, locked off and his weight lowered onto it. The rescuer can now reattach himself, recover surplus gear, attach himself to the descender and begin the descent

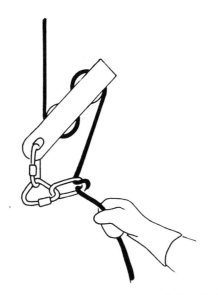

Fig 166 Descenders may provide insufficient friction when double-loaded. Extra friction can be obtained from a single turn around a krab

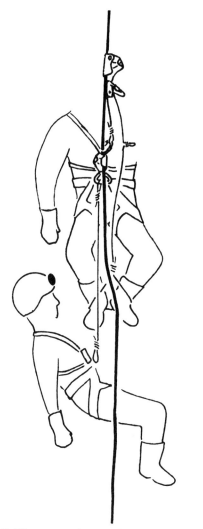

prusik down a little, clip into the same descender as the casualty and abseil down. Additional friction will be required to compensate for the increased weight.

It may sometimes be better to lift the casualty to the top of the pitch rather than go down; for instance in a flooding cave or when perhaps only a short distance from the top of a long pitch. Here, if necessary, the climbing system may be modified to make this easier by running the footloop cord over a krab (and/or a pulley) on the upper jammer and attaching it to the top of the body-jammer (Fig 168). It will probably be necessary to adjust the length of the cord for maximum gain, but this arrangement provides some mechanical advantage; climbing becomes less strenuous but slower. This technique might be essential where the casualty is noticeably heavier than the rescuer, or the lift is for more than a few metres. To maintain the necessary connection to both jammers, you can either clip a long cow's-tail to the upper jammer, place a bulky knot in the cord which will not pass through the pulley, or use the casualty's footloop jammer as a third point of attachment.

Reaching the top of the pitch now becomes a matter of perseverance, but once at the top it may still prove difficult to get the casualty off the rope. A high belay point is helpful, and it may be best to transfer the casualty back to the rope somewhere just below the pitch lip, leaving the rescuer free to arrange some other means of dragging him to safety.

Fig 168 When upward rescue is necessary, a pulley attached to footloop and jammer makes the ascent easier, and can be vital when the load is heavy

Hauling

It is possible to haul on the main rope by using an inverted jammer attached to the body-harness, for example a 'Croll' rigged into the harness upside down. Then by squatting and standing up the powerful leg muscles are sufficient to raise the loaded rope a short distance (Fig 169a). A second inverted jammer is attached to the anchor and installed on the rope so as to retain the slack gained with each cycle. For safety the rescuer is solidly fastened to the belay by a cow's-tail. This manoeuvre is possible either standing on ledges overlooking the pitch, or hanging from the main belay and standing in the footloop. The slack rope must be pulled through the upper jammer, which is often made easier by weighting the jammer (Fig 169b). This is the simplest method – also the most strenuous.

casualty. The rescuer reaches and links himself to the casualty with cow's-tails, before rearranging the casualty's upper jammer on the rope above and running the footloop or a cord through this to his own harness. By releasing his own body-jammer he can then use his weight to counterbalance the casualty's and thereby lift him a short distance to free the body jammer. He then installs the casualty's descender on the rope immediately below the body-jammer and locks it off securely (Fig 167) before lowering the casualty onto it. It is now a simple matter for the rescuer to reattach himself while recovering the surplus gear, then to

Fig 169 Basic hauling methods: strenuous   *Fig 170* Basic hauling methods: less strenuous

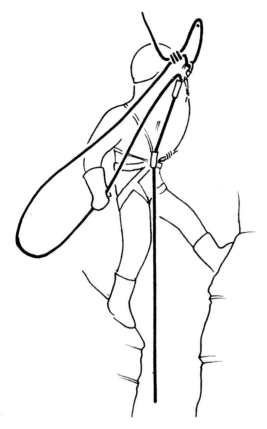

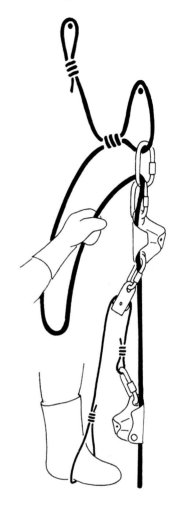

An inverted jammer is installed after the rescuer is attached to a belay point with a cow's-tail and an inverted jammer attached in place of his body jammer. A 'squat-stand' technique will raise the load. The top, inverted, jammer is used to retain the slack rope.

The operation is eased by weighting it with spare gear or a sack containing some rocks

A counter-balance system reduces the effort required. Two inverted jammers are used so that pulling on the lower jammer is made easier while standing in or hanging from the footloop. Slack can then be pulled through the upper jammer with the other hand

Where the pitch head permits, a counter-balance system makes the job easier. Attach yourself to the belay with a short cow's-tail and install an inverted jammer (here a Croll) on the rope with two karabiners above and a third krab (and pulley) below. A second inverted jammer is installed beneath this attached to a footloop running over the krab/pulley (Fig 170). A combination of standing in the footloop while pulling on the lower jammer with one hand is used to raise the loaded rope, and the slack rope is pulled through the upper jammer with the

Figs 171 – 2 More efficient hauling methods

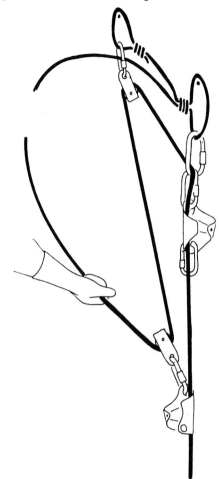

Pulley lift: inverted jammers/pulleys are used

Prusik lift: an inverted jammer is used at the pulley, the rescuer climbing up the slack

free hand. Again this is possible either stood on a ledge or hanging from the main belay. Slightly more technical – much less strenuous.

Once sufficient slack rope has been gained and provided that the extra equipment is available (a pulley and/or third jammer) it may be worth altering the system to one that works better. Two such possibilities are a straight-forward 'pulley-lift' (Fig 171), or a counter-balance technique involving climbing up the slack rope (Fig 172).

Lowering

Lowering from the pitch head is possible only if an extra rope is available and some slack is introduced (by hauling) into the loaded rope, so that it can be undone (or cut) and tied onto the lowering rope. The technique is to run the

lowering rope through an anchored descender and lock it off (Fig 173a). The main rope is tied to the lowering rope and then released so that the load is transferred to the descender, which is subsequently unlocked and the casualty lowered (Fig 173b).

Mid-rope Lower A variation of this technique allows lowering from a mid-rope position where the main rope is fastened to intermediate anchors in the pitch. A counterbalance tech-nique is used to disengage the casualty, who is then lowered from a descender (his own) attached to the main rope by a jammer (also his own).

From above, the rescuer abseils down the lowering rope (which must be at least as long as the pitch and can be clipped into the same belay

Fig 173 Methods of lowering: from the pitch head

Figs 174 – 6 Methods of lowering: from mid-rope (*below and opposite page*)

The loaded rope has first to be raised so that slack is obtained that can be cut or untied. The lowering rope is passed through a descender and locked off.

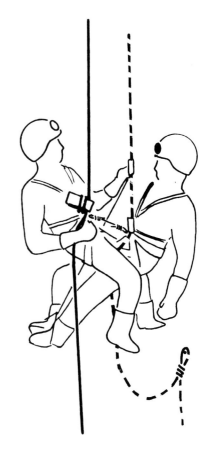

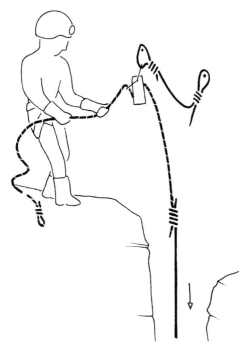

The lowering rope is now attached to the loaded rope, the jammers released and the victim lowered

The rescuer abseils down to the victim, locks off and connects himself (long cow's-tail).

points as the main rope), locks off and connects himself to the casualty with cow's-tails (Fig 174). He now removes the casualty's upper jammer, descender and two krabs, and attaches these to the main rope (Fig 175). The end of the lowering rope is tied to the casualty's harness, threaded through the descender leaving as little slack as possible and locked off. The casualty's footloop is threaded over a krab (and/or pulley) clipped to the descender and used to release the body-jammer. The descender is unlocked and the casualty lowered (Fig 176); the rescuer collects the spare gear and follows down the same rope.

From below the manoeuvre is similar, except that the rescuer is attached by jammers rather than a descender and works entirely on the main rope.

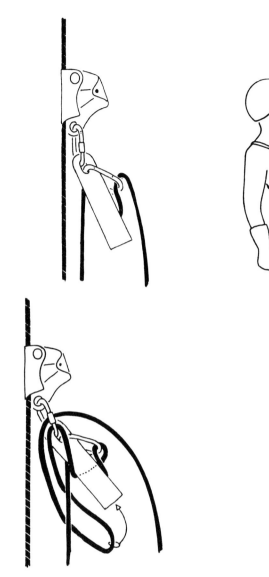

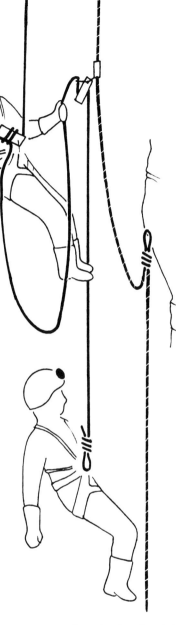

The victim's descender is installed on the main rope with his upper jammer. The lowering rope is attached to the victim, then threaded through the descender and locked off.

Lowering can commence after releasing the victim's body jammer

97

Fig 177 Hauling the full length of a pitch: (above) hauling with two people at the top or (opposite) a combination of counter-balance and hauling

Self-rescue

Once safely landed at the foot of the pitch, the situation can be weighed up and a decision made whether to attempt a self-rescue, send for help, or both. With sufficient tackle, manpower and a little practice, it is not difficult to haul someone up a straightforward pitch. Most of the problems can be overcome by brute force; where muscles are not available they can often be replaced by skill. Fig 177 shows two examples.

Faced with serious injuries perhaps requiring a stretcher, or where there is any doubt about the expertise of the hauling party, the job is best left to an experienced rescue team. This option might not be open to cavers in remote regions, and even in Britain it would not be good to leave a caver with a broken arm at the foot of a short entrance pitch or in a flooding cave. Before embarking upon a course of action, you must be absolutely confident of what the outcome will be; a mistake may kill the person you are attempting to rescue, and you will not help anybody by killing yourself!

5 Discovering Caves

DAVID JUDSON

The World's Caving Regions

Britain and Europe

Caves and potholes were first discovered by either walking, crawling, squeezing or boating in through a horizontal entrance, or by throwing a rope ladder down a shaft. In Britain, by the 1920s and 1930s all the open caves and potholes had been discovered. A similar stage was reached in Ireland in the 1960s and 1970s.

There are many areas of Europe where caves and potholes are undiscovered and unexplored: many parts of the Alps from France through Switzerland to Austria; in Italy and in Spain, north and south; in Yugoslavia, Hungary, Czechoslovakia and Bulgaria. These areas are either so vast, or rugged, or both, that it is likely to be a long time before every nook and cranny is fully investigated.

The Rest of the World

Further afield there are many areas still to be explored by cavers. The Zagros Mountains stretch for over 2,000km from the Persian Gulf near Bandar Abbas in the south into the wild country of north-east Iraq. They reach altitudes of over 4,000m, and for the most part consist of limestones of one sort or another. Only two small areas of this wild terrain have been visited by cavers.

Some areas of the world have not been looked at on account of their political problems but many more because of the expense of getting there. The mountains of central New Guinea and the tropical karst of Sarawak, Borneo, have been opened up only in the past few years, largely because of the logistical and cost problems associated with their locations.

The greatest karst area in the world – an area greater than that of the British Isles – lies in the Kwangsi Province of South China. None of its caves has been properly explored, and even today the local people are interested in them only as a source of water and power. The problems and logistics of organising caving expeditions abroad are looked at in Chapter 13.

In the British Isles today new caves are entered and known caves extended most commonly by means of some form of 'pushing'. This will either be through a surface dig, often initiated at an obvious natural feature, say a 'shakehole' or blocked shaft, or by an underground dig, or else through climbing up avens or passage walls, or through cave diving (Chapter 6).

Surface Digs

The first step, side by side with thinking out the logistics of a proposed dig, is to investigate land ownership and obtain permission. Except in a few rare circumstances, permission of the land-owner and/or tenant is *essential* before any work is carried out on the surface at a digging site. This task should not be underestimated – it may take months of patient negotiation. If the project is an ambitious one it may be worth attempting to buy or lease a small plot of land containing the proposed site.

Every dig has its problems related to situation, local geology, etc. But there are general principles which always apply:

1 The labour situation; how strong is your support for this project and for how long can the team be expected to stay together?
2 How isolated is the location of the dig? What are the access problems and will there be suitable transport available?
3 What technical expertise is available and what equipment can be bought, borrowed or otherwise obtained within the financial means available?
4 What are the constraints on time? How often

will it be possible for the team to put in work on the project and for what timespan are you going to plan?

5 What degree of mechanisation should be adopted? This will depend upon the answers to questions 1 to 4 above. It is no good planning on a sophisticated winch if you do not have the finance, the transport or the technical expertise to set it up and run it; equally useless to set up a manual-handling system that will require a minimum of four men to run if your team is going to drop to two or three on most working days.

As soon as the first day's work on any dig has been completed, it should be made fully stockproof. With a small cavity, good sound boarding may be sufficient, but very soon a sturdy fence becomes essential.

Surface digs take two basic forms; essentially either horizontal or vertical.

Horizontal Surface Digs
The simplest form of dig is the horizontal cave passage which merely has to be cleared of clay, rocks or other debris. Horizontal digs are commonly either active sinks or resurgences, or abandoned phreatic tubes (usually old resurgences). With the active resurgences or sinks the problem is one of following a vertical 'joint' or a horizontal 'bedding' along the water course in the hope of entering a section of larger passage or arriving at a confluence. Unless accreted debris, pebbles and mud are the direct cause of the constriction, the problem usually requires enlargement of the natural passage section by the blasting of rock or boulders. In an abandoned phreatic resurgence tube the problem is likely to be more mundane – the removal of clay and/or boulders. Where there is a sound natural cave roof the work will be straightforward, but where a major collapse feature occurs tunnelling and shoring will be required.

Estimating the amount of rock or fill which will need to be removed before a sufficiently large natural cavity can be followed is always difficult. If the passage appears to follow a route within two or three times its own diameter's depth below the surface then it could be worth carrying out either earth resistivity tests or a programme of seismic testing. Both these methods of testing for natural cavities have

proved exceedingly unreliable, particularly in limestone terrain (Hiscock 1976, Myers 1975). They are prone to being confused by shale beds, bedding planes and/or vertical joints, and by natural cavities filled with sand or clay. If the passage is sufficiently near to the surface to make either of these systems workable, it is also most likely to be choked to the roof with glacial fill.

You should set out on the assumption that the dig will be a long one. Establish a sound working system; if appropriate set up a railway line and a small tipping truck, then a stockproof fence should be erected around the dig as well as around the whole site. The dig should always be left fenced or gated. If the location is suitable it can be made into a 'show dig' and a small charge levied to defray expenses. Where blasting is involved, extreme caution must be exercised and a rigid safety procedure adopted. This is especially so with surface digs, where there will often be visitors (invited or otherwise).

When digging out fill in a horizontal passage the roof level will often rise considerably when a cross-joint is met with. If this rise turns out to be a large one, an aven perhaps, you will reach the point where it becomes unwise to excavate upwards any further. Shuttering will be needed if the horizontal progress is to continue safely. Traditional mining principles of shuttering should be followed; the main structure should

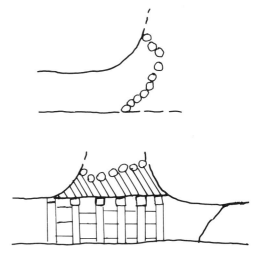

Fig 178 Shuttering and back-packing of 'deads' beneath a filled aven

be of good, sound timber in preference to steel or iron. Timber is not as rigid as steel or iron; it will move a little under pressure and, more importantly, if its stress limit is reached it will normally give some audible warning before final collapse! Steel sheet, corrugated iron, etc, are fine for infilling but should never be used for the main structure.

Where an aven has been partially excavated the resulting gap should be back-filled above the shuttering before work progresses further forward (Fig 178). The excavated material, where suitable, should be placed neatly on top of the shuttering until the space is well packed right up to the top of the previous excavation. If this is not done, blasting or even normal excavation further along the passage might disturb the material in the aven and cause it to drop disastrously from a height onto the shuttering.

Vertical Surface Digs
A vertical dig tends to be a more serious undertaking than a horizontal one because you are working directly against gravity. This not only means that the excavated material has to be lifted out before disposal, but also that the surrounding fill material is constantly attempting to enter the dig. For this latter reason, if there is choice in the precise location of the proposed dig it is usually better to choose a site which has as many solid rock walls as possible (Fig 179).

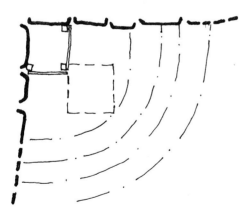

Fig 179 Where there is an element of choice, it may be better if the rock is good, clean and more or less vertical to choose the location offering maximum protection. If the rock is not so good it may be better to pick a central location, even though this will entail a greater amount of timbering

As with horizontal digs, favourite sites tend to be natural features, most often shakeholes, blocked shafts or at a significant point in a stream bed where water is observed to disappear. The stream-bed type of dig will always have water problems and unless the stream can be induced to sink at some other point higher up, or to bypass the dig and sink lower down, the project is likely to be at the mercy of the weather. This will also be true with shakeholes if the feature is large and takes a stream. Even if the shakehole is small with no noticeable stream sink, do not assume that it will be free of weather problems. Where there is clay or soil, even the most sound dig can become a sea of liquid mud after prolonged wet weather or a short spell of heavy rain.

Timbering/Shuttering

It is easy to produce neat drawings showing how to timber a shaft; the textbook examples are fine for excavating manholes in the high street, but less practical for a wet shakehole containing gritstone boulders, limestone fragments, clay, mud and sand. It is rarely possible to go down any worthwhile distance and then find a good base on which to build the shuttering. Moving-shuttering, which slides down under it own weight or is hammered down, has been tried unsuccessfully in a number of Northern Pennine digs. There are invariably sharp boulders or rock fragments which prevent the movement of the shuttering.

Two examples of traditional shaft timbering or shuttering are shown. They are to be found in most good textbooks on the subject and although the general principles are always applicable they are of limited use in shakehole excavations.

'Wedged shoring' is the simplest construction, using least timber. It is applicable in shallow excavations (not more than 3m in depth) where a small cross-section shaft can be used (not more than 1m maximum internally) and where the ground is stable.

'Keyed shoring' is a much better proposition for most cavers' digs in shakeholes. Although it involves more work and more timber it is infinitely stronger if properly constructed. Additional diagonal struts can be inserted as a secondary strengthening if the pressure on the main struts appears excessive. It will of course

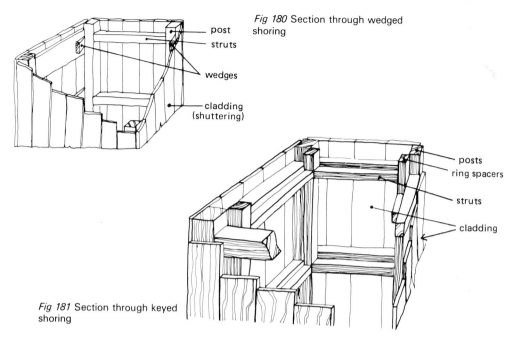

Fig 180 Section through wedged shoring

Fig 181 Section through keyed shoring

be better to anticipate this and put the diagonal struts in at the beginning.

In planning the dig it is advisable to make the initial shaft rather larger than might at first seem necessary for a number of reasons:

1 It will be easier to make successive 'rings' of timber a little smaller each time so that they can be slid down within the upper structure.
2 The addition of diagonal strutting will reduce the working area of the shaft.
3 If a failure of the structure seems likely, there will be the possibility of inserting additional reinforcement or an entirely new structure within the original one before collapse occurs.

The structure should also be designed so that it can be extended vertically upwards as well as downwards. In most shakehole digs the best place for the spoil will be the immediate vicinity of the shaft. By tipping in this handy way the immediate surrounds of the shaft will rise, making lifts in the timbering necessary.

Winches

Once a vertical dig has progressed to a depth of 8 or 10m it will be getting beyond the 'three-legs, rope and bucket' stage and will require a hand winch. Whereas rope clamps can be used as protection for hand-hauling buckets, a winch will provide better protection with a ratchet brake for the ascent and a friction brake for the descent, so that larger buckets, skips and rocks can be hauled out safely. Also there may be a requirement for heavy objects to be sent down, hand-tools, power tools or timber.

Set up the winch in as high a location as possible so that it will not have to be moved regularly as tipping proceeds. As digging progresses not only will the shaft become deeper, but also the top will rise as the spoil accumulates.

Heavy wrought-iron-framed miners' winches were once commonly used for surface shakehole digs but, as well as being extremely heavy, they tend to be scarce today. A lightweight winch with aluminium drum and angle-frame is much better if one can be put together, borrowed or otherwise obtained. In constructing such a winch, design it with a particular power source in mind. The power could be petrol or diesel engine, or an electric or hydraulic unit with remote power source. A remote power source is useful if the dig is internal but within a reasonable distance of a surface access point. It is a means of avoiding the dangerous fumes which are a by-product of petrol and diesel engines. If the engineering expertise is not available, consult one of the larger caving clubs

103

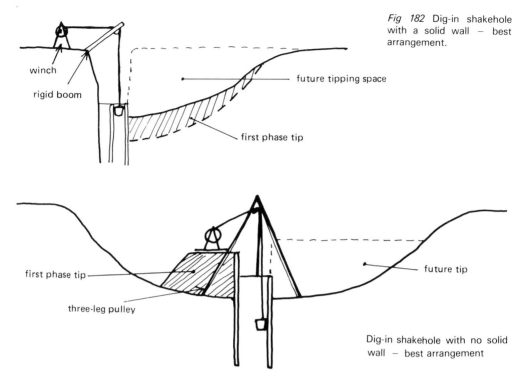

Fig 182 Dig-in shakehole with a solid wall — best arrangement.

winch

rigid boom

future tipping space

first phase tip

first phase tip

three-leg pulley

future tip

Dig-in shakehole with no solid wall — best arrangement

locally, most of which have designed and operated winches.

Once the dig is in excess of 12 or 15m of lift the idea of applying power to the winch will become an attractive one. This should be avoided for as long as possible. Even with a good engineer on hand the powered winch is likely to become a novelty and progress will be slowed rather than speeded up. However, if the dig is to continue, there will come a time when a powered winch is essential. The great Malham dig of the Craven Pothole Club in the 1950s and the Waun Fignen Felin dig of the South Wales Caving Club in the 1960s both reached over 30m (100ft) in depth.

Whatever the mechansim, choose simplicity – the less there is to go wrong the better. A four-stroke petrol or single-cylinder diesel engine is a cheap and easily obtainable solution. Diesels can be run from commercial 'gas-oil' which carries little tax and is less than half the price of petrol. There must be some form of clutch arrangement and a fail-safe brake. For digging it is best to adopt a free (hand-braked) descent rather than a driven descent, since the descending load will normally be small. For smaller digs and for portability an air-cooled motorbike

engine may be preferable.

The SWCC adopted a novel system at the above-mentioned dig. They obtained a lorry rear axle complete with bearings and brake drum, stood it on end and embedded almost half of it in the ground. A large capstan drum with four 2.6m (8ft) scaffold poles was bolted to the top. This provided a steady means of hauling, but required at least three people to operate it.

Underground Digs

Only a few basic types of feature bring about the end of exploration in a cave passage. These are the features which present themselves as cave-digs or as diving locations:

1 Passage (bedding plane) becomes too low to pass.
2 Passage (rift) becames too narrow to pass.
3 Route blocked by boulders.
4 Route blocked by fill of sand, clay or gravel.
5 Passage roof dips below water level.

Removal of Passage Constrictions
The first two situations require the removal of rock. Two factors should be evaluated here

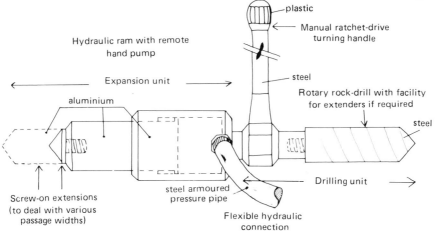

plastic

Manual ratchet-drive
turning handle

Hydraulic ram with remote
hand pump

Expansion unit

steel

aluminium

Rotary rock-drill with facility
for extenders if required

steel

Drilling unit

Screw-on extensions
(to deal with various
passage widths)

steel armoured
pressure pipe

Flexible hydraulic
connection

Fig 183 Hand-powered hydraulic rock drill

before a serious digging project is started. Is there any real prospect of the bedding plane or rift becoming higher or wider within a reasonable distance? If the answer to this is 'yes', then it must be considered whether explosives will be needed or whether the rock will allow removal with a bar or with lump-hammer and chisel.

If explosives are required you will need to seek assistance from someone with an explosives licence. To have obtained this licence (usually a 'private use' licence under the Explosives Act 1888) he is likely to be competent in the use of explosives and the techniques, but a few principles and techniques are worth looking at in detail here.

If anything other than very small-scale blasting is to be attempted then shot-holes should be drilled. Unless the constriction is an extremely abrupt affair the passage will have narrowed gradually and the working space will be constricted. This usually puts the use of lump-hammer and stardrill out of the question. The most valuable tool for most constricted rock-removal is the expanding drill. This is a development of the primitive tool used in mining before the onset of present-day automation; a rotating hand-powered drill with a facility, mechanical or hydraulic, for pushing against the opposite wall, the floor or the roof. These are being developed by cavers and are owned by most of the regional cave-rescue organisations. They cannot be purchased off the shelf at reasonable cost, or in a sufficiently compact or robust form to be of use in caving. The hydraulic version of the 'pushing unit' is considered the most suitable since the pump

can be located remote from the drill and if necessary operated by a second person. The unit must have a number of extension pieces so that it can be used in a variety of passage cross-sections. The parts of the drill should be designed to knockdown easily and pack away into an ammunition box for carrying through the cave. Although it is usual to choose a drill size appropriate to one of the gelignite pack diameters (according to local availability), with plaster gelatine a smaller-sized hole could be used and special packs made up in advance. In a small-scale operation this could dramatically speed up the drilling task.

Where it is practicable to drill more than one shot-hole at one session this should be done and multiple firing practised. It will save time and effort with the firing procedure, and is particularly attractive if the immediately preceding section of cave passage is constricted or unpleasant – more often than not the case! It will also be a good ploy if the air conditions are fairly static or the draught is incoming from the dig and the whole cave has to be evacuated until the fumes clear.

If detonation is not possible from outside the cave entrance, before choosing a site for detonation, bear in mind the following:
1 Rock fragments can rebound around corners – always pass at least four distinct corners before choosing a site.
2 Double check to ensure that there is not another passage or a window, perhaps at high level, which could act as a bypass for the airwave or for the flying rock debris.

Fig 184

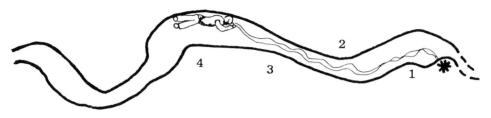

Danger from rock debris. Pass at least four corners

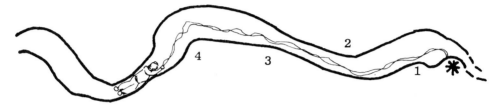

Danger from air-wave. Do NOT fire from a constricted location

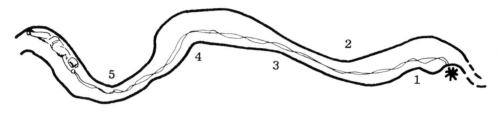

Good location; around five corners and beyond two constrictions

3 In a constricted passage the 'corners rule' can give a location still very close to the explosion. Eardrums can be damaged by the air-wave. Do not fire a charge whilst you are situated in a constriction in the passage – choose a point where there is a considerable widening so that the airwave can pass without harm. If in doubt move further away!

4 Take notice of air currents. If a draught shows any sign of coming out towards you from the dig then fire from a long distance away – preferably in a large space where the fumes will disperse. Do not allow previous experience at the same dig to influence your thoughts; air currents change with external weather conditions, not only in a seasonal way but sometimes from hour to hour (Williams 1975). If in doubt move out!

5 Finally, examine the chosen firing location

for structural stability. This is particularly important if it is quite close to the blast or if you are still within the active area of a large boulder choke.

Using Explosives

Initiation

Two methods are available for the initiation of explosives: (1) plain detonator and slow fuse and (2) electric detonator.

It is preferable to equip for electric firing. The method is safer and more versatile than slow fuse detonation, but there are a few exceptions. Where only one shot is required and the route of 'escape' is spacious and unobstructed, the use of plain detonator and slow fuse could be the more straightforward approach. Here a carbide lamp for igniting the slow fuse will be

Fig 185

Plaster charge placed as far forward as can be reached
– unlikely to be effective

One shot-hole as far forward as possible; difficult to drill
and not very effective on its own

Two shot-holes in easy-to-drill locations; likely to be
very effective

Fig 186

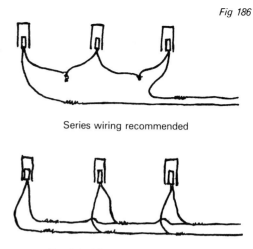

Series wiring recommended

Parallel wiring not recommended

useful, and far better than any type of match. Slow fuse is designed to burn at 100–160 seconds per metre. *Never* use less than one metre, even in the most favourable 'escape' conditions. If there is any doubt concerning the time required to reach a safe firing position, then allow at least twice your estimated time.

For most cave work the instantaneous electric detonator is used. The Nobel No 6 type with 180cm copper leads is probably the most suitable. It is powerful enough to initiate all the commonly available permitted explosives and presents a low electrical resistance (quoted by the manufacturer as between 1.0 ohms and 2.2 ohms).

Where multiple charges are to be fired these are connected either electrically (one detonator for each charge) or physically by the use of instantaneous-detonating fuse. This latter method causes fewer problems in the usual grotty cave environment.

Electrically Fired Multiple Charges – Series Wiring Multiple shot charges should *never* be wired in parallel. There will be a high risk of

one or other of the electrical connections (in the example in Fig 186 there are six) being less good than the rest. Thus there would be a high risk of one, or even two, of the charges not firing. Partial misfires of this type can lead to all sorts of danger. Somewhere beneath the debris of the blast will be an explosive charge complete with detonator and wires. With surface work this tends to be less serious, but the risk of a partial misfire can also be greatly reduced with the use of a large 'professional exploder'. These are too large, heavy and electrically dangerous to be recommended for normal cave use. Thus series wiring is essential.

With series wiring the voltage required in order to be certain of a firing can be calculated as follows:

Where
number of detonators = d
resistance of each detonator = 2 ohms
minimum current required = 1.5 amps
resistance of firing wire = 5 ohms
Voltage = total resistance by current by number of detonators = $(5 \times 2d) \times 1.5$

If a safety factor of 2 is introduced, then minimum voltages required will be:

Number of detonators	Minimum voltage
1	21
2	27
3	33
4	39
5	45
6	51

Fig 187

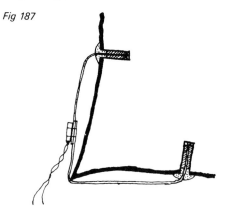

Always avoid sharp bends in the Cordtex

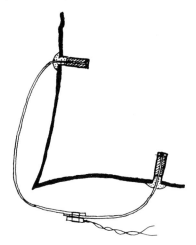

Satisfactory

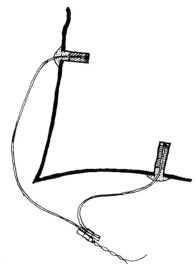

Satisfactory

These are the worst (highest) voltages likely to be required for certain firing. With a thicker firing cable or a shorter length of cable (here assumed as 100m) and clean conditions the voltages required *could* be much less. Since detonator fusehead resistance can vary with manufacture between 0.9 and 1.6 ohms, the above figures could be halved for a batch of good detonators. However, there is no means of knowing this unless a circuit resistance tester is used every time. A suitable meter is available from the Nobel Company, but it is better to employ a system of operation where there can be little need for it.

It can be seen that if multiple firing by this method using two or more detonators is to be employed, then it will be essential to use a small professional exploder (or a similar home-made device) such as the Marston type M.E.12 Kk 2. This can handle up to twelve detonators in series and will deliver a consistent current flow of 1.4 amps at about 80 volts over a 4-millisecond pulse. This could give a painful shock in damp conditions if abused or misused. The larger exploders such as the Schaffler type 750, type 770 or the Beethoven cannot be recommended; not only are they heavy and bulky but with output voltages of 600 or even 1200 volts they can be lethal!

Instantaneous Fuse With this method only one electric (or even plain No 6) detonator is used for each multiple-shot firing. The individual charges are linked together with instantaneous-detonating fuse. This fuse is waterproof, having a thick plastic covering around a core of very high-speed explosive powder. Its detonation speed of 6500m per second is generally regarded as 'instantaneous'!

A 150m/500ft roll of this material, Cordtex or Pentoflex, is the equivalent of 3½lb of explosives, for licence purposes. It is an efficient blasting accessory with a wide range of uses.

Individual charges should be made up and placed first, except that instead of a detonator being located within the charge, the fuse is threaded all the way through it and knotted beyond.

Connections should then be made between the individual charges using adhesive tape or spent detonator wire, and the detonator should be taped to the end of the final length of fuse or fuses. Take care to ensure that all junctions

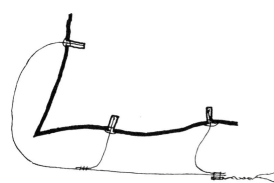

Fig 188
WRONG! This will not work, one line is in reverse direction

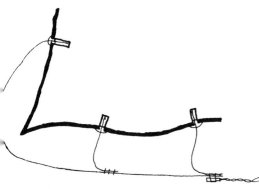

Satisfactory

instantaneous fuse 'Cordtex'

charge   clay stemming

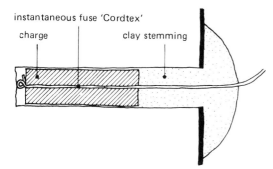

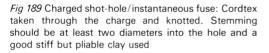

Fig 189 Charged shot-hole/instantaneous fuse: Cordtex taken through the charge and knotted. Stemming should be at least two diameters into the hole and a good stiff but pliable clay used

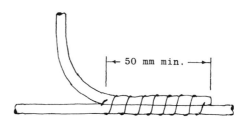

Fig 190 Two Cordtex lines may be joined with adhesive tape or with wire

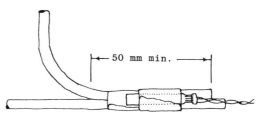

Where the detonator is located it is safer to use only adhesive tape

diverge in the direction of the blast and not against it, and that there are no sharp bends involved. For further reading see ICI 'Nobel' advisory booklets.

Blasting Accessories

The crimping pliers/cutters as supplied by Nobel are useful. The longest leg of the handle has a copper-covered end designed for safely making a hole through a pack of explosive for insertion of the detonator, or for the instantaneous fuse to be passed through. There are sharp cutting blades below the crimper for trimming slow or instantaneous fuse (Fig 191). A pocket-sized exploder/circuit-tester will make the firing routine safer and easier. For single or twin-detonator firings a small robust unit can be made up, based on one of the smaller diecast aluminium boxes available from DIY electronics shops. The device has the same circuitry as the capacitor flashgun used in photography, and the principle is identical to that of the flash-

copper end

cutter crimper

Fig 191 Nobel Special crimping pliers

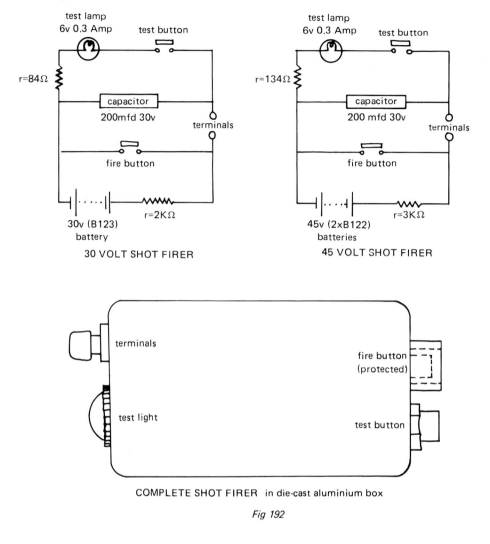

test lamp
6v 0.3 Amp

test button

r=84Ω

capacitor
200mfd 30v

terminals

fire button

r=2KΩ

30v (B123)
battery

30 VOLT SHOT FIRER

test lamp
6v 0.3 Amp

test button

r=134Ω

capacitor
200 mfd 30v

terminals

fire button

r=3KΩ

45v (2xB122)
batteries

45 VOLT SHOT FIRER

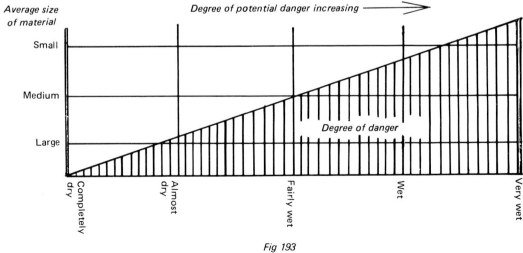

terminals

fire button
(protected)

test light

test button

COMPLETE SHOT FIRER   in die-cast aluminium box

Fig 192

Average size
of material

Degree of potential danger increasing

Small

Medium

Large

Degree of danger

Completely
dry

Almost
dry

Fairly wet

Wet

Very wet

Fig 193

gun, with test bulb and button, firing button and a pair of sprung terminals in place of the bulbholder; but the whole thing needs to be 'beefed-up' a little to give more power and a higher working voltage.

The unit can be based on two Ever Ready type B122 batteries (2×22.5 volts), or on a single type B123 (30-volt) battery. Two suitable circuits are shown (Fig 192).

If the special pliers are not to be used, ie where no slow fusework is contemplated, then a pointed wood or plastic piercing tool will suffice, and a sharp penknife will be required for cutting fuse. A roll of drawing-board tape, masking tape or insulating tape will be useful for making the instantaneous fuse connections, and essential for connecting the fuse to the detonator. Thin rubber gloves are strongly recommended if there is any likelihood of handling the explosive outside of its pack, ie for awkward face-blasting or for use with very small-diameter shot-holes. Direct skin contact with plaster gelatines can have effects similar to, and as serious as, breathing the fumes created by detonation (Williams 1975).

Boulder Chokes

The 'digging' of boulder chokes inside caves is possibly the most dangerous activity outside of cave diving. Every boulder choke is different. In the British Isles over the last twenty-five years the 'pushing' of boulder chokes has led to the discovery of more cave passages than any other exploration activity, namely all of Agen Allwedd, Ogof Craig a Ffynnon, and in Ogof Ffynnon Ddu, Dan-yr-Ogof, Mongo Gill Hole and St Cuthberts Swallet. The risks are great but the rewards may be considerable.

Three basic factors affect the stability of a boulder choke:

1 Average size of the material.
2 Degree of wetness or dryness.
3 Length of time since last settlement.

For classification purposes we can use three definitions for average size of material:

Small – most will pass a 150mm ring
Medium – most will pass a 600mm ring
Large – most will not pass a 600mm ring

Definitions for wetness are more difficult; there are boulder chokes which are completely dry (they have no running water vertically or horizontally) and others have torrential amounts of water running through them from top to bottom. Many others might be described as relatively dry – they may have small trickles of water in average weather conditions and more in heavy flood. Still others have small streams running across their base, and these are potentially very dangerous. Such a stream may appear insignificant; it may never be seen, but is always there, undermining the foundations of the structure. In heavy flood it may cause serious undermining and leave the choke hanging in mid-air awaiting the arrival of the next caver to trigger off collapse!

Generally the larger the average size of the material, the drier it is, and the longer it has been there then the safer it is likely to be. Age is the most difficult factor – unless there are obvious scratch-marks from recent movement of large boulders there can be little evidence. Fig 193 illustrates the relative dangers of boulder chokes, but must be regarded as only a general guide; there are many other factors which may also come into play. When was this boulder choke last interfered with by a caver? Has there been any blasting in this vicinity recently? What is the total height of the collapse – does it go all the way to the surface? Have there been any recent earth tremors in the area?

Methods of Working
Establish a safe working position. Where there is a possibility of following one solid feature this should be done; it might be a partial tube (wall and part roof), a vertical wall or at worst just solid floor. This solid feature can be used for propping against. Where there is a stream running across the base of the choke, follow it. In this way you can see and act against any undermining that it is tending to perform. Dexion duckboards can be used to keep diggers out of the water, with legs adjusted to suit the flow – thus the propping can be made direct from the solid floor and be known to be safe.

Poking and prodding should be done with a long bar or stick, with the digger remaining in the safe position. As soon as a space has been made and the fallen boulders removed, that space should be protected by further propping and shoring. The biggest danger is to advance too far without protection. It is always tempting to do this – to squeeze into the new space and look further ahead. Always resist the temptation until adequate propping has been completed.

There is no substitute for heavy timber sections for initial propping and temporary shuttering (see page 102). Heavy steel sections and/or reinforced concrete are more appropriate for permanent support once a route through has been safely established. Since forces can never be accurately known always assume the worst possible case. Some idea can be obtained by assessing the total width of the choke. As with an opening in a stone wall, there will be a bridging effect – similar to the angle of repose. Although this will be affected by the average size of the material and the angularity of it, it can be assumed to be about 40 to 50° from the horizontal. By assessing the weight of material within this triangle you can get an approximation of the maximum forces (Fig 194).

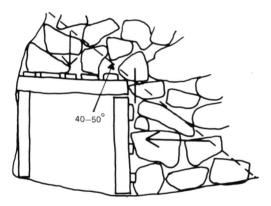

Fig 194 Rough method of estimating maximum weight likely to be acting on an excavation

Vertical Boulder Chokes

The vertical excavation of boulder chokes is the most dangerous pursuit of all. Digging upwards through a boulder choke is never safe. For a distance of up to 2 or 3m a long pole for dislodging rocks, and/or small explosive charges placed on key boulders, can sometimes achieve a successful result. But if the choke has any great height, and no higher series of passages are found within a few metres of digging, then the excavation must be abandoned.

Digging downwards into a boulder collapse is different. The same principles apply here as with a surface shaft excavation, but such excavations are always likely to be well lubricated with water. There have been many such

digs in Yorkshire potholes in recent years – Long Kin East Pot, Boggarts Roaring Hole, Ireby Fell Cavern and Lost Pot. The water always presents the greatest danger, both during the excavations and, if the venture is successful, to all those who pass that way afterwards. At Lost Pot on Leck Fell, water recently undermined the base of an excavation and resulted in a major collapse and a very serious accident to one of the diggers.

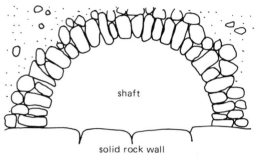

Fig 195 Dry-stone-walling technique used to protect vertical-shaft dig

Dry-stone walling in the form of an arch has been used successfully in a number of Northern Pennine Club digs. Even with weak-mix cement slurry pumped in afterwards to assist with stabilisation, this technique requires skill and practice and is unsuitable for general use. Failure can be sudden and disastrous.

Tools and Equipment (*see table opposite*)

Roof Passages and Aven Climbing

An oft-overlooked means of gaining new ground is through 'roof exploration'. In high cave passages, such as the Master Caves in the Northern Pennines and the large river passages in South Wales, the roof may be difficult to observe. It is often worth a special caving trip with high-powered lighting – a cine lighting unit, or something smaller with a good reflector and a narrow-width beam – to confirm roof passages and investigate easy climbing routes. Eventually you will need to choose a place to begin climbing. Depending upon the scale of the aven, or the width of the passage, one of three techniques (or a combination) is used.

Tools and Equipment

Lump-hammer and chisel	Useful in all digging operations
Plugs and feathers	Rock and boulder splitting
Short bar (horsehead)	Useful in all digging operations
Long (heavy) bar	Useful in all large-scale operations
Entrenching tool	Horizontal digs in sand or fine fill
Short shovel or spade	Ditto, also shaft sinking in fine material
Trowel	General use; confined spaces
Saws (various)	Essential for any dig requiring timbering
5kg hammer	Rock splitting/general timbering work
Buckets/tubs	Mainly shaft sinking
Trolleys/sleds	Horizontal digs
Block and tackle	Shaft sinking
Pulleys	Ditto
Vehicle inner tubes with pre-sealed ends	For transporting cement underground
Rope nets	Shaft sinking; large rocks
Scaffold poles	Shaft sinking and for support of boulders
A-frames and tripods	Shaft sinking
Tirfors	Large-scale boulder digs
Rock drill	Underground digs where rock-blasting or fixing holes are required
Power drill	Surface digs where fumes will not be a problem (and underground digs near to entrance)
Hand winch	Deep/large-scale shaft sinking
Power winch	Deeper/large-scale shaft sinking
Capstan winch	Ditto
Smoke bombs	Testing draughting passages; cave to cave; cave to surface, etc
Inductorphones (Molephones)	Position checking; surface to cave; cave to cave, etc
Ropes (synthetic fibre)	Hauling, protection, etc, all digs
Pipes (plastic)	Diversion of water, all digs
Timber (all sizes)	Tunnelling and shaft work
Hydraulic jacks	Making minor adjustments, all digs
Adjustable props (Acro props)	Propping (not recommended for general use)

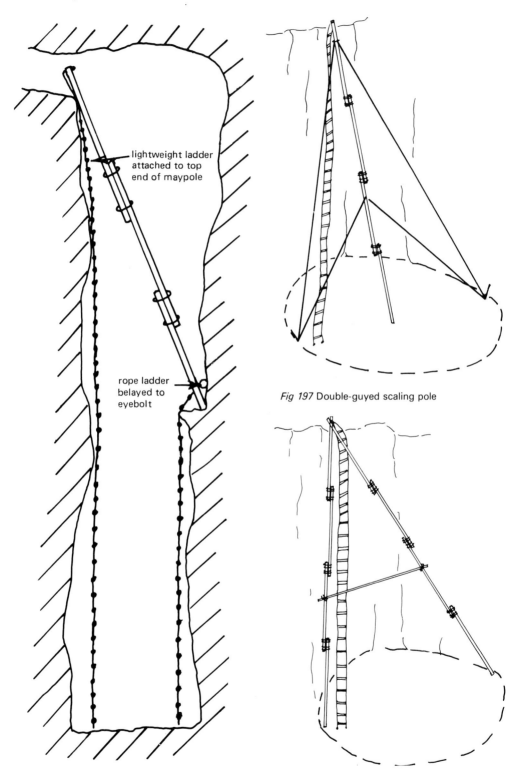

lightweight ladder
attached to top
end of maypole

rope ladder
belayed to
eyebolt

Fig 197 Double-guyed scaling pole

Fig 196 Use of a maypole

Fig 198 A-frame structure

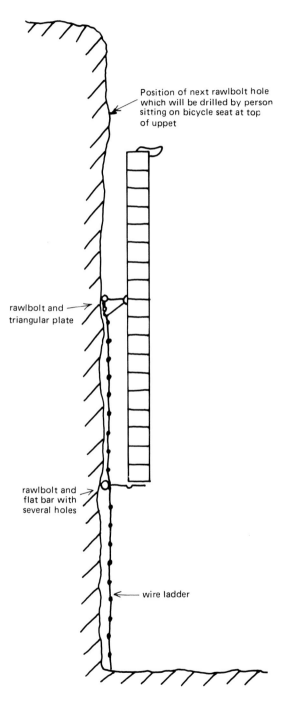

Position of next rawlbolt hole which will be drilled by person sitting on bicycle seat at top of uppet

rawlbolt and triangular plate

rawlbolt and flat bar with several holes

wire ladder

Fig 199 Uppet in position for drilling third hole

Rock-climbing Techniques

Where there are ledges, joints or projections, it may be possible to use standard open-face rock-climbing techniques or a more speleological chimneying/bridging technique. Either way, as with outdoor rock-climbing, it is wise to put in some kind of protection every 2 or 3m. This should take the form of pitons, threads or chockstones, or where there are no suitable natural features small 'red-head' bolts. Bolting equipment is described in Chapter 3, but smaller sizes – down to those which will take a ¼in high-tensile bolt – will suffice.

If you do not have rock-climbing experience within your group or club, try to encourage an experienced rock-climber to join you for the exercise.

Scaling Poles

For a specific task of reaching a promising ledge high up in a cave passage, or climbing an aven which is well broken with ledges, a scaling pole can be useful. There are two types, either built up from standard 50mm scaffold pole and fittings, or purpose-made with sleeve joints or other patent connectors. The simpler the system the better. Sleeve joint connectors tend to suffer physical damage in transit and also become clogged with mud. With scaffold poles the internal 'banana'-type connectors tend to be too sloppy, and it is better to use simple external-angle connectors with bolts through the poles, or with external clamps.

Where scaling poles are extended to more than 5 or 6m, you will need to use one or more tensioning guys on each side to reduce the bending effect and make the structure more rigid. A supply of duralamin scaffold poles can be put to a number of uses, and for a high climb it might be better to construct an A-frame out of these alone.

Bolting Platforms

In the early 1960s the South Wales Caving Club developed a short rigid ladder system (the Uppet), as a means of climbing passage walls and high avens (Cullingford 1969). This was a useful but cumbersome piece of equipment. Recently a lightweight device called a bolting platform has been developed. It is compact enough to fit into a tackle-bag and is a considerable advance over unaided bolting – each bolt takes the climber a further 1.4 or 2m.

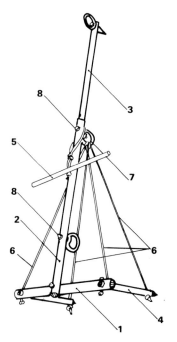

Main frame (2) Tube 26—30mm

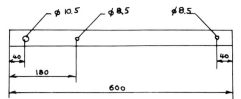

Main frame extension (3) Tube 21—25mm

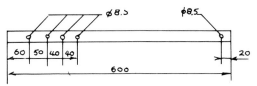

Cross member (1) Tube 26—30mm

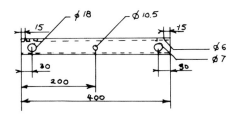

Rock struts (4) Tube 16—18mm

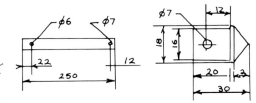

Knee support (5) Tube 16—18mm

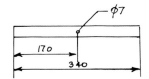

Bolting platform

(1) cross member; (2) main frame;
(3) main frame extension; (4) rock struts;
(5) knee support; (6) main tension
cords; (7) 7mm ring; (8) 8 x 50mm ring
main anchorage

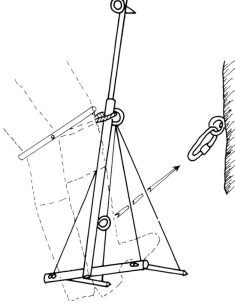

Fig 200

6 Cave Diving

MARTYN FARR

Cave diving, the exploration of totally submerged cave passages, is the most specialised caving technique. It involves the highest level of risk of any caving activity. The hazards of open-water aqualung diving, together with most of the objective dangers met with by cavers, are here combined in the one activity; a cave diver must be thoroughly competent at both.

Motivation for cave diving came originally from the same source as for all the other caving activities; a desire to explore the unknown. Until recent years the passing of a 'sump' or a sumped section of cave passage was merely a means to an end, the same way that the digging out of a boulder choke or the blasting away of a rock constriction was. Since about 1977 a new motivation has emerged. Much of the emphasis is now placed upon cave diving for its own sake – record-breaking dives of length, depth or duration, but principally length (Farr 1980).

History

The history of cave diving in Britain is essentially that of the Cave Diving Group. The CDG was formed in 1946 largely as a result of the early work of Graham Balcombe. The evolution of cave diving is closely linked with improvements in diving equipment. Prior to World War II the only form of diving apparatus available was 'standard diving equipment' – the 'hard-hat' surface demand apparatus. This was used with limited success at Wookey Hole in 1935, and a scaled-down version was used the following year when Sump I was passed in Swildon's Hole. Any form of apparatus that involves air being pumped down to the diver gave serious problems for caving use.

The first major advance came with closed-circuit oxygen rebreathing apparatus, developed during the war years. For the first time divers became independent of surface links, and for sump exploration this equipment was to be used almost exclusively from 1945–60. Models included the DSEA, P-Party, UBA and Sgamtu, but the principle of operation was the same. Divers breathed 100 per cent oxygen from a breathing bag while the carbon dioxide produced during respiration was removed by allowing the gas to pass through a canister of soda lime. A great deal of training was required to operate this equipment competently and divers had to be aware of all manner of hazards that do not exist with contemporary equipment. Oxygen poisoning (a sudden blackout with no warning) was a major risk if the diver went below a depth of 10m. This limit proved to be a severe restraint upon exploration until the late 1950s when oxygen/nitrogen mixtures were used for the deeper dives. Using 50/50 oxygen/nitrogen it is possible to dive to 30m in safety; but such apparatus was more specialised and required a greater level of proficiency in its use.

The method of underwater movement during this period was predominantly bottom-walking. Difficulties existed in achieving neutral buoyancy due to the varying quantity of gas in the breathing bag and the air in the dry-suit. Consequently it was more practicable for divers to weight themselves heavily and walk along the sump floor rather than attempt to use fins.

In 1962 there was a significant change; Mike Boon was largely responsible for the introduction of open-circuit aqualung techniques to cave diving. Boon's early kit consisted of a single 26cu ft (750 litre) cylinder of compressed air and a demand valve – the suit and method of movement were not much altered. The aqualung had been pioneered by Cousteau and Gagnon in the war years and had been widely adopted for cave-diving explorations on the Continent since that time. Once a diver had achieved proficiency with this apparatus the

hazards were appreciably less than those involved with oxygen apparatus. The most important consideration now became the duration of the air supply. By the open-circuit principle, the air, once breathed, is blown to waste; thus for the same volume of gas the duration of this type of equipment is much less than that of the closed-circuit type. Provided that the diver maintained a close watch upon his pressure gauge, the new apparatus fulfilled the desired role; it was portable, flexible and relatively uncomplicated. Adoption of this equipment by the Cave Diving Group was accelerated by a fatal accident to a cave diver using oxygen.

During the early 1960s the use of open-circuit apparatus became universal among cave divers. The wet-suit superseded the dry-suit, and without the problem of varying or shifting buoyancy the use of fins also caught on. By 1964 all these items of diving equipment were available commercially, and the practice of cave diving spread. The 26cu ft bottles became obsolete by the early 1970s and larger cylinders took their place. The use of a second, completely separate reserve system was normal by 1971 together with a range of complimentary equipment.

In the 1970s cave-diving equipment and techniques were continually being reappraised. Spare lighting in the form of helmet-mounted torches became standard after 1976 whilst in the previous year Geoff Yeadon and the late Oliver Statham pioneered underground use of the neoprene dry-suit. This enables the diver to remain warmer and, via a pair of valves in the suit, to adjust his buoyancy at will. In this way considerable quantities of air may be transported, allowing divers to achieve much longer penetrations. Other than for the major dives that have been undertaken in Keld Head, the use of such dry-suits is comparatively rare at the present time, and for the majority of underground explorations the wet-suit (possibly incorporating several layers of neoprene) is usual.

Physiological Aspects

The physiological aspects of diving are of prime importance. The more common occurrences

(opposite) A cave diver explores

affecting the cave diver are discussed here, and prospective cave divers should read the section on anatomy, physiology and relevant hazards in *A Cave Diver's Training Manual* (Lloyd 1975).

Ear Clearing
As the diver descends, the pressure on either side of the eardrums must be equalised or the drums will distort and rupture, causing severe pain. Ear clearing may be achieved by opening the Eustachian tubes connecting the middle ear to the respiratory tract. Gentle jaw-movements, swallowing or pinching the nose and blowing slightly will usually prove successful. This action should begin as soon as the dive commences. Under no circumstances should the diver attempt to descend if he feels increasing pain in the ears.

Air Embolism (Burst Lung)
As the diver ascends in the water the air in his lungs expands. If this is not allowed to escape in the normal manner it will overfill the lungs and be forced into the surrounding tissue and blood, with serious results. It is essential that the diver breathes normally on ascent. On no account should he hold his breath.

Decompression Sickness
Decompression sickness – the 'bends' – occurs if a diver ascends too rapidly from depth. It is due to the formation of bubbles of nitrogen in the blood, which block small blood vessels and so cause the death of tissue supplied by those vessels. Shortage of blood to nervous tissue can result in paralysis. The occurrence of decompression sickness depends solely upon a diver's length of stay at depth and the speed of his subsequent ascent. If a diver remains at depth for a long time his body fat absorbs nitrogen; when he reascends, if all goes correctly, the nitrogen comes out of solution in the body and dissolves in the blood, later to be voided harmlessly via the lungs. This process takes time. If decompression occurs too rapidly, the nitrogen coming out of solution in the body may form into bubbles in the blood stream, with damaging results. If a diver does contract the bends, the only safe recourse is for him to undergo a rapid recompression, followed by a slow decompression; this is usually done in a special chamber under medical supervision.

The important factor in avoiding decompression sickness lies in making an accurate assessment of the amount of nitrogen that has been absorbed into the body during a dive. Shallow dives, less than 10m, involve little risk, but at 30m depth a twenty-minute dive is all that you can safely undertake before the need for careful decompression procedures arises. If you exceed this time, a decompression 'stop' must be made during the ascent.

Tables have been published (Lloyd 1975) dealing with this problem. If you wish to make long dives at great depths it is essential to plan the dives beforehand and take down a reliable watch, depth gauge and submersible tables. Never rely on guesswork; decompression meters can be unreliable.

Nitrogen Narcosis
Nitrogen narcosis is a disturbing affliction associated with diving to depth. Sometimes known as the 'rapture of the deep', the effect is to blunt the diver's awareness and to instil in him a false and irresponsible euphoria. Occasionally the symptoms of narcosis include depression or blackout. There is no way of preventing this hazard, but a diver is immediately cured as he ascends from depth. Although individual limits of tolerance vary (and this tolerance can be built up by making regular deep dives) the reaction is rarely significant at depths of less than 36m.

Equipment

The compressed-air equipment available for cave diving is that used for open-water diving; no breathing apparatus has yet been designed specifically for underground use. A wide selection of demand valves and air cylinders is available and to some extent the kit used depends on the preference of the diver – provided that it is reliable, tough, simple and portable.

Cylinders
Bottle sizes used by cave divers vary in capacity from approximately 12–110cu ft (340–3100 litres) and they should be made of steel rather than aluminium. Steel is much better for withstanding abrasion. For safety reasons all cylinders must receive a regular pressure test. Perhaps the most common cylinders currently used are those in the 45–50cu ft range (1270–

1400 litres). When fully charged these have a normal pressure rating of 3000lb per sq in or slightly less (approximately 200 bars), and are 14cm in diameter. Such bottles can be expected to give a duration of forty-five to fifty minutes at shallow depth. For anything but the shortest of dives a completely separate reserve cylinder and demand valve would be used. A pillar valve, or alternative, will be fitted to the bottle outlet, the type depending on whether the attachment to the demand valve is by a screw thread or an A-clamp.

The cylinder is attached to the diver by a cylinder-band and webbing harness. A quick-release harness is to be preferred, as kit may have to be removed under water on occasions. The bottle is normally worn on the diver's side to give maximum protection to the valve and seating; the diver is also far more streamlined than if he wore a cylinder on his back, and he is in a much better position to pass low sections encountered on the dive.

Demand Valves
The demand valve reduces the high pressure of air in the cylinder to ambient pressure and supplies the diver with air 'on demand' when he inhales. This reduction to ambient pressure is normally carried out in two stages. All the available types of demand valve utilise a single hose for the delivery of air to the mouthpiece. The most important feature is reliability; with the adverse conditions experienced underground not all valves possess this quality. Get advice from experienced cave divers before purchasing any model. The valve you choose should also possess a strong neckstrap fixed to the mouthpiece to prevent the gag drifting out of reach if lost under water. As with all items of diving equipment the demand valve should be treated with great respect, particularly when being transported, assembled and cleaned. Servicing should be undertaken regularly and is best left to an expert.

Ancillary Equipment
A face mask covering at least the eyes and nose is essential. The mask must present an effective seal, be comfortable, possess a strong securing headstrap and have a window of shatterproof glass. Preferably it should also be of a 'low-profile' design.

A robust and reliable pressure gauge must

always be used. This is connected to the first stage of the demand valve by a length of high-pressure tubing. You must consult the pressure gauge regularly during the course of a dive so that you are constantly aware of the amount of air remaining in the bottles. Ensure that this gauge is always easily accessible.

To compensate for the buoyancy of the wet-suit, lead weights must be worn. These are slotted onto a 5cm wide webbing belt and worn around the waist. The amount of lead needed will generally lie within the range 3–6kg. The optimum state is usually that of neutral buoyancy. Quick-release belts should not be worn unless they are of a type that cannot come undone accidentally. The potential dangers involved with the loss of your weights under water outweigh any advantages to be gained by being able to jettison the belt quickly.

The most suitable clothing is a 6 or 7mm wet-suit, supplemented if required by another layer of neoprene for the trunk. A hood of the same material is essential. At accessible sites a drysuit is a consideration but great care is needed to avoid damage. This type of suit is generally not suitable for wear through a normal 'dry' cave.

The main source of illumination for cave diving is a miners' caplamp. Lead-acid battery packs are not recommended unless you are confident that they have been thoroughly water-proofed. The most common power-pack is probably the 20Ah nickel-cadmium cell, or the Nife cell. This is normally worn upon the weight belt. It is helpful to waterproof the head-piece, but not essential. Whatever caplamp you use it is essential also to carry reserve lighting, for example the Spirotechnique Aquaflash. One or more of these waterproofed units may be attached to the side of your helmet. If recharge-able 4Ah D-size batteries (HP2) are used, up to thirteen hours illumination may be achieved from each light unit.

A diving knife or alternative form of cutter is essential. In the case of a knife this should be compact and attached by a length of nylon cord to the forearm – not to the leg, as in this posi-tion it may prove difficult to locate or replace. There would also be a high probability of entanglement with the diving line.

Many forms of diving fin are now available. For most British cave diving the type with the moulded one-piece foot is preferable. If the design involves the use of a strap to attach the fin to the foot then care must be taken with the buckles, as these can foul the guideline. Whatever design of fin you adopt, a fin-retaining strap is recommended.

A line reel is essential for all exploratory dives. These are normally home-made. A significant innovation in the early 1980s has been the introduction of very small 'emergency reels' holding perhaps 5–10m of thin diving line. Should a diver lose the main guideline for any reason, then by tying onto a small block of lead he can commence a local search of the passage until the original line is found.

Equipment Summary
Essential
Wetsuit and hood
Electric light and one or more reserve units
Air cylinders
Cylinder harnesses
Demand valves and pressure gauges
Face mask
Weight belt and weights
Fins and retainers
Diving knife or cutters
Line reel
Compass
Spare O-rings, tools, etc

Useful
Depth gauge
Watch
Filling adaptor, depending upon type of cylinder valve and demand valve being used
Formica slate and two pencils
One or more lead blocks, for weighting the line or tying off at the terminal point
Emergency line reel (very small)
Haul bags or boxes to transport equipment
Decompression tables, possibly a spare bottle for decompression
Drysuit

Techniques

Possibly the primary consideration in this hazardous activity is that in an emergency the cave diver cannot normally jettison his weight belt and ascend to safety; it may take time to reach the nearest usable air space. Failure of equipment which may not be fatal in open-water diving may well be so in cave diving. The sump environment is adverse, and if a diver gets into serious difficulties the chances of his being successfully rescued are slight; the intending cave diver must therefore be completely self-reliant and satisfy himself that his preparations have been absolutely thorough. Equipment should be checked and double-checked before a dive, air pressure noted and a return to base made once a third of the supply has been used. The routine checks should always be undertaken irrespective of conditions or of the nature of the sump. Do not dive if you are not completely fit.

The techniques adopted in sump exploration are flexible, varying with the conditions. In spacious sumps it may be possible for divers to operate in pairs, one following behind the other, while at more constricted sites a solo operation is preferable. As a general rule solo diving is better; less sediment is disturbed and there is only one person to worry about.

Wherever possible always carry reserve equipment. To ensure your safe return, when the visibility is greatly reduced, it is vital to lay a guideline (or maintain firm contact with one laid on a previous exploration). This line may be fed out from base, in the case of a very restricted sump, or paid out by the diver from a line reel. The use of a reel is always preferable, as otherwise difficulties can arise with communication. The line should be a bright colour and at least 4mm in diameter. It is also advantageous if the line incorporates a two-colour 'safety tag' system of markings at 5m intervals. By this method not only can an accurate survey be effected but, far more important, you are always aware of which direction leads out of the sump.

The misfortunes most likely to befall the cave diver are:

1 Stress.
2 Running out of air.
3 Failure or difficulties with equipment.
4 Problems with the guideline; for example positioning, loss or entanglement.

You should always be mentally prepared for any of these; provided that prompt action is taken, problems can usually be overcome. Remaining calm and collected is essential.

The techniques outlined above are suitable for the British Isles and are not typical of the sport worldwide. This approach has evolved in response to limited visibility, restricted size of passage and cold water. Conditions vary considerably in other parts of the world; in Florida or certain areas of Australia the environment is the antithesis of that in Britain, with excellent visibility, spacious tunnels and warm water. Consequently cave divers in their own areas have a different approach. For a fuller account of the development of the sport worldwide, see *The Darkness Beckons* (Farr, 1980).

Training and Qualifications

Training programmes in Britain are laid down by the Cave Diving Group, and prospective candidates are advised to contact experienced divers of the group before attempting to dive any sump. Training facilities are run by the four regional sections: Northern, Derbyshire, Welsh and Somerset. You must be known to members of the section through which you wish to join the group; the only other prerequisites are that you are a competent caver, over the age of eighteen and medically fit. You must then be elected by the diving members of the regional section and are normally admitted as a probationary trainee. Trainees should acquire the basic skills of diving by joining a local branch of the British Sub-Aqua Club, but this is not obligatory. The standards set by the Cave Diving Group are high, and the tests concerned with lifesaving are the most demanding, but with sufficient practice most trainees can master them. Mental attitude is a major factor in performance; you should be completely at home under water but not over confident. The main purpose of the tests is to assess how you are likely to react when something goes wrong. Your life may depend on this.

In the past ten years great advances have been made into sumps all over the world. The key to this success has been the resourcefulness of individuals and constant improvements in technology. Today techniques and equipment exist to permit underwater communication, relatively high-grade survey, first-class photographs, motorised transport and even blasting away blockages. With the adoption of higher-pressure bottles or a sophisticated rebreathing system further advances are assured.

Cave diving is not a sport to take up light-heartedly; it is a serious, potentially lethal pursuit that you should embark upon only after a sober assessment of the risks.

7 The Exploration of Abandoned Mine Workings

MIKE GILL

Like caves, abandoned mines are 'explored' for numerous reasons, besides exploration for its own sake. Common reasons are interest in geology, mineralogy, biology and industrial archaeology.

Anyone wishing to explore abandoned mines should join one of the many local societies. Each of the areas where abandoned metalliferous mines are common has at least one such society or research group based there. In the late 1970s most of these societies came together and established the National Association of Mining History Organisations (NAMHO) in an effort to promote interest in the subject and provide a forum for discussion. Information on local clubs and societies can be obtained from NAMHO (see Appendix 2). The association aims to encourage in its members a more informed, as well as a safe, approach to their endeavours.

The exploration of abandoned mine workings should never be undertaken lightly by the inexperienced (eg as a casual pursuit for a wet Saturday afternoon when such-and-such a cave might be too wet). To be proficient in the skills and techniques required by the potholer is insufficient – the addition of a sixth sense is necessary. Whilst this can be fully acquired only by progressive exploration of mines, the right approach, with an outline of the most likely dangers and problems, is set out here.

Knowledge of a Mining Area

Before setting out to explore a mine it is a good idea to read about the area in question, its geology and the methods that were employed in its exploitation. In this way you will be forewarned of the likely hazards. In the mining fields situated in high areas, the veins will usually have been reached by driving near-horizontal passages or 'adits'. In many cases

these will remain open, or partially open, and may occasionally be used as water supplies. Some mines were served by vertical shafts only, others by a combination of both. When workings progressed below the lowest free-draining horizon it became necessary to pump. The method adopted depended upon the amount or 'make' of water in the mine, the availability of a power supply and the state of technology at that time. Many northern mines employed water-wheels driving flat-rods along adits or pump rods down the shafts. In the deeper mines and those with large makes of water, steam engines were employed. Now all such mine workings are flooded to the water table, but access is sometimes possible as far as the pumping engines. For the experienced industrial archaeologist the surface layout of a mining site, by careful examination, will reveal fascinating information concerning the working methods employed underground.

In metalliferous mines veins are commonly found as slightly off-vertical, or 'hading' veins, or pipes. These would first be worked where they outcropped at the surface, then shafts or adits would be driven in as the workings became deeper. With rake veins where a workable ore body continued for some distance, large vertical fissures would be developed as the ore was removed. It was common practice to back-fill these cavities with waste material or 'deads'. A few stemples, usually well rotted, may now be found supporting huge piles of deads. In limestone areas these deads may become loosely calcited together with time and hang there without any stemples. They must be viewed with suspicion (Fig 201).

Rare in the Northern Pennines, but common in Derbyshire and other areas, veins can be found as horizontal pipes. When worked out, these take on the form of natural caverns. They are usually relatively stable.

Fig 201

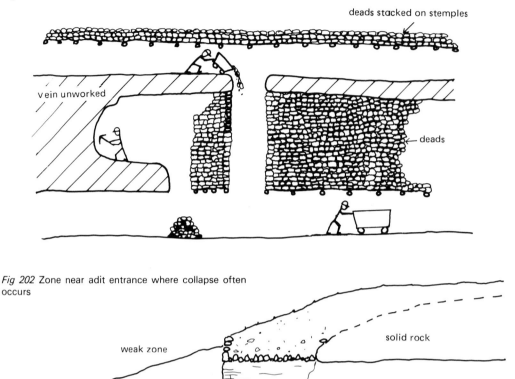

Fig 202 Zone near adit entrance where collapse often occurs

Hazards

In exploring any mine take special care at the entrance. At this point the shaft or level is likely to have been driven through superficial strata overlying the rockhead. This makes it very liable to deterioration by weather and surface water movement and is the reason for many partial and/or complete collapses, and the flooding of adit entrances (Fig 202).

An adit will often have been driven for considerable distances within a bed or beds of soft strata. This will have been done to facilitate ease of driving and to reduce development costs. Such beds, often shales or other thinly bedded strata, are prone to stress zones which may cause the shale to sag away from the overlying beds of harder rock. The vibrations and changes in water level or temperature caused by the passage of an exploring party may cause final collapse. Collapse may also be induced by the proximity of faults, veins or other mine workings.

Falls from shafts, hoppers or stowed ground are a serious danger; they are more likely to occur than falls of shale, far more difficult to control and usually of uncertain size. Such falls commonly comprise loose material, often lubricated by water, and once they have started moving they are very difficult to halt. Such an incident occurred recently in the Geevor tin mine in Cornwall; even in this modern working mine, with all materials and expertise to hand, it took most of two days to rescue the miner trapped at the wrong side of a run-in hopper.

When exploring shafts, take care also at the lip or 'eye' where a cone of ground extending beyond the shaft lining may have been undermined by collapsed ground further down. It was common practice to rest the base of the ginging or stone lining of shafts on a timber crib, which in most cases will have rotted away (Fig 203).

Seathwaite plumbago mines: early L-shaped plateway in very sound level (*J.J. Rowland, FRPS*)

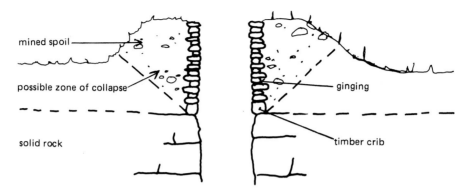

Fig 203 Danger zone at shaft top where collapse often starts

Other obstructions commonly encountered in shafts are the remains of climbing ladders, pump rods, collapsed stagings and partitions. They will usually be dangerously rotted and may support other loose material. Miscellaneous iron pipes, cables, etc, often hang down shafts, a touch may send them crashing down.

Gas in Mines
It is not common to find explosive gas, ie methane or firedamp, in abandoned metalliferous mines, but it can occur in those mines with coal seams or with carbonaceous shales. A commonly found gas is carbon dioxide, 'black damp', which may occur at a shaft foot, down sumps or in badly ventilated headings – it is heavier than air. Again, its occurrence is most common in those mines which have been worked in the grit or shale beds, rather than in limestone or igneous/metamorphic rocks.

Concentrations of gas often vary with the season, with prevailing weather conditions or even with the barometric pressure. A naked flame will not be supported by carbon dioxide; but beware, a carbide lamp will continue to burn in dangerously high concentrations of it! The best test is an upright dry candle. If this gutters, then it is time to leave. Hydrogen sulphide, 'stink damp', is caused by rotting timber or vegetable matter and may be present. The characteristic odour of rotten eggs is soon lost to the sense of smell, which can lead to a false sense of security. This gas is very poisonous.

Hydrogen sulphide and carbon dioxide may accumulate where there are large quantities of rotting timber, vegetable matter or carcasses.

Take special care where ventilation is not good.

The oxides of nitrogen, and carbon monoxide, are produced mainly as the result of explosives and incomplete combustion and will not normally be found in an abandoned mine. The latter may be present in coal workings which are subject to spontaneous combustion. Unused explosives are occasionally found in old mine workings; they should be left alone and reported to the nearest police station.

Guidelines for Safe Exploration

Remember the following points at all times if you venture into abandoned mine workings:

1 Bad air is often present in old mine workings. Its effects are often gradual and not appreciated until it is too late to escape.
2 Many of the older mines were driven in soft ground for ease of driving – such ground may now be unstable and ready to collapse.
3 An accumulation of mud or gravel on the floor may disguise open but water-filled workings beneath or even 'hanging' stoped ground ready to collapse.
4 Where a section of passage is dry underfoot the floor may be based upon open stopes on rotted timbering which is ready to collapse.
5 Ladders and stagings have probably been in place in damp conditions for years and could be dangerously rotted.

Ystrad Einion mine: waterwheel and decaying timbers in a large, mined chamber (*J.J. Rowland, FRPS*)

126

SYMBOLS FOR USE WITH THE N.A.M.H.O. STANDARD PLAN FOR ABANDONED METAL MINES.

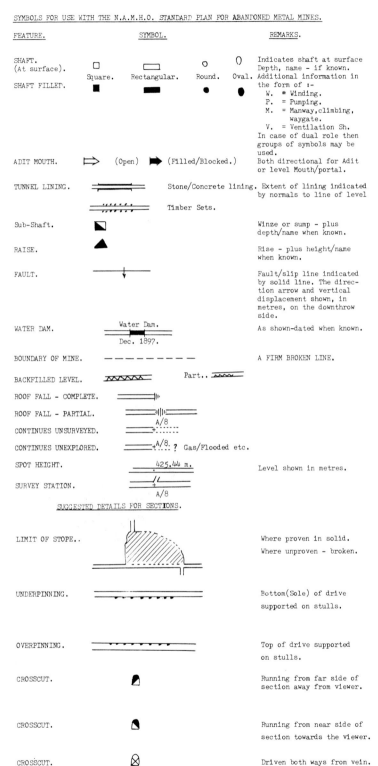

FEATURE.	SYMBOL.	REMARKS.

SHAFT. (At surface).   Square.   Rectangular.   Round.   Oval.

SHAFT FILLED.

Indicates shaft at surface Depth, name - if known. Additional information in the form of :-
W. = Winding.
P. = Pumping.
M. = Manway, climbing, waygate.
V. = Ventilation Sh.
In case of dual role then groups of symbols may be used.

ADIT MOUTH.   (Open)   (Filled/Blocked.)   Both directional for Adit or level Mouth/portal.

TUNNEL LINING.   Stone/Concrete lining.   Extent of lining indicated by normals to line of level

Timber Sets.

Sub-Shaft.   Winze or sump - plus depth/name when known.

RAISE.   Rise - plus height/name when known.

FAULT.   Fault/slip line indicated by solid line. The direction arrow and vertical displacement shown, in metres, on the downthrow side.

WATER DAM.   Water Dam.   Dec. 1897.   As shown-dated when known.

BOUNDARY OF MINE.   A FIRM BROKEN LINE.

BACKFILLED LEVEL.   Part..

ROOF FALL - COMPLETE.

ROOF FALL - PARTIAL.

CONTINUES UNSURVEYED.   A/8

CONTINUES UNEXPLORED.   A/8. ? Gas/Flooded etc.

SPOT HEIGHT.   425.44 m.   Level shown in metres.

SURVEY STATION.   A/8

SUGGESTED DETAILS FOR SECTIONS.

LIMIT OF STOPE..   Where proven in solid.   Where unproven - broken.

UNDERPINNING.   Bottom(Sole) of drive supported on stulls.

OVERPINNING.   Top of drive supported on stulls.

CROSSCUT.   Running from far side of section away from viewer.

CROSSCUT.   Running from near side of section towards the viewer.

CROSSCUT.   Driven both ways from vein.

N.B. When this Code does not have the required symbol refer to those used by the N.C.B. Code or in the case of surface features, the Ordnance Survey,

Fig 204

SKETCH OF N.A.M.H.O. STANDARD MINE PLAN.

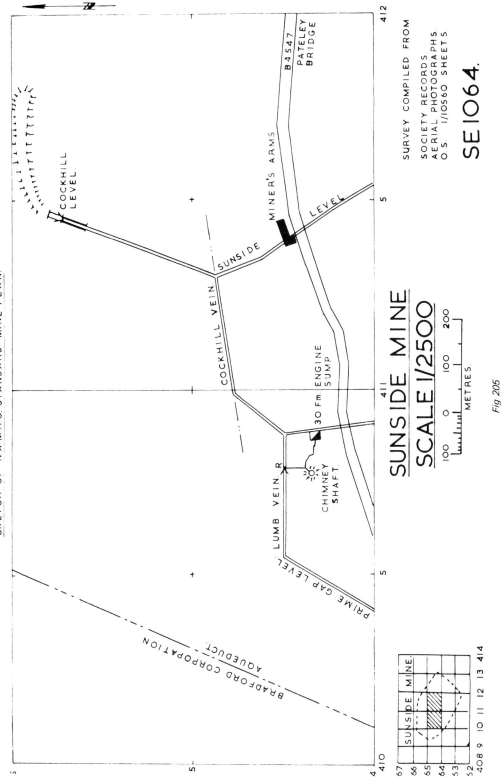

SUNSIDE MINE
SCALE 1/2500

METRES.

SURVEY COMPILED FROM

SOCIETY RECORDS
AERIAL PHOTOGRAPHS
O.S. 1/10560 SHEETS

SE1064.

Fig 205

6 Beware of old shaft tops. The ginging may be inadequately supported on a rotted crib which is ready to collapse and undermine the whole structure (Fig 205).

Adhere to the following guidelines rigidly on *all* explorations of abandoned mine workings (abstracted from the *Handbook of the Northern Mine Research Society*):

1 Never explore old mine workings alone.
2 Always tell someone responsible outside where you are going and what you hope to achieve.
3 Always carry a candle or flame lamp if you are using electric lights; carry dry matches in a suitable container.
4 Test the atmosphere by lighting a candle or oil safety-lamp at any point where ventilation appears to be restricted. If the candle will not burn *get out at once*. A carbide lamp will not suffice for this purpose. Naked lights are not usually dangerous in metalliferous mines since accumulations of explosive gases are rare.
5 Never interfere with old hopper-mouths or timbers – they may be rotten, and disturbance may cause a serious collapse or run-in of loose rock.
6 Keep a check on the floor of the passage as well as the roof. There can be false floors, and timbers near the top of shafts may be rotten.
7 Carry a stick for poking into doubtful pools in the floor ahead. It might be a flooded shaft or sump.
8 Never try to climb up or down old ladders, even when they appear to be quite sound.
9 Never descend an old shaft or winze until you have lowered a flame lamp or candle to ascertain that the air is breathable.
10 Always carry food and drink with you in case you are trapped and have to await rescue.
11 Always wear suitable clothing to protect against mud, cold or wet; wear a hard-hat at all times.

12 Remember that your carelessness in omitting any reasonable precautions may endanger not only your own life, but also the lives of those who will have to attempt your rescue. Persuade a more experienced person to accompany you whenever possible.

Mining Terminology

Many of the mine exploration/research societies produce publications on their activities. Some of these set a high standard of report writing and general presentation. If you wish to write up your fieldwork or present a report a knowledge of correct mining terminology is useful.

The following hypothetical example demonstrates a common mistake: 'We entered Speculation Level which we followed for 175m in a southerly direction. At this point we found cross-cuts going east and west, and there were workings in Lucky Vein in both directions.' This cannot be correct – it must be that Speculation Level itself is the cross-cut, and that east and west levels on Lucky Vein are drifts in the vein. It is important to recognise that a cross-cut is a tunnel driven in barren rock in order to intersect a vein, while tunnels driven in the vein itself are known as drives or drifts. The above should therefore have been written: 'Speculation Level, which we followed for 175m in a south-easterly direction, is a cross-cut to the Lucky Vein. At its intersection with the vein we found that drifts had been driven east and west of the cross-cut and the vein worked in both directions.'

Presentation of Plans

The National Association of Mining History Organisations has recently published guidelines for the presentation of plans of abandoned metal mines. The following table of symbols (Fig 204), and specimen plan have been extracted from these, with the consent of NAMHO.

8 Water Tracing and Flow Recording

DR PETER A. BULL

The study of water tracing and flow recording in limestone regions concerns only part of the cycle of water movement around the earth. The hydrological cycle is a continuous, if simplified, course of water movement, initiated when water is drawn up by evaporation into the clouds over the oceans, precipitated over the land and then drained over or through the rock substratum to the sea again.

In limestone areas this underground movement of water gives rise to caves, and the nature of these caves and fissures in part accounts for the course, duration and quantity of water which eventually emerges in springs and resurgences. This simple model of water movement is complicated by the nature of the limestone through which the water flows. Rock structure and rock type are important determinants of water flow as is the degree of karstification and the history of water base level fluctuations in the area. Further factors include the means of water introduction and movement in the drainage system (percolation or conduit flow) and also the water table concept in limestone aquifers (Smith et al 1976). These are not the only problems affecting water tracing and recording. Under different flow conditions water routes may vary, even within the same horizontal level in a cave.

The use of tracers is only a late stage in the understanding of the hydrology of a region; normally it is necessary to have a likely resurgence area in mind before any tracer can be used to detect it. Even when the trace is successful, there are problems in understanding the nature of water movement from input to output. Bogli (1980) explains how water flow based on the Holloch in Switzerland can be shown to have multi-tracer peaks at a monitored resurgence due to the different water courses utilised by the flow (even within one water flow level). Various delay times are then recorded as discrete peaks as a direct function of the distance of water travel. This technique of tracer diagram analysis provides an accurate prediction of unknown water-course characteristics and has been used with great success, notably in the Gelben Brunnen on Thunersee

Fig 206 Water-tracing methods

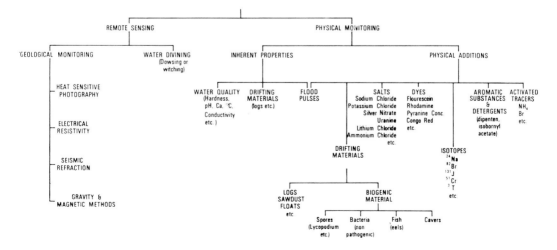

131

in Switzerland (Bogli 1980 provides a review).

Such a profusion of different tracing and recording techniques exists, ranging from simple floats through to the highly technical radio isotope tracers (Fig 206), that almost any area can be investigated by the enthusiastic amateur or serious professional who can call up much technical and logistical help (Drew and Smith 1969). Nevertheless a number of pre-requisites and limitations to each method need to be considered. Following the synopsis of water tracing methods two of the more common (and successful) techniques are described in detail.

Note: before carrying out any water tracing in the United Kingdom the local river authority must be contacted. Elsewhere, the relevant water authorities must also be consulted, and remember that their regulations may be different to those in the United Kingdom.

Water Tracers

The science of water tracing has progressed from an initial inquiry often fired by a need to predict the reliability of a water course for agricultural or domestic use. Many different means are now open to the water tracer (Fig 206). These range from the indirect (remote) methods of water divining, and the simple float experiments often favoured by small boys racing sticks under bridges and through culverts, to the more exacting methods of radio isotope dating. There are a number of qualities that theoretically all tracers should exhibit, although no one method exhibits them all. Drew and Smith (1969), Sweeting (1972) and Todd (1980) together lay out some eleven pre-requisites (Table 8.1).

Table 8.1

Tracers should ideally be:

1 Susceptible to quantitative detection in low concentrations.
2 Absent (or nearly so) from natural water.
3 Chemically non-reactive with natural water.
4 Not absorbed by a porous media (Ca CO_3, for example).
5 Safe in terms of human and animal health.
6 Non-objectionable.
7 Absolutely certain to be detected.
8 Not likely to cause soil or clay coagulation.

9 Inexpensive and readily available.
10 Not needing continuous monitoring.
11 Able to be used simultaneously in various parts of the catchment.

Compiled from Todd (1980), Sweeting (1972), Drew and Smith (1969).

Not all of the water-tracing methods outlined in Fig 208 fit these requirements, but their use in specific areas is due to local physical restraint and, more increasingly, to public pressure versus commercial necessity (see Table 8.2).

The remote sensing methods of water tracing are mostly concerned with large-scale environmental monitoring – beyond the means of the casually interested individual. However, subterranean water courses and general groundwater aquifer monitoring are increasingly being identified by heat-sensitive photography (high-resolution infra-red photographs taken by planes and satellites over vast areas of ground). More direct ground measurements using sensors and transmitters are obtained from electrical resistivity methods (which can monitor rock types: lithified and unlithified), seismic refraction (which easily determines the depth below the surface of the water table) and gravity and magnetic methods (which measure the density of rock within the substratum, and can be used to identify subterranean water bodies – Zohdy 1974). All these methods are very expensive!

Other remote sensing methods include water divining, arguably a seventh sense but regarded by many as 'just a curious quirk' (Riddick 1952). The method does work in some instances.

The most relevant methods of water tracing are those which are physically monitored (Fig 206). These include methods that utilise the inherent qualities of the water at the spring and at the envisaged resurgence. Properties of hardness, pH, calcium content, temperature and conductivity are all signatures of particular water bodies. These properties can often be traced underground or used inferentially as a means of determining rates of throughflow, the nature of the unknown water course and the volume of discharge. This is because it is assumed that each sink and cave passage has its own characteristic water quality. The introduction of a flood pulse alters these attributes within the water and the resultant changes can be monitored at the spring (Fig 207). Unfortun-

Table 8.2

	Flow rate similar to water	Enables subsidiary statistics	Simplicity	High sensitivity	Continuous monitoring not needed	Ability for simultaneous trace	No effect on water	Not naturally present	Detectable at low concentrations	Inexpensive	Not time consuming	Not objectionable	Toxicity	Not absorbed in transit	Soluble in or unaffected by acid or alkaline soln
TRACERS															
Floats: Polypropylene, Dog Biscuits, logs, etc	−	+	++	−	++	++	++	++	++	++	++	++	++	−	++
Lycopodium	++	++	−	++	++	++	++	++	++	−	−	++	++	+	++
Radioactive tracers	−	−	−	+	−	−	−	++	++	−	−	−	−	+	++
Bacteria	−	−	−	−	−	−	+	++	++	+	−	+	++	+	+
Potassium salts	+	−	−	+	−	−	+	+	++	+	+	++	++	+	++
Ammonium chloride	+	−	+	−	−	−	+	+	+	+	+	++	++	+	++
Inorganic salts	+	−	++	−	−	−	+	+	+	+	+	++	++	+	++
Tritium	++	+	−	++	−	−	+	−	++	−	−	+	+	+	++
DYES															
Fluorescein: direct observation	++	−	++	−	+	−	++	++	++	+	−	−	++	+	+
Fluorescein: charcoal method	++	−	++	−	++	−	++	++	++	++	++	++	++	+	+
Pyramine: direct observation	++	−	++	+	+	−	++	++	++	−	−	−	++	++	++
Pyramine: charcoal method	++	−	++	+	++	−	++	++	++	+	++	++	++	++	++
Rhodamine B: direct observation	++	−	++	−	+	−	+	++	++	−	−	−	−	+	++
Rhodamine B: cotton detectors	++	−	++	−	++	−	+	++	++	++	+	+	−	+	++
Congo red	++	−	++	−	+	−	++	++	+	−	−	−	++	+	++

Key: − poor, + fair, ++ good.

Fig 207

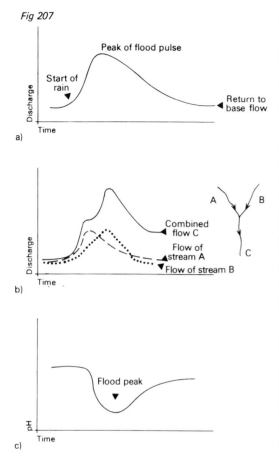

a)
b)
c)

materials (Fig 206). Spores (notably *Lycopodium*), nonpathogenic bacteria and higher life forms are all commonly used for tracing water flow (Table 8.2). Of the higher life forms, tagged eels have been used by Wagner (1954). Bogli (1980) notes that they took fifty-five days to cover 50km. Even cave divers provide water-tracing records by direct observation (reviewed by Farr 1980). Most of these latter techniques need discrete cave passages to float or swim through so the advantages of using smaller particles such as spores and bacteria are immediately recognised, even if they require careful collecting at the resurgence. *Lycopodium* spores (*Lycopodium clavatum* is widely used) can also be dyed different colours. This helps if repeated tests are needed in an area or if complicated water routes need working out. There are a number of disadvantages to the method, which are outlined later.

In the use of bacteria for water tracing, Bogli (1980, page 141) cites a successful tracing in the Danube, but the thought of 'introducing 30 trillion bacteria' into a stream that feeds, say, Bristol or Leeds does not court good press! This highlights the need for permission from water authorities and the problem of public prejudice aroused by terms such as 'bacteria' or 'radioactive', even if the tracing method is perfectly safe.

Other common additives to sinks include salts: common salts (sodium chloride), potassium chloride, silver nitrate, lithium chloride and uranine (a sodium fluorescein compound). The method involves the addition of the salt (often in large amounts) into the sink and the collecting of water at the resurgence for testing for the additive. The classic case of water tracing using common salt (and ammonium sulphate) was reported by Carter and Dwerryhouse (1905). They show how, in 1899, three tons of salt were tipped into a sink in the Malham Tarn area in NW Yorkshire and were eventually traced to Airehead Springs 3,400m away.

More recent use of dye substances has cut down the need for such amounts of tracer. Fluorescein, a commercially available organic-compound dye, is the most usually used. It is green, fluorescent in light and can be detected in small amounts: one part in 40 million is normal, whilst one part in 100 million can

ately this method requires continuous monitoring at the resurgence, can be complicated by multisource dilution, can be interrupted by water storage within the system and, above all, is 'black box' in design (that is, input and output are known, but the processes in between are often not known, nor are they sought).

Other water-tracing methods employed that are a part of the fabric of the water body include chance materials such as logs or vegetation. In Papua New Guinea carved logs were placed in sinks and then observed to come out of resurgences. Obviously large cave passage connections must exist before this can be attempted elsewhere!

Perhaps the most common methods of water tracing, at least for the informed caver rather than the speleologist, are by adding various substances to sinks and recording their reappearance at resurgences. Such substances include drifting materials like plastic floats, dog biscuits (just the right buoyancy!) and biogenic

sometimes be identified. Other dyes can also be used; Brown and Ford (1971) used Rhodamine WT with great success in the Canadian Rockies, whilst Drew used pyramine concentrate with equal success in the Mendips (Drew 1970) and in Jamaica (Drew 1969b).

Sweeting (1972) reviews the successful use of uranine, the sodium fluorescein compound, in Yugoslavia; with 33kg of uranine, the subterranean water course was traced over a distance of 20km. For successful tracing it was calculated that from 2–5kg of uranine were needed for every cumec (m^3/sec) observed at the rising. Lesser amounts can be used if activated charcoal is available as an absorbing agent (see below).

Aromatic substances can also be used. A celebrated example exists of the inadvertent powers of tracing by smell: Bogli (1980) cites a case where a Pernod-distilling factory caught fire and the heat caused the barrels to explode; some days later a nearby and hitherto unknown connected spring smelled strongly of aniseed. Deliberately introduced aromatic substances also exist for tracing: dipenten smells of lemons; isobornyl acetate gives off a spruce aroma.

Rather than turning a spring into a bubbling froth of foam, detergents can be used quite subtly in small quantities. Apart from visual identification they can also be detected by colorimetry methods in the laboratory.

Finally, isotopes and activated tracers; these are not for the casual user. Many isotopes can be used for tracing as well as for accurately assessing throughflow times in limestone aquifers (resonance times) and ultimately to identify the complicated pattern of flow and storage in a catchment.

Comparison of Methods

None of the methods of water tracing outlined above satisfies all eleven pre-requisites set out in Table 8.1. However, depending upon terrain and the degree of commitment of the speleologist or caver, at least one method should be suitable. A fuller assessment of the pros and cons of techniques for different conditions is presented in Table 8.2. These data are taken from *Techniques for the Tracing of Subterranean Drainage* (Drew and Smith 1969), essential reading for anyone seriously interested in water tracing in limestone areas.

Dyes

The best methods of tracing using dyes involve placing detectors at resurgences rather than depending upon visual assessment. Fluorescein, pyramine and rhodamine all rate well when used with detectors at the resurgence rather than with visual observations. Without detectors, tracing is time-consuming. Furthermore, greater quantities of the dye are needed for visual observations; this increases cost, toxicity and the degree of objection that would arise to the material's use. They also prevent the unnecessary use of excessive amounts of dye.

A research student testing for a stream connection between sink and resurgence in the River Ilston, Gower, South Wales, gained a positive visual result at the expense of turning the water supply of the village of Ilston bright green and, when it drained through the village, turned the sea green at the mouth of the river. Such orders of magnitude error can be prevented if detectors are used.

None of the dyes presented in Fig 206 provides any means of subsidiary statistics and none allows more than one test to be run at once. Rhodamine B, which is harmful to man and animals, should not be used in areas where water may enter public supplies. It is not allowed as a tracer in America. Normally fluorescein is used, particularly in temperate regions; in tropical conditions it is adversely affected by strong sunlight and peaty humic waters and so pyramine concentrate is used.

'Physical Addition'

Of the various 'physical addition' methods (after Fig 206) summarised in Table 8.2, perhaps the best is *Lycopodium* spores. Their only disadvantages are their time-consuming preparation, their expense (up to four times the cost of dyestuffs) and complicated use. These disadvantages are easily outweighed by their advantages; the spores, if dyed, can be used for simultaneous tracing in a number of streams at once, and also provide an accurate assessment of water flow (dyes travel at only 80 per cent of water flow, whilst spores travel at almost the same speed as water flow) and can be used successfully over long distances and in heavily contaminated waters. The most important points that come out of Table 8.2 are:

1 Ability for simultaneous trace.
2 Need for continuous monitoring.
3 Relative cost.
4 Ability for subsidiary statistics.
5 Estimates of water flow rates.

Techniques

Preparation of Fluorescein and Pyramine Concentrate
Input Powder or water solution, or in alcohol; in one phase or drip fed. Amount varies due to local factors. Drew and Smith (1969) give, as an approximation, 60g dye/km of underground travel/0.15 cumec discharge at the largest resurgence.

Detection Visually – water turns green. Detectors – activated charcoal (this deactivates in air after two or three weeks; to reactivate, heat in an oven at 150°C for about two hours). 20g of charcoal should be placed in nylon bags, connected to a rock by nylon cord, at the resurgence. Make sure you do not miss the dye pulse!

Analysis A hot solution of 10 per cent potassium hydroxide (beware: this is very caustic) in ethanol to be poured over 10g of charcoal (do not heat over a naked flame). The dye becomes visible within thirty minutes. (Ultraviolet lights aid identification, but beware of damage to the eyes.)

Procedure for Using Lycopodium *Spores*
This is strongly recommended by Drew and Smith (1969, page 13) as the only satisfactory mechanical method for tracing underground water flow.

Input Add spores to sink and collect at resurgence. *Lycopodium clavatum* are recommended; they should be coloured as required by one of the following dyes: methyl violet, safranine, malachite green, bismarck brown or magenta.
   Amount varies according to local factors. Drew and Smith (1969) advocate 600g/km of underground travel/0.3 cumec discharge at the largest rising in the catchment. Spore preparation involves adding 100ml of detergent and 1.5 litres of water to every kg of spores used. The mixture is boiled, stirring continuously, for ten to fifteen minutes. A pre-dissolved (in methy-

lated spirit) dye is added in the quantity 200ml per 15g of mixture. The whole is then heated (and stirred) at 90°C for another one or two hours. To avoid mould growing, 10–20ml of formaldehyde per kg of spores is added before the mixture cools. Store spores as a slurry after evaporating the mixture in shallow trays heated at 70°C (no naked flames). Beware: *Lycopodium* spores, when dry and in dust, are highly inflammable.

Detection Funnel nets made of 25-micron mesh. Open end of the funnel is strengthened by a canvas collar and wire hoop. The apex is glued to a rubber tube outlet which has a screw clamp fastened to the tube. Support the nets on a Dexion frame.

Pre-analysis Treatment To remove excessive organic content 0.5g urea and an equally small amount of formaldehyde are added to the sample with 1ml of 10 per cent potassium hydroxide. The whole is then heated in a container in a water bath, containing gently boiling water, for ten minutes. To remove calcite debris, treat spores with urea and formaldehyde as above and add a few drops of concentrated hydrochloric acid (this is corrosive!). Centrifuge treated sample at 3000rpm for one hour and run off excess liquid.

Analysis Add material to microscope slide. View at about 100×. Count spores of each colour. Spore concentration gives added detail of underground flow conditions.

Flow Recording

Bearing in mind the constraints outlined above, it is possible to trace the course of underground water flow from spring to resurgence. Many of these tracing techniques are borrowed from surface hydrological procedures. Similarly, the recording of water flow in a karst region owes much in technique to 'surface' hydrology studies, although problems of unknown routes and the three-dimensional nature of karst water drainage make the study of water flow in these regions complicated.
   The different ways of recording water flow data depend upon which component is required. We will consider here three components: velocity, discharge estimates and water

level (height) recording. Information on past flow conditions can be gauged from flotsam in branches, flattening of grass and other vegetation on river banks, or more scientifically by noting the size, shape and spacing of sediment ripples on the river bed. Historical records, too, reflect the extreme event, but without a detailed study such records are little more than cosmetic. Perhaps the most important means of flow recording is via the estimation of average (mean) channel velocity and river discharge. Here the velocity of the river is measured (see Table 8.2) and this is multiplied by the cross-section dimension of the river (width versus depth). This gives a quantification of the water being discharged by a river expressed in cubic metres of water per second or m^3s^{-1}.

These measurements can be assessed using current meters, sophisticated electro-magnetic or ultrasonic devices. For small streams the easiest method of determining water discharge rates is to channel the whole stream through a pipe into a bucket of known volume and observe the time required to fill the bucket. Although crude, this is an accurate means of assessing flow so long as the operation does not cause too much water back-up upstream of the gauging point. More sophisticated automatic devices can be made with a bucket which tips and empties on filling. A counting device can record the number of bucket tips in a set time, giving an automatic gauging record.

A second simple method of determining water discharge involves injecting a solution of known strength into a stream. The solution, normally a salt, is sampled and measured downstream to record the degree of dilution. This reflects natural stream discharge rates. Similar 'tracer' methods (pulse or gulp techniques) are discussed in more detail by Smart and Laidlaw (1977).

The most permanent and conventional method of recording flow discharges above and below ground is by a weir or flume. Weirs are usually V-notched or crested; they record accurately the amount of discharge against a calibrated scale. They can be used for flows up to 240 litres per second, whilst for larger discharges flumes are needed (Gregory and Walling 1973). The advantages of using a weir or flume is accuracy; the disadvantage is that a properly built structure can be expensive (also they can clog up with sediment if left unattended for long periods). Overall the advantages outweigh the disadvantages, and for permanent water records a weir or flume should be used.

A third component of flow recording is assessing the fluctuations in water level. This is perhaps the most obvious visual component of water flow. The height of the river or stream is normally related to the amount of water discharge. An assessment of water level is easily obtained by erecting a painted staff, graduated in centimetres and metres, on the edge of a stream or bank (above or below ground). Automatic (autographic) recorders are commercially available, or university and polytechnic geography departments can be coerced into lending them. Failing this, visual recordings will give approximations; cavers can be asked to record water flow readings in caves – this works well so long as they register the time of observation as well as the depth.

Alternatively cheap technology now allows us to use multi-channel data-loggers which are battery powered, storing information on magnetic tape. This gets over problems of clockwork devices running down, or rusting up in the cave environment.

The aim of the hydrologist in recording discharge, flow rates or flow levels is to construct a hydrograph (or water flow characteristics) for a given river. By plotting the reaction of a stream to different rainfall events a pattern of response can be built up. Some streams take a long time to rise, others reach maximum discharge quickly; some have more than one peak indicating multi-source inputs; each has its own signature or response. Thus with the characteristics of the flow regime worked out it might be possible to predict the response of a stream to a given input. It might seem simple, but it never is (Ward 1975 and Smith et al 1976).

9 Instructed Caving in Britain

M.K. LYON

Many cavers regard instruction with suspicion. This results from the long-standing idea that caving should be exclusively practised by caving clubs, and the status of caver only conferred on those able to break into the brotherhood of the club system. Also cavers like to pursue their business unfettered by rules and regulations, and they suspect that instruction will eventually lead to certification and total control.

Caves are an only too finite and vulnerable resource, which will be destroyed if caving is popularised on a 'caving for all' basis; there is much logic in the 'caves for the committed only' point of view. If caving instruction were to inject the youth of the country *en masse* into our caves, then it should rightly be condemned. Guidance on the place of caving within the educational system has been produced by the training committee of the National Caving Association (NCA), and this advice, reproduced here, is commended to everyone concerned with the introduction of young people to caving.

NCA Guidelines

The philosophy of caving

In the past, considerable misunderstanding has occured over the nature of caving. It is extremely dangerous to treat caving as a sport since it is in no way a competitive activity – co-operation is an essential spirit when caving.

Caving is the exploration of natural underground passages, and its primary motive is the desire to learn about such passages. A vital element in caving is the satisfaction and fun obtained by discovery, not the defeat of other people or the mere overcoming of a natural obstacle.

It follows that people, young or old, should only be caving from a personal desire to do so. It is vital that no pressure be used in encouraging people to go caving.

The exploration of a cave is a group activity – but the group should be small, both for mobility underground and so that each person should feel an important part of the group. So far as possible each member of the party should be self-reliant at the level of difficulty attempted.

. . . Before being introduced to caving young people should have some experience of other activities making similar physical demands, eg a child unwilling to walk say eight miles is unlikely to benefit from, or be safe, when caving. Caves are *not* a suitable environment in which to subject young people to conditions which could result in exhaustion or exposure.

The practice and method of the introduction of young people to caving

. . . Participants should be underground of their own volition. It is thus suggested that teachers and other leaders should normally wait for an approach from young people before assisting them to obtain experience of caving. It is desirable for the young people to make a preparation for the experience themselves. (For example to follow up references to caving literature, or to obtain appropriate clothing.) Apart from the check on the pupil's motivations and the increased educational content of the exercise, this allows an honourable outlet from peer-group pressure for the young person who may dislike or genuinely fear the idea of caving but not wish to lose face. Inability to procure a pair of boots or something similar gives a suitable let-out for such youngsters, but it is unlikely to prove an insuperable problem to even the poorest child who *wants* to go.

It is inappropriate here to give a detailed account of relevant codes of practice for caving. If the leader requires such information from this booklet he is not fit to take parties underground. Possession of a set of rules can be used as a dangerous alternative to good judgement. Hence we outline the ways in which caving can be conducted for the guidance of head teachers and others who may be asked to authorise activities, and give more detail on what is required of the teachers who may be taking parties caving.

There are basically three ways of introducing young people to caving:

1 For the group to go caving on their own, with appropriate advice and discussion before and after the experience. Such an approach requires a very high degree of caving judgement and teaching skill from the leader. Its advantage is to give a grounding based on immediate and important lessons in self-reliance and personal discovery. Its dangers are obvious if misapplied, but that does not detract from its basic merit. An argued case for this approach is contained in *Caving for Beginners* published by the Council of Southern Caving Clubs and available from the CSCC, 40 Wells Road, Wookey Hole, Wells, Somerset, price 15p.

2 For the group to be accompanied and led by competent leaders. This has the advantage of closer contact with the leader, and will be more appropriate for training in vertical pitch techniques as opposed to straightforward caving. Its disadvantages are in the diminution of the spontaneity of discovery and experience which is part of the essence of caving and, in the hands of less experienced or wrongly motivated leaders, a danger of stretching a group beyond their own limits. A code for parties conducted underground by leaders is contained in *The Organisation of Novice Caving Trips*. Information Sheet 1 of the British Association of Caving Instructors and available from BACI (see Appendix 2) at 3p per copy.

3 A roughly equal ratio of experienced cavers to novices is maintained on an apprentice basis. This method is favoured by old established caving clubs. It tends to assume that an experienced caver is capable of looking after an inexperienced one. Information about local caving organisations is available from the National Caving Association Hon Secretary (see Appendix 2).

As it is the first two methods which will tend to be most appropriate to parties of young people it should be observed that they are not incompatible and that elements of both can be combined to good effect. Young people who wish to continue caving should be encouraged to join a club, where method 3 often becomes applicable.

The leader
By far the most important requirement is that the leader should be a dedicated and experienced caver. Evidence of such interest and experience is usually shown in his being an active member of a recognised caving club, but careful note should always be taken of the reliability and judgement of the person in question. Some regional bodies in caving are prepared to arrange that references from fellow cavers may be given when requested. A recognised certificate – the Cave Instructor Certificate – is available and can be of value, but it should be remembered that whilst the testing of personal technique and skill is comparatively easy, leadership, common sense and judgement are far more difficult to assess.

Outdoor centres
'Outdoor centres' covers many different types of organisation, from just buildings used by a group accompanied by their usual teaching staff to highly specialised single activity organisations with very competent resident staff.

The primary motivation of children who volunteer for courses at a centre may be other than a desire to experience the activities. A child may find the informal social content of the course attractive, may wish to escape from school for a period, or from a stressful home. Even greater care is needed in a multi-activity centre to avoid peer-group pressures and to ensure that alternative activities are available.

Children often attend such centres only once and the caving they undertake must be of extremely simple type. The repetitive nature of such caving can be extremely tedious for the instructors and calls for a high degree of dedication if any enthusiasm is to be passed to the children. Further, when the centre operates over weekends, the instructors become divorced from the main stream of active caving. It is important that instructors at centres be encouraged to cave with local clubs and the time tables organised to permit this. The improved quality of their work resulting from broadening of the instructors' outlook should amply repay the inconvenience.

Multi-activity centres should further be aware of the dangers of asking non-caving instructors to supervise caving activities until they have acquired sufficient experience under the guidance of a caving specialist.
(October 1977)

Instruction Methods

Instruction in caving, then, should be given only to those who have shown a very positive interest. How should such introductory training/instruction be given?

The 'heuristic approach' – learning through direct experiment – finds its most articulate exponents in the Mendip caving region. Young people wanting to go caving are told to go away. If they persist, they can be told the whereabouts of an easy cave and left to organise their own visit. If they return with bumps on their heads and stories of broken torches, they can be given suggestions on helmets and headlamps. Thus experience will be gained slowly but well, with novices learning self-reliance. To be successful this type of instruction requires suitable caves relatively near at hand and a very experienced adviser. There are risks of damage to cave and novice alike, and the method is difficult to apply in a predominantly pothole, as opposed to cave, region. Its strong point, which deserves high rating, is that the small number of cavers coming through this process are likely to be committed and resourceful. The 'club line' takes an opposite view, emphasising the dangers of allowing the innocent to wander into caves on their own. A beginner fortunate enough to find a club that will accept him or her as a trainee member will be able to learn caving as a passenger on normal club trips, sandwiched between and looked after by experienced cavers. In this approach a small ratio of trainees to experienced cavers is essential. The trainee is 'carried' through situations over which he has no control, and that control must be provided by others. This can be a successful approach, or dangerous and stultifying. Unfortunately some influential club cavers cannot see the merits of any other training method. 'Total responsibility' – the third method of introduction – is for a group of trainees to be taken caving by one or two experienced cavers. The caves should be within the individual capacity of each member of the group. The 'sandwich' approach, where perhaps ten novices are the filling between two experts, who then take the group through a system quite beyond their capacity without help, is indefensible, and it is this stereotype that worries some club cavers. 'The-leader-takes-total-responsibility-for-the-group' approach is perhaps best embodied in advice for leaders prepared by the British Association of Caving Instructors (BACI).

BACI Guidelines

1 The safety of the party depends primarily on the judgement and skill of the leader. He must be an experienced caver and must be empowered to modify the party's activities in the light of immediate circumstances, to maintain the safety of the party. (For detailed information, refer to the Cave Instructor Certificate.)

2 The leader should choose a trip which is not too extending for the group, in a system with which he is familiar.

3 Each school or youth group party must be accompanied by at least two adults. The minimum standard of capability of the assistant leader is that in an emergency he would be competent to bring the party back to the surface safely and that he has a thorough knowledge of the relevant cave rescue procedures.

4 The upper size limit recommended for a party is ten pupils with two adults. This is the maximum safe number with two adult cavers in easy systems – that is, where the party would be able to get out safely at any stage without the adults. The number of

pupils must be reduced if the system demands it. The party must consist of a minimum of four people.

5 The technical difficulties of a group's first trip should be such that one might reasonably expect each individual to successfully overcome them. The leader must be able to exclude from the party anyone who might be prejudicial to its safe and proper conduct. No person should be pressurised unduly to go underground. Throughout the trip novices should be checked for signs of physical weakness, reckless behaviour, claustrophobia, poor reaction to wet or cold and other symptoms likely to hinder their progress on subsequent trips.

6 Before going underground a concise briefing should be given on safety and conservation. Additional information should be given as opportunities arise.

7 The minimum equipment for each individual should be:

(a) warm clothing and protective overgarment;
(b) protective helmet with chinstrap and lamp bracket;
(c) boots without hook lacing, and preferably with commando-type soles;
(d) an efficient headlamp, preferably electric.

The party must carry spare lighting and emergency food in addition to that normally eaten on the trip. Leaders should have a first-aid kit, and a whistle each. A wet-suit, exposure suit or other suitable gear must be worn by all the party if there is any possibility of prolonged exposure to water. Ropes, ladders and other equipment will, of course, be taken as required.

8 Before entering the cave the leader must:

(a) check the equipment and clothing of all members of the party ensuring that helmets fit correctly and lights are working;
(b) check the condition of the party;
(c) leave a note of the passages to be followed and the time of return;
(d) have left an identifying object (or person) at the entrance of the cave whenever necessary with a responsible person;

(e) satisfy himself, by consulting weather forecasts and by direct observation, that there is no chance of the system flooding. A wider margin of safety must be allowed than on a normal caving trip.

9 Conservation measures should be taught and observed. Spent carbide and batteries should never be left underground; litter, even if left by others, should be removed if possible. Stalactites and other formations should never be handled or broken. A respect for caves as irreplaceable natural phenomena should be cultivated at all times.

10 When underground, the leader and his assistant must have a comprehensive awareness of the possible hazards to the party and guard against them. In particular the leader and his assistant should:

(a) be in contact with the front and rear of the party;
(b) be aware of the physical and mental well-being of the party and be prepared to turn back at any stage;
(c) be aware, and warn the party, of specific dangers;
(d) give extra protection and assistance to novices because of their inexperience.

11 *Vertical pitches*

(a) Parties which will encounter ladder pitches or roped sections underground should first be taught and practise the relevant technique. This training, and particularly ladder practice, should be carried out in caving gear, preferably on the surface.
(b) The time each ladder pitch will take should be estimated in advance from the surface practice, and the trip and party-size planned accordingly. Long waits underground should be avoided, particularly under wet conditions.
(c) All ladder pitches must be lifelined using accepted safe techniques. Lifelines should be held by experienced cavers or by competent pupils under constant supervision. No one should ever be allowed on a wire ladder in hook-lacing boots. An experienced caver must descend and ascend first and last.

12 *Mines*

Mines, being man-made, can present totally different dangers and problems from those encountered in cave systems. They must therefore be treated with the greatest respect, and may require additional knowledge and competence on behalf of the leader.

This code must be used with common sense and with due consideration of a number of factors. Foremost is the need to see that the exploratory element of caving is not lost. If a group cannot be given the opportunity to explore at least a small section of cave for themselves on a first trip, the cave is too hard. A good leader will give his group the maximum chance to assess the cave for themselves. He will let a couple of the party go in front to do the route-finding, and be in a position to see what they are doing and to give advice. The leader who stays at the head of his party will have little idea of how they are getting on. Cave surveys and their use will be introduced at an early stage, and the group will be involved in the process of getting permission before going down the cave. Good leadership is about passing on expertise to others, not simply shepherding.

Leadership Training

There is no place in caving instruction for the youth leader or teacher who is not, first and foremost, an experienced caver. Secondly, there must be a desire to pass experience on to others; and thirdly, the ability to understand the fears and limitations of those with less experience than himself. The last requirement rules out many individually expert cavers.

The level of skill required by a leader depends on the nature of the instruction to be undertaken. One common fallacy is that all outdoor centre instructors need to be very experienced at a high caving standard, as opposed to 'amateur' leaders, such as schoolteachers, who take groups caving. Many centres will undertake just one caving day at a low level with each group, and the chief requirement of the instructor, after a modicum of experience, is resistance to boredom and frustration. Starry-eyed young cavers wanting to become instructors should take this into account! The

leader with a group that develops over the course of several years has the opportunity to guide his charges into the most advanced fields.

More caving with groups will be at an introductory level than at any other. Introductory 'wild' cave trips cannot alone be blamed for the increase in numbers of cavers. They are but one of many factors: show caves, caving books and guides, television programmes and the general rise in interest in the outdoors also figure, together with the increase in university and college caving clubs. However, introductory caving trips, though not involving vast numbers of cavers, can have unfortunate effects on caves. The leaders of such parties must see that their activities do not damage caves or obstruct other caving parties.

The introductory trip should be to a flood-prone cave with multiple passages and entrances, though not when it is liable to flood! (A leader incapable of assessing this risk is unfit for the job.) In this way the danger of turning a beautiful fossil passage with stalactites and interesting floor deposits into an untidy, mud-smeared hole is minimised, and other parties will not be held up by bottlenecks. Porth yr Ogof in Wales and Long Churn Caves in the Northern Pennines are good examples of flood-prone caves suitable for novices.

It is too late to do much about many fossil systems heavily used by novices, such as Pridhamsleigh in Devon and many caves on Mendip. Leaders who have to use these caves have a special responsibility to teach their charges that other caves should not be allowed to get into such a deplorable state. Leaders must also see that the techniques they pass on are as good as their attitudes. This is often difficult, as the hard British caver has specialised over the years in letting toughness and 'neck' triumph over good technique and equipment. However, attitudes to training beyond the novice stage are changing, and in most areas there is now a reluctant acceptance that cave leaders should be trained for the job. This may be through club caving alone, or augmented by training courses at Whernside Cave and Fell Centre or elsewhere. There is a national scheme of training and assessment for cave instructors now operated through the National Caving Association's Training Committee. This requires participants to gain experience of the whole spectrum of caving before attending a week's assessment: The syllabus of training for the certificate is given here:

NCA Syllabus
Candidates will be assessed and tested on the following:

1 *Leadership and judgement*
The candidate must satisfy the Board of his ability to make wise decisions with regard to the safety of his party. No specific standards of physical prowess are laid down. It is necessary, however, for candidates to gain experience at a more advanced level than that at which they intend to lead parties underground.

2 *Knowledge of caving hazards*
This refers to natural hazards rather than those arising from the type of party, its equipment and its ability to use this, eg flooding, rock falls, exposure to cold, getting lost, infection, foul air and the difficulty of rescue after even a minor accident. An Instructor should be aware of the real and potential danger of cave systems. He should be able to both assess these and take suitable precautions for the protection of his party by, for example, avoidance, adequate briefing or physical protection.

3 *Limestone topography, origin of caves and the development of cave formations*
The cave instructor should have a general knowledge of the rocks in which caves form, and the deposits they contain, sufficient to be able to discuss these things intelligently with other cavers. They must also be capable of passing this knowledge on to others.

4 *Cave access*
Candidates must be able to locate up-to-date information on access arrangements for caves of their area, and also understand the reasons for the procedures necessary, including the historical perspective. This will include agreed or acceptable routes to caves, as well as access to the entrances themselves.

5 *Cave conservation*
Respect for the caves visited should be a keynote of all cave leaders' activities. They will thus be expected not only to set a good example at all times, but be able to put a totally convincing case to their charges on the need to restrict movement through decorated passages, avoid contamination by carbide, etc, and in general appreciate the conservation problems that visits to caves inevitably pose.

6 *General knowledge of cave surveys*
An instructor should be able to interpret well-drawn surveys using signs and symbols currently in use, and to make an intelligible sketch survey of a cave after a visit to it.

7 *Surface navigation*
An instructor should be able to read Ordnance Survey maps, extract the information they contain relevant to caves, and navigate to and from caves without problem.

8 *Clothing and equipment*
An instructor should show:
A general knowledge of the main types of clothing and equipment used underground including a specific knowledge of the advantages and disadvantages of commonly used items.
A general knowledge of group gear sufficient to be able to choose, use and care for commonly used items of tackle.

9 *The ability to use tackle underground*
An instructor must be able to demonstrate ladder-lifeline techniques and single rope techniques, and be able to teach these to others. The skills required include the ability to rig pitches to best advantage, and to safeguard other people. Care of tackle below ground will be regarded as important.

10 *The organisation and conduct of novice parties*
Instructors must be capable of assessing and if necessary selecting their party before they go underground, be able to handle any difficulties posed by or to the party, and be capable of exercising sufficient control over their party to prevent dangerous situations arising. They must be capable of choosing an appropriate cave and routes, and be able

to convey something of the spirit of caving to their party.

11 *What to do in the event of an accident underground*

An instructor should have a clear idea of his responsibilities both to the casualty and to the rest of his party. He should be able to decide when self-help is possible and be able to organise this, ie he should know some method or methods of aiding a partially incapacitated person along passages of all types including short pitches. He should be certain that if help is sent for there is no possibility of this help not being reached as soon as possible. The solution to the dilemma of either leaving the majority of his party underground or sacrificing speed in reaching help by taking them out is largely dependent on circumstances and a leader must be able to make a sensible decision.

The instructor should be conversant with the function of his area Cave Rescue Organisation, know how to call out the CRO in the event of an accident and know what information will be required.

12 *Underground first-aid*

The Cave Instructor Certificate will not be awarded until the candidate produces a valid adult First-Aid Certificate. Because the cave environment is so different from the normal everyday situation he will be required to demonstrate some first-aid procedures underground.

13 *Exposure to cold (hypothermia)*

An instructor must have an understanding of the causes, symptoms and effects of exposure to cold, its prevention and treatment. The hostility of the cave environment is such that it is, at present, generally considered advisable to remove exposure victims to the surface as soon as possible. A leader should be capable of deciding sensibly when a casualty can be moved, how to do this and when to stop. The accent is on sensible decisions as no clear-cut procedure can be laid down and opinions tend to vary on this matter.

14 *Weather*

The prime concern of the caver with regard to weather is the likelihood of rain, and the effect it may have on the cave to be descended. The leader should thus know where and how to obtain an up-to-date weather forecast and also the general rainfall picture of the area in which they are caving, so that the forecast can be interpreted as accurately as possible. He should have a knowledge of factors affecting run-off, types of run-off and the characteristics of flood-water flow before and after reaching caves. Background knowledge of other aspects of cave weather, for instance temperatures to be expected, draughting, etc, will be regarded as useful.

15 *Caving interests*

The instructor should have a real interest in caves over and above the desire to take others underground. It is expected that this should be reflected in a special interest and knowledge of one or more of the wider aspects of caves and caving. Topics looked for under this section might range through cave photography, expedition caving, club organisation, cave science and many others.

The level of the certificate is that needed by leaders or instructors requiring a carte blanche to make all their own decisions in running a programme of caving instruction.

Local cave leader assessments, based on guidelines set by the NCA Training Committee, are also available. The candidates must show that they are safe and competent leaders in caves both of their own choice and in more difficult caves.

Who Needs Instruction?

The first cavers in Britain to recognise the need for training were the cave divers. The Cave Diving Group has its own training manual and testing system, recognising that expertise must be acquired by every individual if he is to be safe. Now that the old methods of safeguarding pitches have been largely replaced by SRT, the same consideration applies to cavers in general. Training is no longer only for novices but for all cavers.

Perhaps the greatest need of all is for general

training of members of university and similar clubs. We now have numerous caving clubs of young, inexperienced but keen individuals without the restraining and guiding influence of older, more experienced members. As long as these groups operate without recourse to better training than can be provided from within their own ranks, they will head the lists of incidents dealt with by rescue teams.

The National Cave Training Centre

The UK is unique in having a permanent year-round training centre for cavers. This is the Whernside Cave and Fell Centre at Dent in the Yorkshire Dales National Park. Its services include courses at all levels up to instructor assessment, with a wide range of technical tuition covering equipment, rope techniques, rigging, self-rescue, cave rescue, surveying and photography. Back-up services include equipment hire and sales, equipment testing and weather forecasting. Special training is available to suit the requirements of specific groups, such as pre-expedition training, etc.

This centre has been the launching-pad for many cavers, and provides the best introduction to caving for those not fortunate enough to have an immediate entrée into a good, established club.

10 Photographing Caves

J.J. ROWLAND, FRPS

The satisfaction and challenge of cave photography lies in the careful and creative use of lighting under difficult conditions. The importance of lighting makes cave photography in some ways similar to studio photography. The similarity does not go very much further! The studio is a comfortable environment for the photographer and his models, and there are no serious limitations on the weight and bulk of his equipment. In contrast, the cave photographer works in cold, wet and often muddy surroundings, his helpers quickly become cold and bored, and dust and damp get into the equipment. He has to carry and use his camera and lighting in constricted passages, and this leads him to compromise on its size and weight.

To overcome these difficulties gives immense satisfaction and produces photographs completely different from anything achieved on the surface.

In this chapter some general knowledge of photography is assumed.

Equipment

The Camera

The ideal caving camera does not exist. Any camera can be used in caves, provided it has a shutter which can be held open (on a 'B' or 'T' setting) or a flash synchronisation socket. If it has both, so much the better.

In the cave, everyone's preference will be for a camera which is small and lightweight, but the quality sought in the results usually eliminates formats smaller than full-frame 35mm. Medium-format cameras (eg 6×6cm or 6×4.5cm) can have advantages in terms of picture

Pi Chamber, Ogof Ffynnon Ddu: a single flash slightly above and to one side of the camera (*J.J. Rowland, FRPS*)

quality but their extra weight and size are an encumbrance. Rangefinder cameras are more compact than single-lens reflex cameras, but do not offer the same ease of focusing and composition, nor the same range of lenses. Single-lens reflex cameras are particularly well suited to photographing helictites, cave fauna and so on in close-up.

Most cave photographers find the 35mm single-lens reflex camera the best compromise, while those striving for extra quality, particularly in producing prints, favour medium-format reflexes. Compact 35mm rangefinder cameras are used where minimum size and weight are important, and the watertight Nikonos is suited to extremely severe conditions, in particular cave diving photography.

A common view is that the 'standard' lens is of little use in caves and that a wide-angle lens is essential. This is not true; many superb shots have been taken in caves with a standard lens. A wide-angle can, however, provide dramatic results otherwise impossible to achieve. Long-focus lenses are normally of benefit only in close-up work where, used with extension tubes or bellows, or on 'macro' setting in the case of a zoom, the longer focal length helps keep the camera at a safe distance from delicate straws and helictites.

Electronic Flashguns

Virtually any form of artificial lighting can be used for photographing caves, but the most practical general-purpose light source is electronic flash.

When selecting a flashgun you must compromise between weight and bulk and light output. A convenient means of comparing the power of flashguns is provided by the guide number quoted by the maker. When using guide numbers in this way take care to note whether they refer to distances in feet or in

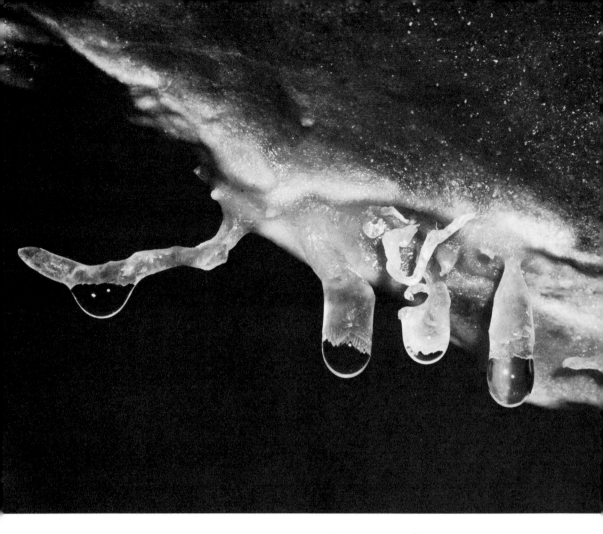

Helictites: single flash carefully positioned to give the best effect (*J.J. Rowland, FRPS*)

metres, and ensure that you are comparing the guide numbers for similar film speeds. (Use of guide numbers for determining exposure is covered later.) Flashguns with a guide number of less than about 35 (metres) for 100ASA film will be barely adequate for cave use, although many flashguns of this power or greater are large and heavy.

Important features on any flashgun for cave use are an 'open flash' pushbutton (which fires the flash when pressed) and a facility which enables the gun to be connected via an extension lead to the synchronisation socket of the camera. A low power switch, fitted to some flashguns, can be useful in balancing the lighting when using several flashes. The various 'automatic exposure' facilities offered by many flashguns are of little use to the cave photographer, who almost always needs as much light as he can get.

To select a powerful, yet compact and otherwise suitable flashgun is difficult, and examination of the products of a range of manufacturers will be needed before reaching the best choice.

Flashbulbs
Flashbulbs are well suited to cave photography. Although they are no longer manufactured, they do occasionally become available, and for this reason some mention is made of them here (see also 'Determining the Exposure').

Flashbulbs were manufactured in two versions, blue and clear. Daylight type colour film requires blue bulbs, although clear bulbs may be used if a Wratten 80B (blue) filter is fitted to the camera lens.

The larger sizes of flashbulb are powerful compared with compact electronic flash units, and they are useful for photographing large passages and chambers.

Flashbulbs can also be used to good effect when photographing moving water. The duration of the flash from a bulb is considerably longer (1/30th second or more) than the duration of an electronic flash (1/500th to 1/2000th second). The bulb flash therefore gives a soft, flowing appearance to the water, whereas an electronic flash produces a frozen effect. A mixture of the two types of flash in the same picture can be very effective.

A further advantage of bulbs is that they require only a low voltage to fire them and so can be used successfully in very wet situations, such as beneath waterfalls and even under water.

Containers/Transportation

The most suitable containers for equipment are ex-government ammunition boxes which can be obtained in various sizes from specialist caving shops. They are robust and, if lined with 2 or 3cm of foam rubber, will help protect your camera even if the box is dropped. Provided the seal is clean and in good condition, an ammunition box is watertight, even when completely immersed.

Tripods

As we will see later, the tripod is an essential item of equipment for 'open flash' photography and also an important aid to composing your picture. When you are setting up a shot it is rarely possible to see the whole scene clearly through the viewfinder: it is usually necessary to direct a caplamp beam to various parts of the scene and to frame the picture required by successive adjustments of the tripod head, which can then be locked in position.

Tripods for cave use should have channel-section legs rather than a tubular or other enclosed section. It is difficult to clean out mud and grit from the latter type and this can lead to early failure of the locking devices on the legs. Tripods whose legs can be raised independently, almost to the horizontal, and then locked in position are very useful in straddling the camera over traverses and in other awkward places. A cable release is required when working with a tripod and a good length is 20 or 25cm.

Insurance

A good insurance policy to cover your equipment against 'all risks' (loss, theft and accidental damage) is essential – and very reassuring when using expensive equipment underground. Good insurance companies do not impose extra premium or special conditions when insuring equipment to be used in caves provided it is not being used for commercial gain.

Film

Black-and-white, colour-negative and colour-reversal films may all be used successfully in caves. Colour-reversal films are available in 'daylight' and 'artificial light' versions and it is the daylight type which is appropriate for use with electronic flash and with blue flashbulbs.

The choice of a particular colour film, either reversal or negative, is a compromise between film speed and quality of results. Faster films normally give more grainy results and also tend to have poorer colour rendition. However, faster films make cave photography easier in that less light is required or more depth of field is obtained for the same amount of light.

In the case of black-and-white film, the choice is not governed purely by the speed/quality compromise because there are two fundamentally different types of film available. There is the conventional type which has been used for many years, and there is the much newer 'chromogenic' film. The chromogenic film can be used over the range of speeds from 125ASA to 1600ASA and produces results with a grain similar to a conventional film a quarter of its speed. For example, a chromogenic film at 400ASA will give results with grain similar to that of a conventional film rated at 100ASA. The advantage is obvious – more quality for less light! Chromogenic films have a slight disadvantage in that they need to be processed in the same way as colour-negative film, which is not as simple a process as for conventional black-and-white film.

Choice between nominally equivalent films from different manufacturers should be the result of your own experiments.

(*overleaf*) Silhouette: a single flash behind the figure (*J.J. Rowland, FRPS*)

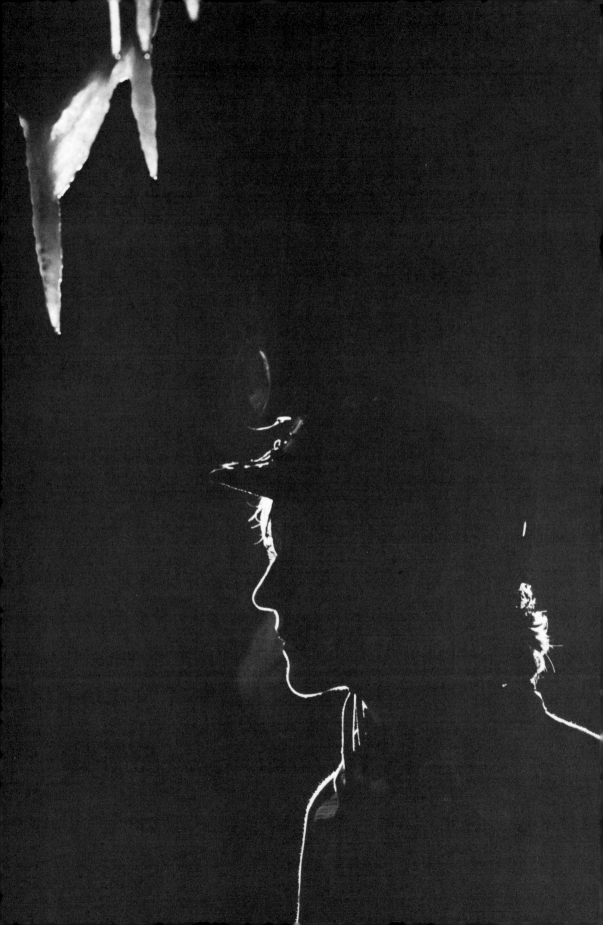

Working with Flash

'Open flash' Photography

The shutter is held open on 'B' or 'T', the flashes are fired by pressing the 'open flash' buttons and the shutter is then closed. This method generally requires one helper for each flash to be fired plus, of course, any 'models' needed. There are two limitations of open-flash; firstly, when more than one flash is used, if the flashes do not occur simultaneously (as is likely!) and there is any movement of your models there will be multiple images produced which can spoil the picture. Secondly, the cap-lamps of people in the picture must be extinguished to prevent their slight movements from producing streaks on the film during the time the shutter is open. Both these problems arise from the unavoidable movement of people in your picture; always attempt to minimise its effect.

Synchronised Flash

Both the limitations of the open-flash method may be avoided if the flashes are synchronised with the shutter. As soon as the shutter is fully open, all the flashes fire simultaneously and the shutter immediately closes again – hence no multiple images. If the shutter speed is fast, then the problem of 'streaking' from caplamps can also be avoided, removing the need to extinguish them.

Cameras which have focal plane shutters normally have an 'X' on the shutter speed dial to indicate the fastest speed at which they will synchronise with electronic flash. This is usually in the range 1/40th to 1/150th of a second, depending on camera model. Cameras with leaf shutters will synchronise with electronic flash at any speed and are particularly useful where rapid movement of the subject's caplamp is expected, such as in a true action shot. The speed of the electronic flash is sufficient to 'freeze' the motion of the subject himself.

With either type of shutter, flashbulbs will properly synchronise only at speeds below

(*previous page*) Long Crawl, Dan-yr-Ogof: single flash held as far away from the camera as space allows (*J.J. Rowland, FRPS*)

(*opposite*) Traversing: a single synchronised flash (*J.J. Rowland, FRPS*)

about 1/30 of a second, and synchronisation is therefore less beneficial than in the case of electronic flash, although it can still sometimes be convenient.

To synchronise the flashes with the shutter, the simplest arrangement of connecting the flashguns and camera is to mount a flashgun on the camera's accessory shoe, with electrical connection made via the 'hot shoe' itself or via a short lead which plugs into the camera's 'X' synchronisation socket. We will see later that 'flash on camera' is not a satisfactory means of lighting cave photographs; the flash is better situated away from the camera and connected to it by an extension lead. We will also see that many pictures benefit from the use of two or more flashguns, some of which may be a distance from the camera. All the flashguns can be joined to the camera by extension leads and 'Y' adaptors (which can be bought or made up from extension leads), but the consequent tangle of wires can be impractical, and an alternative means of firing is required.

Slave Units

These provide a convenient method of firing flashes remote from the camera. A slave unit is a small light-sensitive device which is connected to a flashgun via a lead. The slave unit is sensitive only to the light of an electronic flash unit, and when it detects another flash being fired, it fires the flash to which it is attached. The delay between the slave unit detecting the incoming light and firing its own flash is so short that the flashes appear to fire simultaneously. One electronic flashgun connected directly to the camera may therefore be used to fire simultaneously any number of remote flashguns fitted with slave units. The slave unit, being sensitive only to the high speed flash of an electronic gun, is virtually impossible to fire accidentally with a caplamp.

Slave units can be bought, although the cheaper types are too insensitive for use in caves. The more expensive types are very useful, although their range is limited, particularly where there is not a direct line of sight between the slave unit and the first flash.

The most serious problems in using synchronised flash in caves result from moisture finding its way into the connectors of the extension leads and slave units. With electronic flash there are several hundred volts between the

Top view

Side view

Fig 208 An example of backlighting

inner and outer contacts of the plugs and sockets, so that even slight moisture is enough to prevent the flashes from recycling properly. Silicone grease and other water repellents can help but there is no substitute for care in keeping the connections away from water. This is easier if the number of connectors is minimised, which can be achieved by using slave units.

Lighting Techniques

Single Flash

The simplest lighting arrangement is a single flashgun mounted on the camera. At best this gives flat lighting with no 'modelling' of the subject. Matters are made worse by the mist and dust usually present in cave air. This reflects the light from the flash directly back into the camera lens and gives a result low in contrast. A dramatic improvement in picture quality can be obtained by holding the flash about a metre away from the camera, slightly above and to one side of it. This emphasises the texture of formations and provides slight shadowing which adds realism to faces and

clothing. The light from the flash no longer bounces back into the camera, which therefore 'sees' through the murk. Once you have used your flash off the camera in this way you will never put it back!

For special effects the single flash can be placed in any desired position, and for certain subjects, particularly formations, and even in macro work, side or back lighting can be effective. An idea of the effect which will be obtained can be gained by holding a caplamp in various positions; the best position for the flash should be found in this way.

Multiple Flash

The use of two or more flashes can add tremendously to atmosphere and feeling of depth. The most frequent use of multiple flash is in the addition of a back light to a conventionally lit shot; many shots which are taken with a single

Edward's Short Cut, Ogof Ffynnon Ddu: flash behind the figure giving most of the light, with a fill-in flash near the camera (*J.J. Rowland, FRPS*)

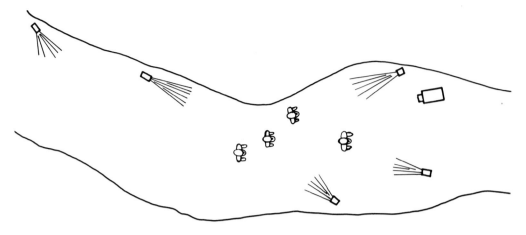

Fig 209 A multiple-flash arrangement for photographing a party in a large passage. Note the use of two backlights: one directed at the figures, the other at the wall behind them to add shadow detail

flash could be greatly improved by the addition of a back light.

A back light is a flash placed directly behind, or behind and to one side, of the subject so that the flashgun is not directly visible to the camera (Fig 208). This produces a pleasing highlighting effect on the subject and can also give attractive reflections from walls, floor and roof, particularly if these surfaces are wet or highly textured. Back lighting can also give the impression that the cave goes on beyond the section being photographed and so add interest.

Further uses of multiple flash are in lighting up large passages or chambers. Helpers with flashguns can be placed to illuminate each other, or they can illuminate a section of wall behind them so that they appear in silhouette. Alternatively flashes fitted with slave units can be used to light a party moving through a large passage or chamber; Fig 209 gives a possible lighting arrangement for this type of shot.

Determining the Exposure

We have seen that the shutter will be fully open for the entire duration of the flash or flashes. The aperture rather than the shutter speed determines the exposure.

The 'guide number' quoted by the manufacturer of the electronic flashgun (or bulb) for the speed of film being used is the starting point for calculating the exposure. The guide number relates the aperture setting required and the flash-to-subject distance (*not* the camera-to-subject distance) as follows:

$$\text{f/no} = \frac{\text{guide number}}{\text{flash-to-subject distance}}$$

Remember to note whether the guide number assumes distances in metres or in feet.

The guide number will depend on the speed of the film being used, and there is normally a calculator dial fitted to electronic flashguns which gives the guide numbers for the various film speeds. Alternatively the calculator will give the aperture/distance combinations appropriate to the film speed in use. Guide numbers for flashbulbs are shown below:

Type	Guide no (metres)	
	100ASA	400ASA
PF1	40	80
PF5	56	110
PF60	110	220
PF100	150	300

The guide number for electronic flash or for bulbs is just a guide, and the aperture calculated may need to be adjusted for particularly light or dark subjects. Furthermore the quoted guide number assumes that you are working in a normal room where light reflects well from the walls. In a cave the walls absorb most of the light and you will usually need to use an aperture around two stops wider than that indicated by the guide number. A way of making this correction is to use as your starting point the guide number quoted for a film one quarter of the speed you are actually using, which is equivalent to opening up two stops.

Traversing a pool: a subtle back-light synchronised with
the main flash adds depth to this photograph (*J.J.
Rowland, FRPS*)

(*overleaf*) Dan-yr-Ogof, the Green Canal: two synchronised flashes used (*J.J. Rowland, FRPS*)

(*above*) Boulder fall: three synchronised flashes used here (*J. J. Rowland, FRPS*)

(*previous page left*) Ogof Ffynnon Ddu stream passage: action shot, with main flash and a back-light both synchronised and (*right*) Photographer at work: several unsynchronised flashes used here (*both J.J. Rowland, FRPS*)

(*right*) Arête chamber, Ogof Ffynnon Ddu: a combination of back-light (silouette) and fill-in flash used here (*J. J. Rowland, FRPS*)

For example, when using 400ASA film use the guide number for 100ASA.

When you have calculated the aperture, make any further correction for a light or dark subject, and then take two extra shots with exposure settings one each side of the calculated setting; you are likely to get one shot with just the effect you want.

With multiple flash, calculate the aperture setting as already described, using the distance from the 'main' flash to the particular part of the scene you wish it to illuminate. Then place the remaining flashes at appropriate distances from their own subjects, again using the modified guide number, but this time the other way around:

$$\text{flash-to-subject distance} = \frac{\text{guide number}}{\text{f/no}}$$

This method enables you to balance the lighting even when using flashguns of differing light output. The distance you calculate should again be modified to take account of light or dark subject matter for each of the additional flashguns.

Ultimately, successful exposure determination relies on accurate judgement of the conditions and is best achieved by experiment and practice.

Photographing People in Caves

It is often difficult to get your models to pose so that they look natural in the final picture. It can be helpful to use synchronised flash and to ask them to walk a few paces, during which you take the picture. A few attempts should produce a picture with quite natural-looking figures.

The clothing worn by your models can make the difference between a good and bad shot. A light-coloured overall which does not darken when wet will, whether you are using colour or black-and-white, prevent people from blending with the walls in the way that they often do when wearing old clothes or a wet-suit.

Do not forget the welfare of your helpers; they are essential to your photography! One can suffice, but two or three make life very much easier, and for large passages and chambers more will be needed. Your helpers will not be as fanatical about standing around cold and wet as you are about taking pictures of them, so work as fast as you reasonably can. Have a rough idea before you go into the cave of the type of pictures you want and where you are likely to get them. Indecision on your part will bring you pictures of bored-looking people.

Cave Conservation (see also Chapter 15)

Damage is often done to cave formations and other features by careless photographers; a tripod leg is placed on an unspoilt section of floor because 'it will not go anywhere else', a stalactite is carelessly knocked off by someone photographing near it. One photographer crossing a tape to get to a good viewpoint will lead to others doing the same and thus to the ruin of part of a 'protected' area. Do not take photographs at the expense of caves!

Results and Picture Quality

If you honestly and critically judge your cave photography, you will achieve a high failure rate. In order to improve, study other people's work. If you think it is better than your own, decide precisely why, and what you can do about it. If you think yours is better than theirs then you may still be able to glean new ideas from them.

Study books on appropriate aspects of photography. If you process your own work, polish your darkroom technique. If you take slides, polish your presentation. Cave photography is done under difficult conditions; by comparison, slide presentation and darkroom work are done in comfortable surroundings. You should make the most of this and ensure that your darkroom skills and presentation techniques extract every last bit of quality from the pictures you have gone to so much trouble to obtain.

(*previous page*) The Cloud Chamber, Dan Yr Ogof
(*J. J. Rowland, FRPS*)

11 Surveying a Cave

BRYAN M. ELLIS

Grades of Survey

Cave surveys are most frequently produced to show other cavers the size and layout of a particular system. Other uses include the presentation of scientific information or to show what tackle is required for a cave. Whatever the original reason for a survey, the result will fall into one of three rough categories based on its accuracy:

a *sketch* with no real pretensions of accuracy;
a *rough survey* made quickly with simple instruments; or
an *accurate survey* where care has been taken to produce a result as accurate as the time and conditions allow.

Cave surveys in the British Isles (and many other countries) are usually graded to give the user an indication of the accuracy that can be expected. Details of the British Cave Research Association (BCRA) grades for this purpose are given in Tables 11.1 and 11.2.

Caves are surveyed by preparing a representation of a line through the passages and then adding detail to show the shape of chambers and passage widths. Table 11.1 deals with the centre line or skeleton of the survey, and Table 11.2 with the accuracy of detail. In this chapter the making of surveys of grades 1A, 3B and 3C is considered. Grade 5C and 5D surveys require specialist skills and sophisticated equipment; anyone intending to make them should start with a lower-grade one to gain experience and then refer to a specialised book on cave surveying, eg Ellis (1976) or Hoseley (1971).

Table 11.1 Grading of the survey centre line

BCRA SURVEY CENTRE LINE GRADINGS

Note: Caving organisations, and others, are encouraged to reproduce tables 1, 2 and 3 in their own publications; the permission of the British Cave Research Association to reproduce these three tables need not be obtained.

Grade 1	A sketch of low accuracy where no measurements have been made.
(Grade 2)	(May be used, if necessary, to describe a sketch that is intermediate in accuracy between grade 1 and grade 3.)
Grade 3	A rough magnetic survey. Horizontal and vertical angles measured to ± 2½°; distances measured to ± 50cm; station position error less than ± 50cm.
(Grade 4)	(May be used, if necessary, to describe a survey that fails to attain all the requirements of grade 5 but is more accurate than a grade 3 survey.)
Grade 5	A magnetic survey. Horizontal and vertical angles *accurate* to ± 1°; distances *accurate* to ± 10cm; station position error less than ± 10cm.
Grade 6	A magnetic survey that is more accurate than grade 5.
Grade X	A survey that is based primarily on the use of a theodolite instead of a compass.

Notes:
1 The above table is a summary and is intended only as an aide memoire; the definitions of survey grades given above must be read in conjunction with the additional comments made in the BCRA book *Surveying Caves* (Ellis, 1976). The more important comments are summarised below.
2 In all cases it is necessary to follow the spirit of the definition and not just the letter.
3 The term accuracy, used in the definitions, means the nearness of a result to the **true** value; it must

not be confused with precision which is the nearness of a number of repeat results to each other, irrespective of their accuracy.

4 To attain grade 3 it is necessary to use a clinometer in passages having an appreciable slope.

5 It is essential for instruments to be **properly** calibrated to attain grade 5 – details of calibration are given in *Surveying Caves*.

6 A grade 6 survey requires the compass to be used at the limit of possible accuracy, i.e. accurate to ± ½°; clinometer readings must be to same accuracy. Distances and station position must be accurate to at least ± 2½cm and will require the use of tripods or similar techniques.

7 A grade X survey must include on the drawing notes on the type of instruments and techniques used, together with an estimate of the probable accuracy of the survey compared with grade 3, 5 or 6 surveys.

8 Grades 2 and 4 are for use only when, at some stage of the survey, physical conditions have prevented the surveyor from attaining all of the requirements for the next higher grade and it is not practical to survey again.

9 The tabular summary above must not be republished without these notes.

Methods and Equipment

Grade 1 surveys include anything from the sketch of a new cave drawn in beer on a bar counter, through the rough drawing on the back of an envelope, to the well-presented drawing published in a journal but where the information is based on memory, not measurement. In other words, the probable accuracy, not the tidiness of presentation, of a survey determines its grading.

For a grade 3 survey it is necessary to use simple instruments so that horizontal and vertical angles can be measured approximately, together with some method of measuring distances. The instrument used almost exclusively for measuring horizontal angles or direction is the compass, and for a grade 3 survey virtually any instrument will be suitable. The instrument recommended for grade 5 surveys is the model K14/360 made by the Finnish firm of Suunto and this is also very suitable for use with a grade 3 if one is available. Magnetic compass readings are subject to many errors, but while these become very important when making accurate surveys (grades 5 and 6) the majority need not concern the surveyor producing a grade 3 survey. Remember that iron and steel objects and electric currents will deflect a compass needle if brought too close and give rise to a false reading – keep them away from the compass. The other likely cause of false readings is tilting the compass when taking a reading thus causing the card to stick. This is particularly likely if one station is appreciably higher or lower than the other.

Table 11.2 Classification of survey detail

Class A All details based on memory.

Class B Passage details estimated and recorded in the cave.

Class C Measurements of detail made at survey stations only.

Class D Measurements of detail made at survey stations and whenever necessary between stations to show significant changes in passage shape, size, direction, etc.

Table 11.3 Recommended grading/ classification combinations

Grade 1A
Grade 3B or 3C
Grade 5C or 5D
Grade 6D
Grade XB, XC or XD

The other essential measurement is that of distance; experiments show that visual estimation is not good enough. A proper measuring tape can be used although there is no need to record the distances to better than the nearest half-metre; if a tape is not available, use a suitably marked length of string. Alternatively, provided care is taken, you can measure distances by counting the number of paces taken between stations, or if the passage is low, by counting body lengths. It is not easy to count regular paces under some conditions, such as clambering over boulders, but with care and practice this method can be accurate enough for a grade 3 survey. If you use a proper tape, which is the easiest method, then the one recommended is the Fibron tape made by Rabone Chesterman; this is a tape of polyvinyl chloride, strengthened with longitudinal glassfibres.

If the cave passage slopes to any appreciable extent you will need to measure the angle of the slope or take special care that you record the horizontal distance between stations and not the sloping distance. This is because the survey of any but the simplest cave should be a true plan

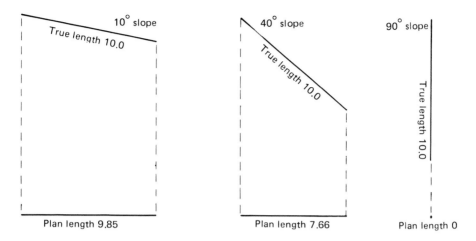

Fig 210 Comparison of true and plan distances at different slopes

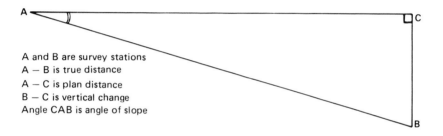

A and B are survey stations
A — B is true distance
A — C is plan distance
B — C is vertical change
Angle CAB is angle of slope

Fig 211 Measurement of passage slope

(accompanied if necessary by a section) showing a view of the cave as seen from vertically above. However, a plan does not show the true length of a cave passage, unless the passage is horizontal, and as the slope increases, so will the difference between the true and plan distances. In the extreme case of a vertical passage, it will have no length on the plan (Fig 210). When making an accurate survey you will need to measure the slope with the same accuracy as you take the compass bearings, but for a rough survey it is not necessary to be so particular. If the cave is virtually horizontal you can ignore the slope, but with a slope in excess of 10 or 15° you will need some form of clinometer to measure it.

The best clinometer available for cave surveying is the Suunto model PM5/360 which matches the recommended compass. Other suitable instruments are the Abney Level and the Watkin clinometer. Any of these is suitable for grade 5 or a lower grade, as would be some form of home-made clinometer. Instead of using a clinometer you can keep the measuring tape level while making readings and then measure additionally the vertical change between the stations – in Fig 211 measure A-C and C-B, instead of A-B and angle CAB.

The only other equipment required for rough surveys is a notebook or some other method of recording the information obtained in the cave. Make sure that everything needed is recorded – it is not always possible to return to the cave to obtain that missing detail.

Procedure and Techniques

Any attempt to make a cave survey consists of recording two related sets of information in the cave, one set for the centre line and the other for the passage detail. A surveying team of at least two is required, one to take the instrument

171

readings and the other to record the readings and make sketches of the cave as the survey progresses. Before starting off, make sure that the team knows exactly what it is expected to do, and how, and what is meant (in the context of the survey being made) by terms such as 'left', and 'backwards'. If this precaution is not taken there can be confusion, mistakes and loss of temper – not the best conditions for surveying.

The survey of the centre line consists of taking measurements along a line through the cave, each section of the line from survey station to survey station being called a leg. On each leg it is necessary to measure the distance, the direction (by compass) and the slope (by clinometer), if it is significant. Of the two basic methods by which this can be done, the more obvious and logical, called the 'forward method', is to start at station 1 and take readings to station 2, then move to station 2 and take readings to the third station and so on. The other method, less logical but cancelling out some inherent surveying errors and also saving time in the cave, is known as the 'leapfrog method'. The surveyor starts at station 2 and takes readings back to station 1, and then forward to station 3. When this is complete he moves to station 4 and takes readings to stations 3 and 5, and so on along the passage. A combination of the two methods, depending on the caving conditions, is the most satisfactory. The disadvantages of the leapfrog method are the need to record whether the readings were taken looking forward or backward, and later to change all backward compass (and clinometer) readings into the equivalent forward readings. The novice should use only the forward method until he has mastered the rudiments, developed his own techniques and with luck formed his own surveying team, and then change to the leapfrog method to save time and improve accuracy.

The exact technique used will depend on the surveyor and the cave but the principle will be as follows. Leaving the assistant at the first station holding the end of the measuring tape, the surveyor will proceed into the cave until he comes to the end of the tape or a bend in the passage. At this point he sets up the second station. He reads the distance between the two stations, then the compass bearing and, if necessary, the clinometer reading. All of these

he calls out aloud for his assistant to write down. Next, the assistant travels along the passage, sketching its shape and size as he does so, past the surveyor and on until he is just about to disappear from sight. Now the surveyor takes the readings forward along this leg before proceeding forward past the assistant again until he reaches the fourth station, and so on. The sketches of passage shape should include measurements of passage height and width at each station if the intention is to produce a grade 3C survey, but these dimensions need only be estimated (and recorded in the cave) for grade 3B.

It is often difficult to return to a cave to obtain forgotten or illegible figures. Care and effort spent in the cave making sure that everything has been written down clearly may save frustration later. Probably the most frequent cause of error in survey notes is writing down the wrong number – it is surprisingly easy to transpose digits. This type of error can be reduced by making it a rule for the assistant to read aloud the number he has just written down; any discrepancy should be noticed by another of the team. Other points are to ensure that decimal points are not 'lost', that a degree symbol is not taken for a zero and that an incorrect figure is crossed out – an altered figure may not be legible.

Compilation

The first task after leaving the cave is to sort out all the damp muddy pieces of paper covered with figures and sketches. A check through the notes shortly after leaving the cave can often rectify an omission or ambiguity while it is still fresh in the mind. Similarly it is a good practice to draw the survey, if only roughly, as soon after the survey trip as possible. If the notes are scruffy make a fair copy before starting drawing, but be careful not to introduce errors at this stage and do not destroy the originals, in case you need to refer back to them. On this fair copy note: the station to which and from which the readings were made; the sloping distance between stations; the compass bearing. If the cave had an appreciable slope you will need to note the clinometer reading and then leave a space in which to enter the calculated horizontal distance between stations. This is found by using the equation:

horizontal distance = slope distance × cosine
of slope angle

The values of cosines of angle can be found
either direct by using a suitable calculator or
from mathematical tables. Finally, if the leapfrog method of taking readings was used,
reverse the compass readings for those bearings
that were taken looking backwards, eg from
station 2 back to station 1, but not the reading
from station 2 forward to station 3. The bearing
is reversed by adding 180° if the bearing is
between 001° and 180°, or by taking away
180° if it is between 181° and 360°. This may
seem complicated but requires only a sheet of
paper ruled in columns (Fig 212).

Presentation

Drawing the survey is simple once these figures
have been obtained and is most easily done on a
sheet of graph paper. First decide on a scale
according to the size of the cave and the
required size of drawing; it is usual to use a
scale of 1/100, 1/250, 1/500 or 1/1000. Now
make a mark on the paper to represent the first
station in such a position that the survey does
not run off the sheet. Taking the graph grid
lines to represent north-south in one direction
and east-west in the other, place a protractor
along the north-south line with the centre on
the position of the first station and with the zero

Readings From Sta	Readings To Sta	Sloping Distance	Compass Bearing	Clinometer Reading	Horizontal Distance	Corrected Bearing

Fig 212 Summary of survey readings

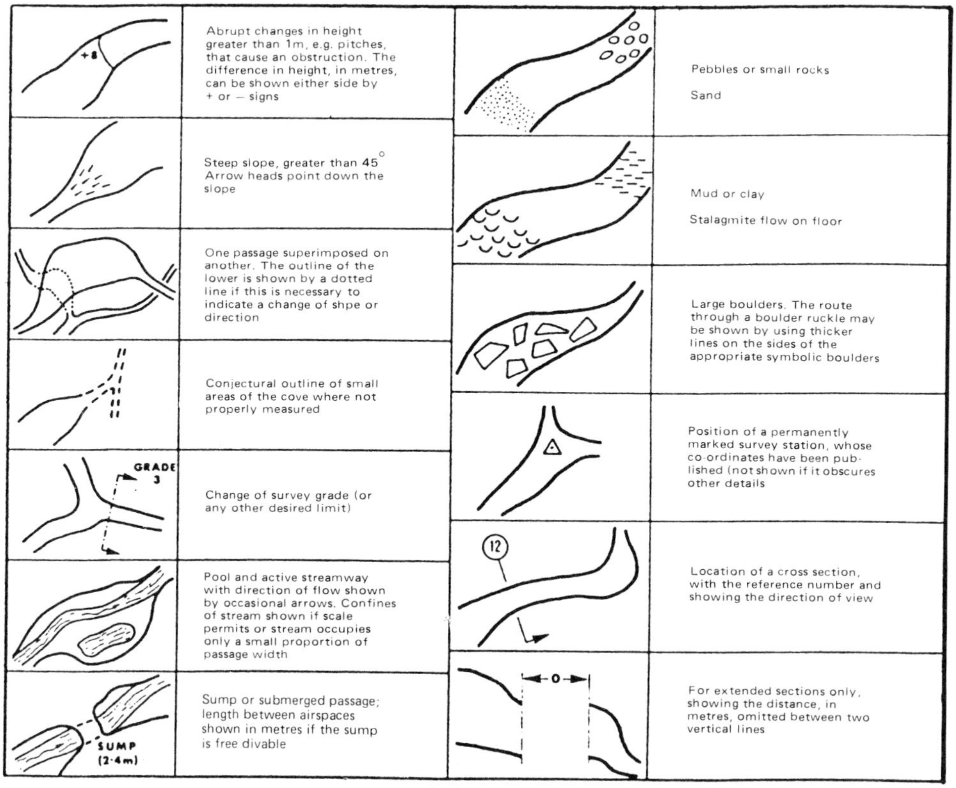

Fig 213 Recommended symbols for use on surveys

graduation to the north. Mark off the (corrected) bearing of the second station from the first against the protractor. After removing the protractor draw a line from the first station along the marked-off bearing. The position of the second station lies along this line at a distance equal to the horizontal distance between the two stations at the chosen scale and is measured off with a scale. With the second station marked, repeat the process to find the position of the third, and so on until all the survey stations are plotted. Do this as carefully as possible, especially if the survey is using a small scale; any error made in marking the position of one station will affect the marked position of all succeeding stations. You next need to add the details of passage shape using the information recorded in the cave. You can add other details, such as active streams and the position of ladder pitches, using the recommended symbols shown in Fig 213.

Only the drawing of the plan view has been considered so far. This is the view drawn in practically all cases, and with surveys of grade 3 often the only view. If the cave has considerable vertical development, it is advantageous also to draw a section or view from the side of the cave. The extended section, the simplest type, is drawn using similar principles as for the plan.

With the draft drawing complete it remains only to trace a fair copy that can be used for the preparation of copies – a survey made but never published serves no useful purpose. Take some trouble over this fair copy – do not spoil all your hard work by producing an untidy drawing. The use of proper drawing pens and dry transfer lettering (eg Letraset) will make so much difference. Finally make sure that your survey includes the following:

1 The name of the cave and its location.
2 The national grid reference (in the UK) or latitude and longitude (abroad) of the entrance, and the altitude.
3 The BCRA grading and classification of the survey.
4 The names of the surveyors/draughtsmen and the date of the survey.
5 The direction of north (if possible show true north; if only magnetic north is given quote the date to which it refers).
6 The scale of the survey in the form of a scale bar.

Anyone wanting ideas on drawing up a survey can do much worse than study existing surveys – a lot, good and bad, can be learnt from them.

Some of the techniques described above are not suitable for making grade 5 and 6 surveys. The rough survey should be thought of as an interim drawing only, made to obtain approximate information as soon as possible after discovery or by an expedition abroad with insufficient time for more accuracy. The grade 3 survey should be replaced by one of grade 5 or 6 as quickly as possible. The principles for making an accurate survey are the same as those for a rough survey but take care to minimise the errors introduced by the underground conditions and magnetic compass inaccuracies. The instruments have to be calibrated to determine their errors, extra care taken when making the readings and effort made to reduce other errors in the cave and when drawing the final plan. Drawing error can also be reduced by plotting the cartesian co-ordinates of stations, and the use of a programmable calculator considerably speeds up the calculation of these (Young 1978). You can progress from grade 3 to more accurate surveys with the help of one of the standard works and perhaps advice from an experienced cave surveyor.

12 Communications

R.O. MACKIN

The only requirement for good communications in many caves is a loud, clear voice (see Signals, Chapter 2). But once deep and wet pitches are encountered, whistles (a referee's whistle is best) are necessary to ensure that the lifeline is held (one blast), taken in (two blasts), paid out (three blasts) or that an SRT rope is free to climb (four blasts). Occasions arise where such simple means of communicating are useless. Verbal communication can be vital between parties separated by hundreds of feet of rock during deep pitch descents, surveying trips, long-stay excursions in flood-prone caves or during rescues. This chapter is concerned with battery-powered devices which can provide such communications through the passages or through the rock.

Telephones

As a reliable and hardy means of surface-to-underground or underground-to-underground communication, telephones are hard to beat. They can be put together simply using surplus handsets, or alternatively military surplus equipment purchased. The circuits to build these handsets are straightforward consisting of interconnecting cable and a battery in the basic form.

The ex-GPO telephone handset consists of an earpiece (a small speaker) and a carbon microphone. This microphone is a capsule containing granules of carbon between two plates of metal which, when subjected to the vibration caused by speaking at one plate, are compressed together and released in sympathy with the speech. This causes a corresponding change in the resistance of the microphone and thus in any current passing through it. If this current flows through an earpiece it attracts and repels the diaphragm in sympathy with the changing current and this movement reproduces the original sound. Fig 214 shows the circuit of the simplest system.

The original interconnections are removed and the handset is rewired in series – one terminal of the microphone connected to one of the earpiece and the other two terminals to the outside world. It is useful if the coiled cables are used to connect the four fine wires in two pairs to make them more reliable, but it is better to fit terminals straight onto the telephone. These devices are not polarised, so it is unimportant which way round they are connected. One handset is connected directly to a two-core wire and the other wired in series with a four to six-volt battery. This circuit will allow two people to speak over several kilometres. The wire need not be 'telephone wire' but the two cores must be reliably insulated. 'Figure-eight twin' as sold for table lamps and loudspeakers is cheap and suitable. The exact battery voltage for long

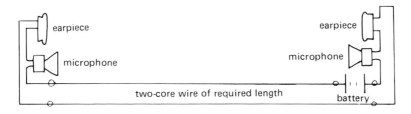

Fig 214

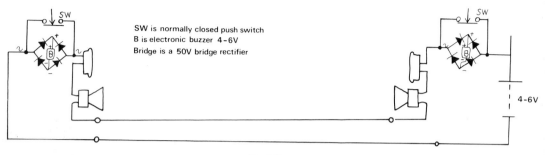

SW is normally closed push switch
B is electronic buzzer 4-6V
Bridge is a 50V bridge rectifier

4-6V

Fig 215

cable lengths is best found by trial and error but must be the minimum required for adequate volume. The circuit consumes power all the time it is connected but one Oldham battery or two in series on very long cables would run the system for about twenty hours. The main disadvantage of this system is that no signalling is provided to attract attention.

A modification can provide a signalling facility. The circuit is wired as before but an electronic buzzer is connected in series in each handset. These are available from component shops such as Tandy, and one which will work from four to six volts is ideal. A normally closed push switch is wired across the buzzer so that unless the switch is pressed the buzzer is short-circuited and does not operate (Fig 215). The disadvantage is that power is consumed all of the time. The buzzer must be in a bridge rectifier to enable it to operate from either polarity. The buzzer is connected plus to plus and minus to minus on the bridge and the AC terminals may be connected either way round.

Radio and Inductive-loop Systems

Radio Equipment
The design of systems for non-wire communication through ground is difficult. In large caves where communication is required through air across large areas, or down big shafts, 'walkie talkie' can be used with mixed, sometimes very good, results. These sets can be private mobile radio or citizens' band types and hand portables, usually of one or two watts output. Choice of site is important and if poor results are obtained moving one or both radios may optimise performance.

A lower operating frequency is advantageous,

and therefore citizens' band radios operating at 27mHz are superior to low-band or high-band VHF sets – provided they are superhetrodyne types of good quality. The cheap 100mw super-generative sets are not suitable. Radio equipment is suitable only along line-of-sight and will not work reliably round corners.

All radio equipment is covered by licensing legislation. Take care that you comply with this to avoid possible prosecution and confiscation of equipment. This is especially necessary when crossing national frontiers.

Guidewire Systems
Guidewire systems are worth considering for communicating down long ladders or winch ropes. They are a radio transmitter-receiver much like walkie talkies, but operate at very low frequencies and are coupled by a single wire like a common aerial. They must be directly coupled to the wire, or an aerial from them must be close to the wire ladder or winch rope that is to go between them.

If you want to experiment with this system they are available in the form of 'wireless intercoms' which work down the mains wiring without connecting wires. These units take their power from the mains, but the actual circuit uses about ten volts and is thus easily modified to work off batteries. They feed their radio frequency output and take their input from the line of the mains. This would have to be brought out to an aerial terminal. These units usually operate at about 450 kHz and are frequency-modulated. The range is dependent on conditions (which can be enhanced by connecting the negative battery terminal to earth) but should extend from hundreds to a thousand metres.

Inductive-loop Systems

Inductive-loop systems fall into two main categories, audio frequency and radio frequency.

In an audio frequency system a high-power audio amplifier is fed into a coil typically 100 turns, 30m in diameter, and a sensitive amplifier's input connected to a similar coil. If the output of this is connected to headphones or a loudspeaker the transmitted signal will be heard up to about 200m depth depending on power output and coil size.

Many suitable integrated circuits are available to build this type of system; integrated power-amps can be run in bridge configuration to deliver 50 watts of power (about the minimum required) and low noise preamplifiers are available (intended for use in tape recorders) suitable for the receiver's front end.

These systems will work reliably but suffer from interference from power lines and natural phenomena like thunder; the coils must be as large as possible making them heavy and bulky; they also consume a great amount of power and need large, heavy-duty batteries. They are, however, easily constructed and tested without extensive knowledge of telecommunications or expensive equipment and give useful results at moderate depths.

For surveying, units can be constructed easily and cheaply, transmitting 1kHz tone only, using high Q tuned coils of 200–300 turns of around 0.3m diameter. With these units, clear of man-made noise such as overhead power cables, locations and depth measurements can be made up to 60–90m (200–300ft).

Radio-frequency Inductive-loop Systems

In a radio-frequency inductive-loop system the audio tone or speech is not transmitted in simple form but is used to influence a much higher-frequency signal called a carrier. This influence is as described for guidewire systems where the amplitude of frequency of the carrier is changed in sympathy with the information. This process is known as modulation.

Although based on simple facts the implementation is difficult, mainly due to the limitations of aerial size and licensing regulations. There is no propagation from these devices; whereas a torch sends out light which travels forwards even when the source is turned off, the inductive-loop system is linked only by the magnetic field which does not propagate. The significant fact is that both ends are linked by a returning medium which, if broken, breaks the link – unlike light or radio where power is sent out at the same rate whether intercepted or not. The significance of this is that the received signal power falls as $1/D^6$ instead of the familiar $1/D^2$ inverse square law.

This puts severe limitations on the modes and techniques which can be employed, and requires expensive equipment to construct, service and ensure that it is operating within licensing requirements. This is why little development has been made with RF systems. Reasonable results can be obtained from amplitude-modulated systems operating around 100kHz. Running about 5w into tuned coils, these systems will work to about 100–150m depth and provide speech communication and survey facilities.

The best systems use single side-band – although they are the most difficult to implement. The problem is that expensive instrumentation is necessary to ensure that the carrier and unwanted side-band are correctly suppressed, and that the receiver alignment is correct. Because of the phenomenal change in signal power, the receivers must have a dynamic range many orders of magnitude greater than telecom systems and therefore unconventional design is necessary.

Such a system is now commercially available. Known as the Molefone, it uses open coils of 1m sq, or loaded coils in tubes 14cm long for short range in confined spaces. It has a range of 200–300m depending on the circumstances. Information available from the University of Lancaster Engineering Services (see Appendix 2).

Principles of Operation and Surveying

To obtain the best results from inductive-loop systems, and to obtain results at all when surveying, an understanding of the principles involved is necessary.

The transformer in Fig 216 has two coils connected magnetically by an iron circuit. If an alternating voltage is applied to the primary of N1 turns a magnetic flux will be established round the iron linking the secondary N2 and inducing a voltage in it. Unless the secondary is loaded and current drawn from it, the only current flowing in N1 will be that necessary to establish the field and overcome the losses. The

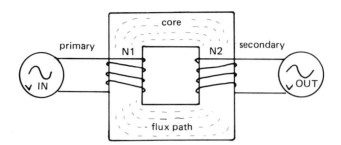

Fig 216 Transformer

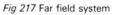

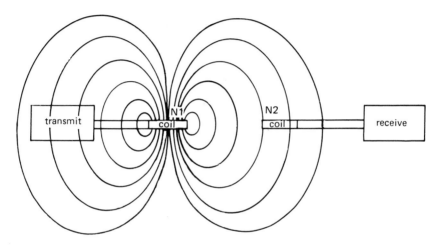

Fig 217 Far field system

$$\text{Depth} = \frac{2L}{\sqrt{(9 \tan^2 \alpha) + 8} - 3 \tan \alpha}$$

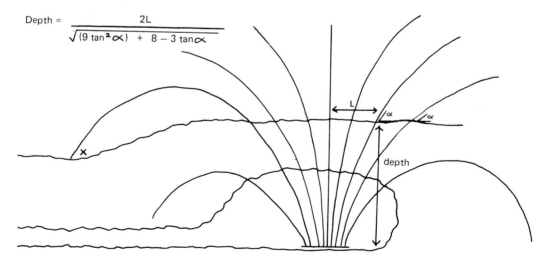

Fig 218

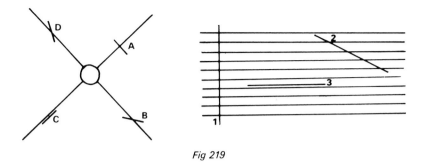

Fig 219

voltage induced in N2 will be Vin×N2/N1. This is the basic transformer where nearly all the primary flux links the secondary; simple laws apply.

If the iron core is removed the field pattern around N becomes the familiar pattern of a bar magnet and only a small amount of the flux links the second coil. Once the range is more than a few coil diameters the receiving coil is in the far field where its loading effect on the primary is negligible. Therefore the only power used by the primary is to overcome the losses, mainly coil resistance and eddy current loss. This is why the system is non-radiating with the voltage induced in the receiver coil being proportional to $1/D^6$.

To use these systems as a survey tool the field must be explored and several parameters noted. Reference to Fig 218, with its underground coil and the resulting field at the surface, shows that the field is vertical above the coil centre and slopes with a predictable angle as the observer moves away from this point. If the surveyor is far away (especially if the terrain dips) he can be in the return field path at point X and, if relying on field declination, would move in the wrong direction. Therefore the initial search must be based on standard radio direction-finding practice. Fig 219 shows a plan view of an underground coil. If the receiving coil is held vertically as at A, then the maximum amount of flux links the coil shown by 1, and a signal minimum is observed; if it is rotated clockwise to B then a lesser flux linkage is obtained, shown by 2, and a lesser signal received; if rotated to C, shown by 3, no flux links and a signal null is observed; if rotation continues to

D then the signal rises again. So if the coil is held vertically and rotated for a signal null it will point at the underground coil centre. If this is done from two or three positions a rough location of the underground site is obtained.

Once inside this area there will be no danger of being over on the return field and the declination can be used. First obtain a null with the coil vertical then rotate it through 90° as at A, this provides maximum coupling; then dip the coil towards the underground site until a null is observed; then move towards the centre by moving in the direction of the dipped side of the coil, observing the angle steepening; when vertical, check at right angles and correct accordingly. When the coil can be rotated through 360° and a null observed all the way round, it is over the underground coil centre. This is extremely accurate and easily missed; typical accuracy being a 5cm maximum circle for 100m depth.

Depth can be measured by applying one of the many formulae by the following method. Having found the coil centre, a known horizontal distance L is measured, and the angle where the field nulls is noted, hence the declination measured. This should be done in at least two directions possibly with different lengths and avoiding angles greater than 90° or less than 10°. These results should then be applied to one of the published formulae, such as the one shown in Fig 218. A programmable calculator holding this formula gives exact results, alternatively a table can be used. With care you can achieve accuracies of better than 5 per cent.

13 Expedition Planning and Organisation
A.J. EAVIS

Conception

An expedition starts from an idea – somebody's idea to go back to an area they have been to before, or that someone else has been to or flown over, or just a hunch. If the area has already been visited by a caving expedition you can consider organising a venture of some scale. If it has not been visited before, a reconnaissance trip is sensible. Assuming a reconnaissance or earlier visit has shown good speleological potential, you can decide the scale of the expedition. If the originators of the idea are interested in a big multi-disciplinary caving expedition and the speleological possibilities are sizeable you can start planning a large-scale expedition.

If the originators want to keep the group as small as possible there will be certain other factors to consider. In an area at a great distance from a rescue team, the expedition should be able to mount its own rescue, which probably gives an absolute minimum of about six people to a remote place. Economically used vehicles means filling them reasonably full of people; if you drive a four-seater car to the Pyrenees, go in a group of four; if you charter a twenty-seater plane to fly into the centre of Papua New Guinea there will be a case for twenty people.

Once the idea has been born, political permission should be obtained; often there may be a limit on the number of people allowed to visit a particular country or area, or only outline permission given which would preclude setting up a large scale venture.

Resource Planning

Where the objectives are well defined – extending or working in a known cave system, or searching a new but self-contained area, for instance – spend a little time planning the basic resources. Apart from finance, it is equally important to plan two other elements: time and manpower.

The total number of man-days required should be built-up from the totals for each task in the programme: exploration, survey, photography, research, etc.

Time

Too much time is rarely allowed; commonly there is too little. A two-week expedition to Morocco will be likely to have a very short time in the field – one serious vehicle breakdown or accident and it will be reduced to nil. Too long a time allowance will increase food costs, but should not seriously affect the usually larger transportation costs. For an expedition far afield it would be prudent to take a small team for a long period rather than a large team for a short period.

Manpower

Manpower usually has less constraints, but greatly affects costs, in respect of both transportation and food. Neither too few nor too many people should be involved in any project. It makes sense to build in a small 'safety factor' to allow for illness or other incapacity. This is especially important with very compact expeditions and takes on a greater significance in remote regions and with extremes of climate.

Once the area and scale have been decided, make an expedition-costing working on a 'bare bones' basis. This is the minimum amount of money that will enable the number of people concerned to go. They will travel as cheaply as possible and eat inexpensively. This cost should be divided by the number of people and used as a figure to quote to prospective members, showing the expedition to be feasible even without sponsorship. Sponsorship will mean that the expedition does not have to be on a shoe-string; if enough outside money is forthcoming the original suggested expedition contribution *could* be reduced.

Expedition Membership and Administration

Once the above questions have been answered a team can be organised. When a group of friends from one club go on a small scale trip everybody who wants to go usually can. With larger scale expeditions a selection procedure will have to be used. Usually the person or persons who came up with the idea ask their friends or acquaintances to join them. A medium scale, remote and expensive expedition could consist of:

Administrators: leader, doctor or nurse (or both), cook or camp organiser.
Non-scientific personnel each responsible for: food, surface equipment, underground equipment, finances, packing, transport, local liaison and research, insurance, etc.
Scientific personnel each responsible for: geology, biology, geomorphology, hydrology, sedimentology, etc.
Still photographer and film crew.

As many of these people as possible, preferably all, should be good expedition cavers. Such a team is likely to have about ten scientists, ten non-scientist cavers, one or two administrators and a film crew of two or three, giving a total of about twenty-five. All these subjects could still be covered by a smaller group provided people double-up on jobs.

With jobs in mind, individuals can be contacted and a first meeting held. At this stage, or soon after, a returnable deposit should be charged, say 10 per cent of the estimated personal cost. This will commit individual members and give working capital to help finance the next stage.

Publicity and Support

Next think about finance and figureheads. For a large, expensive trip to a remote place, a well-known respectable patron will help in obtaining financial support. Maybe an industrial sponsor will lend his name to the expedition in return for advertising material, etc. Academic bodies

such as universities or the Royal Geographical Society may also give their approval, which helps in obtaining sponsorship.

A brochure should be produced. This should follow after the initial meeting, when duties have been agreed. For a major expedition a small colour booklet should be considered. For a two-man trip to the Alps a single black-and-white sheet should be adequate – either way the effect should be dramatic, comprehensive, readable and well produced.

Once a brochure has been produced possible sponsors can be approached. The most successful applications mostly come from personal contacts. A company that supports an expedition in a small way may, if it is successful and they get some feedback, be prepared to support subsequent expeditions by the same team to a larger degree. Initially, though, it is a question of lots of letter writing and a very low success rate. For the New Guinea 1975 expedition over 20,000 letters were despatched with about a 2 per cent success rate. Potential sponsors/supporters are:

Financial: banks, insurance companies, trust companies, scientific bodies, academic bodies, grant-making bodies; all local firms and possibly large national companies.
Transport: shipping lines, airlines, vehicle-hire companies, vehicle manufacturers.
Food: manufacturers, wholesalers, retailers, importers.
Medical: usually handled by medical personnel; drugs, equipment, money for medical magazine articles.
Equipment: all obvious caving-equipment manufacturers could be considered, and do not forget surface gear.
Logistical help: shipping agents, travel agents, insurance brokers, field-transport haulage companies, radio facilities, medical facilities.
Media: newspapers, periodicals, television, book publishers.

Grant-making Bodies
There are six well-known grant-making bodies which cover caving expeditions:

1 The Ghar Parau Foundation (GPF) makes grants each year to caving expeditions (£800 to £1000 per annum). Emphasis is on scientific studies and/or original exploration

in little-known areas. Closing date for applications is 1 February each year.

2 Sports Council Grant Aid is also administered by the GPF and the closing date is the same. Interviews are usually held in March. Emphasis is on exploration, sporting caving and development of equipment and techniques (up to £6000 per annum in total).

3 The Winston Churchill Memorial Trust offers travelling fellowships each year under various headings. Exploration is usually included but not always. Grants are made to individuals but the individual can be the leader or any member of an expedition. Grants can be up to £1000 or more. The closing date for a submission is 1 November (for an expedition the following year).

4 The Royal Geographical Society offers grants to expeditions and can also give 'support' which can be helpful with other fund-raising, etc. Only expeditions with a considerable scientific programme should apply. Closing dates are 30 January and 30 September.

5 The Mount Everest Foundation is administered by the RGS. Only expeditions to high-altitude areas will be considered. Closing dates are 31 December and 31 August.

6 The World Expeditionary Association (WEXAS) makes a large number of small grants to assist travel each year. Closing date 31 March.

Addresses of the above are in Appendix 2.

Supporters must be treated with respect and there is no point in contacting organisations you know will not give useful help. Successful application for sponsorship is an art helped by hard work and luck. Trade directories are useful and names of the relevant company individual should be obtained whenever possible. The letters should be good, dramatic and short, well produced and complementary to the brochure. Individual letters aimed at the particular company chief are the most successful. Large-scale letter-writing is helped tremendously by word processors, which seem to have been designed with expeditions in mind.

Logistics

For detailed information pertaining to particular problems or types of expedition, a list of expedition reports appears at the end of this chapter.

The helicopter taking supplies to the Mulu 80 base camp

Transport

While the task of seeking sponsorship is under way, you will have to tackle other logistical problems. Of these, transportation is of primary importance and often difficult. The over-riding consideration will usually be cost, with travelling time a close second. Explore every avenue of group discount; often the most obvious form of transport is not the cheapest. It may be cheaper and faster to pay a large lump sum on a car ferry rather than several smaller sums on petrol. Long journeys to distant parts are nearly always cheaper by air than sea and obviously much quicker. Sea-freight charges are usually much lower than air-freight rates, but slow and often unreliable.

The final leg of the journey into the prospective area can prove an interesting logistical problem. On first consideration backpacking the food and equipment would seem the cheapest way, but this is very time-consuming in caver manpower. Local carriers or mules, horses or yaks may be available at surprisingly reasonable rates enabling the cavers to get straight on with the real job they are there for. In some locations it may be possible to hire a helicopter and fly all the gear straight in, although helicopters do not usually come

Unloading at Mulu 80 base camp

cheap. Consult maps and/or air-photographs as to the nearest road, etc. If there are still doubts as to the best approach, organise a reconnaissance. This could take the form of a small-scale expedition the year before, or an advance party reporting back in plenty of time for the main trip.

Timing and Duration

Factors such as holiday periods of expedition members are important to an expedition's timing, but local weather conditions can be critical. In many areas of the world the time will be dictated between the snow melt and the onset of the first snow. In other areas local monsoon periods should be considered. In desert regions midsummer may be unbearably hot, and dry seasons make drinking-water an extra problem.

Field Planning

Where is the camp going to be and will there be a need for more than one? The main camp should be comfortable; if a local five-star hotel is offered free of charge, accept it! As much effort as possible should go into the enjoyable

Building the 'Long House', Mulu 80

Flood-liable kitchen, Mulu 80 base camp

Sub-camp, Mulu 80

parts of the expedition and as little as possible into everything else. If somebody offers to come along and do all the cooking, food buying and camp organising they should be encouraged, particularly if they are a good caver as well.

The position of the camp or camps should if possible be decided *in advance*, and how each camp will be reached; also, how many people are likely to be at each camp and the procedure for inter-camp communication especially in the event of an accident. People travelling on foot are usually adequate to convey urgent messages, but in remote and/or difficult terrain, working without radio communication may be danger-ous unless each camp has sufficient personnel to mount a rescue. Will there be underground camps, and if so how many people will be involved? How will the equipment be packed?

Insurance
Personal insurance to cover rescue, medical fees and repatriation is the absolute minimum. There is no point in overdoing the cover; if free helicopter and free air flights home are available in a country with a national health service this could be quite small. Otherwise these personal insurance items must be covered by the

individuals, possibly in a package with the medical insurance. Expedition-owned equip-ment needs insuring while in transit but usage-cover for equipment in the field is a real hassle and it is difficult to justify the high cost involved.

BCRA has an excellent expedition insurance scheme in operation, enquiries should be made via their Insurance Officer (see Appendix 2).

Equipment
Packing will depend on what transport methods are to be employed and on group size. For air freight, packing cases should be as light as pos-sible; if small river boats are to be used, water-proofing will be sensible. For a final leg of the journey by foot, boxes should be of a size to fit on a packframe or into a rucksack. If you can decide size and number of camps with reason-able certainty in advance, food and equipment can be packed accordingly.

The Mulu 1980 expedition used one cubic metre palletised packing cases, and into these went either eighteen small boxes or eight larger

185

ones; both sizes fitted on a packframe. Heavy tins and equipment went into the small boxes; biscuits, clothing, etc, into the larger ones. Delicate equipment was packed into waterproof polypropylene drums and again fitted onto packframes. These drums were water and vermin-proof and could also be used for water storage. Mulu 1980 planned two main camps so food and equipment were packed accordingly, 60 per cent to base camp and 40 per cent to the main sub-camp. Co-operation between food officer, equipment officers and expedition leaders resulted in most of the food and equipment being in the right places.

After the planning and packing phase is over, if the freight is sent by sea, there is then a lull between the ship leaving and the members leaving by faster transport to catch it up. Customs and transport problems may be numerous and you should allow quite a few days to get equipment through customs. The best organiser on the expedition, probably the leader, should handle it personally and might be wise to employ a professional agent.

Field Organisation
Camps must be set up and supply routes organised before caves can be discovered and pushed. If applicable radio links have to be established, you must obtain local licences in advance; if possible use a radio compatible with the local telephone system. Communication into a telephone system will enable discussion directly with the local supermarket or even with the wife back in Britain!

Approach local contacts for help or advice. There may be appropriate courtesy calls to make to national park headquarters or high commissions. Investigate local medical and emergency services and any other organisations that might be of future help. Large companies often have helicopters and in emergencies might provide them free of charge; they can sometimes be contacted directly by camp radio.

Once in the field, who goes where will have to be decided. Some persuasion from the expedition elder statesman might be necessary to prevent all the keenest cavers disappearing down the most promising hole at the same time. A long and difficult cave-pushing expedition might require careful organisation to send shifts of cavers into the system. Underground camps

require their own level of organisation.

If high-level organisation is necessary there may have to be an expedition administration to look after it. This would normally be the leader and would be centred on base camp. Often medical personnel play a part in the organisation; if the group is lucky enough to have a cook, he or she may be the person to look after camp organisation and radio operating.

Hired labour requires its own administration. Records will have to be kept, wage rates negotiated, facilities provided and order maintained. Foreman labourers may take some of the duties from the cavers, and subdividing into camp men, carriers, boat men, etc, can simplify this. In remote areas where all transport is by foot a number of local helpers equivalent to the number of cavers is a reasonable idea. Local people will be much better at building camps, lighting fires and finding water than foreign cavers and they may well know where some of the cave entrances are.

If a lot of cave is being discovered it is difficult to keep pace with surveying and photography. The time comes when a mutual agreed code has to be adopted. Some expeditions decide that the people making the discovery must do the surveying; another approach is to survey and photograph while exploring. Some extensive caves in New Guinea and Borneo have a grade 5 survey and reasonable photographic record, made on the one-and-only caving trip, by just two people!

Small groups can be more efficient than large ones; three-man teams are usually ideal underground. A good idea is to have multiples of three if a cave or area requires more than one group. Safety must always be borne in mind and small groups can operate safely only with reliable communication between camps and with the outside world.

Film crews should be separately financed, and although given adequate support and co-operation they should not be allowed to dominate the expedition. Some expeditions have done everything twice, once for the sake of the expedition and again for the sake of the film crew. However, if caving expeditions are to get increasing help, film teams must be adequately encouraged.

The journey home will probably be a reversal of the journey out, with due time allowed for packing, customs clearance, etc. Expeditions

have left much valuable equipment behind when everybody has made a beeline for home.

The film crew in Nasib Bagus, Mulu 80

Post-expedition Work

After the expedition there should be nearly as much work as there was before the trip. Sponsors must be looked after if they are going to be encouraged to help in the future. They may want photographs and reports on their equipment, plus press conferences, internal magazine articles, slide shows, etc. The expedition report must be written; there is no point going on an expedition if you do not make its results available. Even if no caves are extended, tell people how you tried and why you were unsuccessful. Large expeditions may warrant a general report and a scientific report. Newspaper and magazine articles might be called for, and if a film

crew were involved they will be editing and may need further material, voices, etc.

Photography and Publications
In my view all film should be bought by the individual expedition members possibly on a group discount deal. After the expedition a slide show should be organised where members show their best slides and other people can order copies. After copying and sorting, the expedition keeps the originals of the copied slides for a period; the owner gets a copy and each member gets the set of copies ordered. The expedition then has a good set of original slides it can use for magazine articles. These can later be exchanged for the copies, and the

expedition ends up with a full set of slide copies.

Individual income from expedition business (slide shows, magazine articles, etc) over a certain figure should be the property of the expedition for a limited period, say one to two years. If a book is written on the expedition by an individual there will have to be some negotiation on splitting the proceeds.

In the case of a very large expedition which has received considerable financial support it is worth every member signing a legal contract in respect of both written and verbal reports and articles, as well as *all* photographic material. This can eliminate difficult situations, particularly after the expedition members have dispersed, and considerable income might be pending.

The expedition may take at least a year to organise before departure and maybe a year to wind up after its return home. Keep these two periods as short as possible within the confines of good organisation and report-writing. As much as possible should go from the expedition back into cave exploration. This will mainly consist of information, but excess proceeds could be put into appropriate financial bodies, particularly Ghar Parau Foundation. Equipment that does not have to be sold for financial reasons could be channelled back into a cave expedition equipment pool (see Appendix 2). All too often an expedition sells gear at knockdown prices one year then pays through the nose for similar the next.

Remember, the planning, execution and writing up of caving expeditions are all about speleological research but, even more importantly, about the enjoyment of cave exploration.

Expedition Reports

Brook, D. B. 'The British Speleological Expedition to Papua New Guinea 1975', *British Cave Research Association Transactions*, Vol 3, 3 & 4 (1976)

Brook, D. B. & Waltham, A. C. (eds). *Caves of Mulu* (Royal Geographical Society, 1978)

Eavis, A. J. *Caves of Mulu 80* (Royal Geographical Society, 1981)

James, J. M. (ed). 'Papua New Guinea Speleological Research Expedition', *N.S.R.E. 1973* (Speleological Research Council, Sydney, Australia, 1974)

James, J. M. & Dyson, H. J. 'Caves and Karst of the Muller Range', Atea 78 (in conjunction with the Speleological Research Council Ltd, Australia, 1980)

Judson, D. *Ghar Parau* (Macmillan Publishing Co Inc, 1973)

Maire, R. *et al.* Spelunca supplement to No 3 Jul–Sept 1981 'Report of the French Speleological Expedition to P.N.G.' (*Federation Française de Speleologie*, 1981)

Matthews, G. (ed). 'Exploration 70', *Report of Nottingham University Students' Union Speleological Expedition to Picos de Europa NW Spain* (University Caving Club, 1970)

Riley, D. *et al. Tresviso 78* (Lancaster University Speleological Society, 1978)

Singleton, J. 'Pozu Del Xitu', *Proceedings of the Oxford University Cave Club*, No 10, 1980–1 (1981)

Waltham, A. C. (ed). *British Karst Research Expedition to the Himalayas 1970* (Trent Polytechnic, 1971)

Watkinson, P. *et al. Expedition 67 to the Gouffre Berger* (The Pegasus Club, 1967)

14 Food for Cavers

DAVID JUDSON

There is no magic diet which will make a caver go on and on! Individual taste plays an important part. The correct planning of food for expeditions is a complicated business, but there are points to note, especially for long-duration or arduous caving trips.

As with long-distance walking, mountaineering, orienteering and ski-mountaineering, caving, when carried out on anything other than a casual basis, involves a high rate of energy consumption and possibly considerable endurance. Energy consumption can be expected to be at a higher rate than for mountain walking or average rock-climbing. Caving often involves the use of many parts of the body simultaneously – particularly in rope-climbing, traversing and crawling – and there will usually be considerable energy loss due to the relatively low temperature of the air, and more particularly of cave water.

With regard to endurance, caving is almost unique. It is usually impossible to opt out at any particular stage, as with most other outdoor activities, and in a pothole there is also the return journey to undertake; the ascent is *always* more strenuous than the descent, often with the additional burden of wet equipment. With a cave system this may not be so pronounced, but progress is usually more difficult when you are wet and tired, whether carrying large amounts of equipment or not.

You should enter a cave having eaten a fair-sized, well-balanced meal with plenty of carbohydrates and sugars, and not too great an amount of protein or food which is difficult to digest. With this precaution you should then need to carry only a fairly small quantity of high-energy rapid-yield foods on the journey. It is easier to carry most of the food inside the body than in an ammunition box!

Among the best readily available high-energy rapid-yield foods are glucose, chocolate, fudge, raisins and dates. These will fit easily into a small or medium-size ammunition box, along with whatever other gear is required for the trip. Alternatively on a lightweight trip they can be put into a polythene bag and placed inside the helmet.

There are many advocates of the flask of hot coffee, tea or soup. The beneficial effects of this tend to be more psychological than real. A cup of strong coffee with plenty of sugar will act as a stimulant and a warmer, and the sugar will provide some energy. But a large mug of beef broth will produce more energy-loss through digestion then any short-term benefit!

With the longer and more arduous trips in British caves, even a working trip in, say, Otter Hole or Langcliffe Pot, it is rare for more than fifteen hours to be spent underground at one stretch. Long-term sustenance is therefore not a problem outside foreign caving expeditions.

Although trips are unlikely to exceed twelve to fifteen hours, many factors may serve to extend a short trip beyond its anticipated duration: failure of equipment, a physical accident involving a member of the party or a member becoming exhausted and having to be assisted out of the cave. In planning food for a trip there should be flexibility and, as a rule, over-provision rather than under-provision.

Energy consumption varies from individual to individual. The rate can be such that demand exceeds supply. Drowsiness and staggering may not be a symptom of hypothermia; they can be brought on by lowering of blood sugar – a sheer lack of energy. If quickly recognised, this can be just as quickly eradicated with the consumption of a high-sugar food, such as chocolate or fudge.

Catering on caving expeditions abroad, or

Deep inside the cave an exploration party pauses for food and a rest, New Guinea 1975

wherever caving is to be carried on more or less continuously for a number of days or weeks, is totally different. Here it is important to keep up a well-balanced diet to maintain a high level of energy output over a protracted period of time – several months in the case of a major expedition. The body's health must be preserved to combat viruses and other diseases not ordinarily met with. A good policy, for instance, is to have a fairly heavy breakfast with a balance of protein, carbohydrate, fats and vitamins, take high-energy food on the trip and follow this up with a relatively high-protein dinner near the end of the day.

Exactly the same principles apply to underground camps and underground stays of several days. Weight and packaging become important, but a balanced diet is the first essential. Bear in mind that the more food needed for consumption underground and the further underground that it is to be consumed, then the more manpower will be involved in its transportation.

15 Cave Conservation

DAVID JUDSON

Cave conservation should be the responsibility of every active caver. It should not be regarded as the special preserve of a few aged armchair cave politicians. Within the British Isles new cave systems are discovered only rarely. A cave destroyed is a cave destroyed for ever. Formations deliberately or carelessly defaced or removed are lost for all time. Each of us must ensure that we do as little damage as possible to the fabric of our caves.

Conservation or Preservation?

Whilst 'preservation' implies that something must be meticulously looked after and maintained in constant state, 'conservation' implies a more flexible approach – that of retaining the best, the most characteristic or salient features. For the most part, the preservation and conservation of caves are closely allied. As much as is *practicably* possible of the character and texture of a cave passage should be retained in its original state – as seen by its original explorers. Thus something of the approach of the better show cave developer must be adopted. Paths should be set out to allow access to as much of the cave as possible whilst in the process destroying as little as possible.

Access Controls

Whilst it has become popular in recent years to link conservation with access as though they were inseparable subjects (the National Caving Association has a Conservation and Access Group) the two do not go well together in many respects and can, on occasions, conflict.

In the more vulnerable caves, with delicate formations and fine fossil features on their floors, access needs to be carefully controlled if conservation is to mean anything at all. It is possible that one hundred cavers, divided into

twenty or so parties of four or five persons each, would do far less damage than they would going in as five groups of twenty. This approach presents a practical problem; is this sort of control to be placed by one group of cavers upon all others? If it is, then who is to make the rules and administer them? Where the entrance passages form a show cave, as at White Scar Cave, Peak Cavern and Dan-yr-Ogof, or where there is an 'external' controlling body, such as the Nature Conservancy Council in the case of National Nature Reserves (Agen Allwedd and Ogof Ffynnon Ddu particularly), the problem is easier. The 'us' and 'them' are clearly defined from the outset – which perhaps makes restrictions on free access more palatable.

Usually, where there is no external agency involved, access restrictions in the interests of conservation should be a tripartite agreement between the landowner, the discoverer (perhaps an individual, more likely a caving club) and representatives of cavers at large – a regional caving council.

Time and time again, when an individual caver, caver/owner or even an individual caving club has tried to establish its own access control over a cave, the attempt has not been well received and has led to misunderstanding and animosity. The gating and locking of Lancaster Hole entrance pitch by the British Speleological Association shortly after its discovery in 1946 is the outstanding example of this sort of ill-conceived conservation approach. It was in practice an attempt by one man, the late Eli Simpson, recorder of the BSA, in agreement with the landowner, to control exploration and research in a major cave system for the benefit of his own chosen few. It has been a useful lesson in showing that this sort of unilateral conservation measure can never work in the UK.

At the extreme, a cave with its entrance

effectively sealed off by the landowner is a cave which is being totally preserved! There should be a happy balance and an agreed solution which must, in the case of the more vulnerable caves, lie somewhere between complete closure and a complete free-for-all. Threats to caves fall into two main categories: the internal threat, as discussed briefly above – from the activities of cavers themselves – and the external threat, principally from quarrying, mineral extraction and various activities of farmers and land-owners (dumping of farm rubbish in shake-holes, animal carcasses, infiltration of pollut-ants, etc).

Internal Threats to Caves

Although it has for a long time been popular amongst the caving fraternity to concentrate upon the external threats to our caves, slow day-to-day wear and tear results in far more damage. It is for the main part insidious and difficult to combat. With many of our more active cave systems, such as most of the classic Yorkshire potholes, there are clean-washed hard limestone floors, few calcite formations and therefore little damage to be done – even from intense pressure of numbers. With the large fossil cave passages of the major Welsh caves, the opposite is true. Floors are often adorned with delicate cracked mud or splash formations. There may be stal formations on floors, walls or ceilings, and crystal pools always seem to occur at the most awkward constrictions in the passage where they are most vulnerable to the muddy boot!

In the first instance responsibility for conser-vation falls upon the members of the original exploring party. There is an onus upon them (and to a lesser extent on the other members of their caving club or group) to return quickly and regularly to their find, not only in order to produce a survey of their discoveries, but to photograph them carefully and then take measures to ensure that others who follow do so with minimum damage.

Where the vulnerable sections of the cave passages are spacious, protection is relatively easy. Brightly coloured plastic tape should be used to direct visitors past and around the most delicate areas. The effect should be to direct visitors to a safe and relatively narrow route rather than the more negative approach of plac-ing the tape close in around particular features.

Tape should not be placed too close to the floor; it will be more effective if a conscious decision has to be made to cross it. It should therefore ideally be placed at about half a metre above the average floor level. In level-floored, mud-covered passages, such as Agen Allwedd main chamber, this is easy – short metal or plastic rods or tubes can be used to maintain location and height. On rocky floors small cairns can be used for this purpose. Elsewhere small holes can be drilled in floor, walls or boulders in which to locate the posts firmly. This sort of protection has been commonplace for many years in caves in Eastern Europe and in certain parts of the United States, and we in Britain should take a similarly keen interest in cave conservation.

Where the going becomes more difficult, such as in the large mud-covered boulder chambers of Montague Cavern, Lancaster Hole and parts of Ogof Craig a Ffynnon, effective taping following discovery becomes more difficult. Discreet but unambiguous notices should be positioned at the start of taped sections particularly at points where they will be first met with by most parties entering the cave system – *not at the cave entrance*, where they will certainly be vandalised. These should explain the need for care and the purpose of the tapes: 'Please keep strictly to the marked path'.

In some of our caving areas it is considered anathema to have any access restrictions at all. In particular this is manifest in the anti-locked-gates policy of northern caving clubs in general and the Council of Northern Caving Clubs in particular. Since the scale and number of cave and pothole entrances in the Northern Pennines area would make restrictions a total impracticability in all but a few isolated examples, this is perhaps not so serious as it might appear. It has, however, already led directly to the blasting in of one cave entrance by an agent of its landowner when gating was specifically called for and refused (Thackthwaite Beck Cave, N. Yorkshire).

Restricted Access Arrangements

Since weight of numbers is responsible for much of the damage to caves, it seems logical to make access restrictions on those vulnerable cave systems that attract the greatest numbers of cavers. If a cave system is sufficiently large, there need be no limit to the number of parties permitted to enter in any one day; but the maximum size of each party should be controlled. Experience has shown at the two National Nature Reserve caves, Agen Allwedd and Ogof Ffynnon Ddu, and also at nearby Dan-yr-Ogof, that restriction of party size does have a real effect in reducing the damage done. It seems that a party of six or less is likely to operate as a close-knit group, so that the more experienced and responsible members keep an eye on the others. This tends to be unpopular amongst parties of university students in particular (who for economy often travel in groups of ten or more), but is becoming more widely accepted as necessary in the interests of conservation.

Access control has proved essential in recent years. Although in the Northern Pennines pressure came first from the large landowners, as protection for their property, gamebirds or stock, it has been shown to have a useful safety spin-off with increasing numbers wishing to descend some of the more constricted potholes. With the large and popular caves of Mendip and South Wales, conservation is overwhelmingly important. Experience at Ogof Ffynnon Ddu 1 has shown that, with increasing numbers, it becoms impossible to meet demand on the basis of a strictly controlled leader system. (It works there now only because the bulk demand has been shunted off following the discovery of OFD 2 and 3.)

The type of access control system whereby all responsible caving clubs are *encouraged* to provide approved leaders from within their own membership appears to be more workable, and must be the way forward. At present it has been adopted for Ogof Ffynnon Ddu 1, Dan-yr-Ogof, Tunnel Cave, Otter Hole and the Fairy Cave Quarry Caves on Mendip.

With Ogof Ffynnon Ddu there are special problems, partly a result of its being the deepest and second longest cave system in the United Kingdom, and partly because of its great variety of passage type and character. It is a cavers' playground *par excellence*. Both extensive and complex, the system is understandably very popular with novices and experienced cavers alike – trips can be arranged varying from very easy to extremely long and strenuous – and it attracts visiting parties from all over the UK and from abroad. It would be beyond the manpower resources of any one caving club to

provide a leader system to satisfy legitimate demand or even to administer one with outside leaders. In these circumstances the unusual step has been taken of having specially restricted access to one particularly vulnerable part of the cave system – the immediate vicinity of The Columns in OFD 2. The locked gate into this section is opened only on a few previously advertised days each year. On these occasions The Columns are closely patrolled by cave wardens to ensure that the tapes are not crossed and that damage is not done either carelessly or otherwise; a drastic step, but one taken only after all other methods had been tried and found lacking.

External Threats

Land Development

The principal external threat to cave conservation is limestone quarrying. There are also many others which are not always quite so conspicuous to the naked eye or the passing caver. Mineral extraction, although less common today in limestone areas, can damage caves and have a detrimental effect upon local streams and water supplies. Some of the practices of farmers and other landowners – the disposal of farm rubbish and dead animals into shafts or shakeholes – whilst not always doing any irreparable physical damage, may cause water pollution which will affect life in a cave and perhaps pollute the resurgence. The gripping of open moorland, whether as a preparation for forestry or merely to improve the 'quality' of the land, can have far-reaching effects on local caves fed by the area. Apart from the danger to cavers from the greatly speeded up run-off after rainfall, there may well be a heightened flood pulse and increased total run-off due to reduced evaporation. These can combine to have serious physical effects upon the charactersisics of a cave – sediments may be removed, average water levels may be increased, etc.

Moorland gripping is often carried out with the aid of a Ministry of Agriculture grant, in which case the Nature Conservancy Council (NCC) would be notified and consultations with local cavers should take place before the event. Use of pesticide on land does not operate in this way; the first knowledge of such activities might be a dramatic loss of cave life. In the lower-lying caving areas the use of karst features for large-scale refuse tipping has been a recent threat. There have been two instances in Devon of a planning authority giving itself planning permission for such an activity, and then later running into problems with access to caves or serious damage to the cave environment.

Regarding 'development' covered by planning legislation the cave registry system may be a route to reduction of such threats. All the caving areas of England and Wales except for the Northern Pennines have a cave registry set-up. Through co-operation with local authorities it has proved possible to establish an early warning system of applications which might be detrimental to caves or karst features. National Park authorities have been particularly helpful in this way, and there is no reason why planning authorities outside the parks should not do the same. Unfortunately there is no statutory power, and a goodwill arrangement may lapse with the departure of a particular officer.

Forestry presents a special problem. Although it does not technically require planning consent, it is rarely carried out on any scale in this country other than with the aid of a Forestry Commission grant. The Forestry Commission have an informal agreement that they will not give such a grant without first consulting with the relevant planning authority. Such consultations will not necessarily bring in either the NCC or the local cavers but are likely to reach the local press. A case at South House Moor, Ingleborough, N. Yorkshire, became public in this way after agreement on consultation had been reached. It was resolved in favour of the *status quo* only after the intervention of the Secretary of State following a press and television debate.

Apart from the visual effect of afforestation upon the karst landscape, there are the same objections as there are to gripping. Additionally the extra run-off in the early stages after planting will usually carry with it a great deal of vegetable debris which can cause blockages within sumps and cave passages.

Limestone Quarrying

Prior to the 1960s limestone quarrying tended to be a small-scale undertaking. There were many small quarries scattered around, and it was fairly common for them to break into undiscovered caves. In the case of the Ogof Ffynnon Ddu system, for instance, this has occurred twice – first with the isolated piece of cave adjacent to the Penwyllt road, and later at Cwm Dwr quarry. If the cave was of reasonable size this tended to be a nuisance to the quarry and it would be likely to be avoided in future working. Modern quarries are much larger and therefore present a greater threat.

Demand for quarry products tends to be geared to economic prosperity and particularly to the state of the building industry and the road construction programme. Output rose steadily up to 1973. Many government and local government statistics predicted a continuous rise in demand with consequent alarming results in terms of quarry size and numbers. In fact there has been a considerable reduction in demand since 1973 and the future is anyone's guess.

Although there may be fewer quarries in the future, there will not be a return to small-scale operations. Apart from direct physical damage and removal of caves there are serious pollution risks to nearby caves. When applications are being looked at for new quarries, or for extensions to existing ones, any known cave which could be affected by water flowing down dip or through a known phreas should be regarded as at risk from the proposed operation. If an outright objection to the planning application is considered unwise, then steps should be taken to get strings attached to the approval to give protection against pollution from diesel fuel, slurry from washing plant, etc. There are examples in Yorkshire and Derbyshire where natural cave passages have been completely silted up as a result of outwash from mineral/quarry workings being pumped directly into shakeholes.

Military Training and Adventure Holidays

Finally there is another type of 'external' threat. This is the use of caves for military training, scout exercises, adventure holidays and the like. If these activities are legitimate (it seems doubtful) then they must be firmly directed by the caving community to caves of low conservation risk. This should be a responsibility of the regional caving council, but is perhaps one which can be achieved only where the high-conservation-risk caves are gated and locked!

Statutory Protection

In the UK (except Ulster) there are two government agencies with responsibilities for the protection and conservation of caves. Within the earth sciences field the Nature Conservancy Council (under the NCC Act 1973) is responsible for giving advice to government and local authorities on all matters relating to the conservation of geological and physiographic features. Although the NCC is best known for flora and fauna conservation, it is very much involved with the conservation of caves and related features. This aspect of its work is dealt with by its Geology and Physiography Section (see Appendix 2). The conservation officers of both the British Cave Research Association, as well as the four regional caving councils, work closely together with Dr G. P. Black (Head of the G and P Section). As a recently completed part of the Geological Conservation Review, the list of cave sites now scheduled as Sites of Special Scientific Interest (SSSI) has been rationalised over the whole country, comprising forty-eight sites (see end of chapter).

Landowners are contacted on first scheduling, and any development which requires planning consent must be notified by the local authority to the NCC before a determination of the planning application is made. This has now been amended and extended by the Wildlife and Countryside Act 1981, so that the landowner is required to notify the NCC additionally of certain operations not requiring a planning application. The precise scope of this depends specifically on development or operations which have been included by the NCC in their notification to the landowner of their proposed declaration of the SSSI. The new Act brings new powers for the protection of limestone pavements with the introduction of Limestone Pavement Orders – made by the Secretary of State or the local authority. This allows the NCC together with the voluntary caving bodies to raise any proper objection to proposed development or operations with the local authority and at any subsequent public or local enquiry.

To date there has been only one major loss of a cave to development in this way. This was the case of Fairy Hole, Weardale, which has now been partially quarried away for cement manufacture. As the battle over this cave was atypical in that local employment was a major issue, it may still be deduced that the protection system works well or that there are very few threats!

In exceptional circumstances the NCC can declare a site to be a National Nature Reserve (NNR). This normally involves land purchase but can be achieved through a legal agreement with the landowner(s). There are only two such NNRs in Britain with caves as their central features: Agen Allwedd and Ogof Ffynnon Ddu, both in South Wales. With Agen Allwedd the surface features and plants were the *raison d'être* for the NNR, but continued discoveries of more cave have now made the cave equal in importance. Ogof Ffynnon Ddu was declared an NNR in 1975 wholly on account of the cave system.

In both cases access and conservation are handled through a cave management committee, administered by the local NCC regional office, but which consists mainly of cavers. Both have worked well to date, and it is to be hoped that, should further cave NNRs be declared in other caving areas, similar management structures will be adopted.

Where caves fall accidentally within NNRs which have been declared for entirely non-speleological reasons, access can be a problem. This should be resolved in the first instance by contact with the appropriate NCC regional office. Where this fails on a personal basis it is usually possible for the regional caving council to resolve the matter satisfactorily.

The NCC covers all cave science fields except cave archaeology. Here responsibility rests with the Ancient Monuments Inspectorate of the Dept of the Environment (see Appendix 2).

In Northern Ireland the NCC does not operate. Its responsibilities are broadly covered by the Department of the Environment for Northern Ireland, Conservation Branch (see Appendix 2). Its powers are derived from the Amenity Lands Act (Northern Ireland) 1965 and it has responsibility for Areas of Scientific Interest as well as for NNRs – for their establishment and management in a similar manner to the NCC in the rest of the UK.

The Cladagh Glen and Marble Arch have been designated as a National Nature Reserve since 1970, but so far there has been no active management of its conservation or access. In co-operation with the DoE for Northern Ireland the local authority (Co Fermanagh District

Council) is currently developing the first part of this cave into a public show cave. With its two river passages and proposed boat trip it could be the finest in the British Isles.

Where a caver learns of a serious external threat to a cave system he should contact either the conservation officer of the relevant regional caving council or the conservation officer of the British Cave Research Association (see Appendix 2).

The greatest threat to caves in the UK, from cavers themselves – through wear and tear, weight of numbers and isolated incidences of vandalism – will be met only by greater caver awareness, vigilance and care, and by the positive protective measures of discovering parties.

Sites of Special Scientific Interest

There follows a list of speleological sites as proposed in the Geological Conservation Review. Forty-eight sites are listed in all, comprising twenty major areas (marked *) and twenty-eight smaller sites. Although the list may appear short, almost half of the sites are large areas which take in either a group of related caves, or a large number of scattered caves, eg the whole of Ingleborough. The Geological Conservation Review has aimed to achieve a rational list of sites which embody the finest examples of all the important features to be found in caves, not to schedule every cave of any size or interest.

Northern Pennines
Birks Fell Caves, Wharfedale
* Birkwith cave systems, Ribblesdale
* Black Keld catchment area, Wharfedale
Boreham Cave, Littondale
* Brants Gill catchment area, Ribblesdale
Crackpot Cave, Swaledale
Dow Cave/Providence Pot system, Wharfedale
Fairy Hole, Weardale
Hale Moss Caves (near Arnside), Cumbria
* Ingleborough Fell
* Kingsdale (East and West)
Knock Fell Caverns, Cumbria
* Leck Beck Head catchment area

Pikedaw Calamine Caverns, Malhamdale
Short Gill, Barbondale
Sleets Gill Cave (inc. Dowkabottom Cave), Littondale
Strans Gill, Langstrothdale
Stump Cross Caverns/Mongo Gill Hole, Greenhow
* Upper Dentdale Caves
* Upper Nidderdale

Derbyshire
Bagshaw Cavern, Bradwell
* Castleton Caves
* Masson Hill Caves, Matlock Bath
* Stoney Middleton area
Stanley Moor/Pool's Cavern, Buxton
* Upper Lathkill Dale, Monyash

Mendips
* Charterhouse Caves
* Cheddar Caves
Lamb Leer Cavern
* Priddy Caves
Thrupe Lane Swallet
* St Dunstan's Well catchment area
Wookey Hole

Wales
Alyn Gorge Caves, near Mold, Clwyd
Minera Caves, Clwyd
Dan-yr-Ogof Caves, Powys
Little Neath River Caves, Powys
* Mynydd Llangattwg Caves, Powys/Gwent (partly National Nature Reserve)
Nant Glais Caves, Mid Glamorgan
* Ogof Ffynnon Ddu area, Powys (partly National Nature Reserve)
Otter Hole, Chepstow, Gwent
Porth-yr-Ogof, Powys
Siambre Ddu (Brynmawr)

Scotland
* Allt Nan Uamh Caves, Inchnadamph, Sutherland
* Traligill Caves, Inchnadamph, Sutherland

Other Areas
Buckfastleigh Caves, Devon
Napps Cave, Devon
Beachy Head Cave, East Sussex

16 Access to Caves

DAVID JUDSON

History

In the early days there were few problems over access. There were far fewer cavers and fewer caves. All cave entrances are situated on somebody's land but, with few cavers around, landowners could be approached on a one-to-one basis, and gentlemen's agreements were made. With the large estates this agreement would usually be made with the man on the spot, either the tenant farmer or, in the open fell locations, the gamekeeper or shepherd. Up to World War II this arrangement worked well. The odd problem, arising from an individual animosity or incident, would occasionally exclude all cavers from a particular area or cave, but this was rare.

After the war the scale of activity began to mushroom. Not only were there many more caving clubs and many more cavers, there was also an influx of cave diggers. Some areas such as Easegill, Stump Cross and many parts of the Derbyshire and Mendip caving areas assumed the appearance of Klondike!

Although this development of the sport is broadly true for all the main caving areas, from this time onwards each area tended to develop its own access problems. This was affected by local conditions: the degree of urbanity, the proximity of the caves to the villages and farmhouses and the varying pressures of numbers of cavers in each area. Many of the remote parts of the Northern Dales are still at the happy 'gentlemen's agreement' stage today.

In the main caving areas of the Northern Pennines, because of their remoteness from farms and villages and the wide-open nature of most of the pothole entrances, a free-for-all went on throughout the 1950s and 1960s, and to a lesser extent persists today. It may be a short-term expedient for some cavers, but in the long term it will be to the detriment of all.

Northern Pennines

Access to two of the main fells, Leck and Casterton, became increasingly difficult in the early 1960s. There had been a spate of irresponsible activities, damaged walls, loss of stock and arguments with tenant farmers, as well as damage and disturbance resulting from cave rescues. The two large landowners concerned pressed for one organisation with which they could deal, instead of the growing number of caving clubs. After several meetings of cavers the Council of Northern Caving Clubs came into being in 1963.

As problems arose with other sub-areas these were gradually taken on board by the CNCC, so that they now administer access to many of the popular caves and potholes on behalf of their member clubs (and clubs from other regional caving councils, through associate membership arrangements). Most of Fountains Fell, Birks Fell Cave and Mongo Gill Hole are administered in this way. For each of these areas a meetings secretary handles all bookings and keeps the farmer/landowner up to date. CNCC publish a booklet, *Northern Caving*, which gives full details of these and all other access arrangements for caves in the Northern Pennines (see Appendix 2).

Mendips

The Mendips, although overcrowded in terms of caving activity, are compact and more densely agricultural than the Northern Pennines; hence a closer spirit of co-operation between farmers and cavers. Where large statutory landowners have been involved problems have arisen. The Bristol Waterworks Company are owners of several square miles of land around the village of Charterhouse-on-Mendip. There are many cave entrances involved but the major ones are Longwood-

197

August system, GB Cave and Rhino Rift. These are gated and locked; access is by arrangement with the Charterhouse Caving Committee, a body made up by representatives of the area's ten main caving clubs. The committee holds a licence to sole caving and archaeological rights in the area. It has to indemnify the company against any claims arising from caving activities and strictly maintains an indemnity permit system for access. Other caving clubs and visitors from outside the area may seek to become affiliated to the CCC or be invited as guests of one of the ten clubs; otherwise they need a permit from the CCC (see Appendix 2).

Closely following the formation of the CNCC in the North, the Council of Southern Caving Clubs came into being in 1964. It arose more from the demand for a national body, and thus for a regional set-up in each main caving area, than from pressing access problems. It does not itself control access to caves, but attempts to coordinate the work of individual clubs and the Southern Caving Clubs Co Ltd. This latter body controls access to Lamb Leer and the disused stone mines at Bathford near Bath – Swan Mine and Brown's Folly Mine. There are many caving clubs controlling access to small caves throughout Mendip. The comparatively few major caves are the caves of Fairy Cave Quarry, controlled by the Cerberus Speleological Society with access on a prior-booking permit basis with a small fee charged, and St Cuthbert's Swallet, where access is controlled by the Bristol Exploration Club and a strict leader system is operated with a maximum party size of five. The CSCC publish a most useful *Handbook and Access Guide* (see Appendix 2).

South Wales

Caves in South Wales occur in widely scattered groups and individual locations. A number of access arrangements have grown up over the years.

The South Wales Caving Club was the first club to be resident in the area (formed 1946) and gradually developed access agreements with landowners in respect of all the major caves within its immediate area. Ogof Ffynnon Ddu, Tunnel Cave, Dan-yr-Ogof, Agen Allwedd and Otter Hole have all been discussed in the previous chapter. A much more open system covers Pant Mawr Pot. Visitors are requested to call at the SWCC HQ on their way to the pot, but there is no lock or gate.

Ogof Craig a Ffynnon is a fairly recent discovery and access is controlled by the original exploring party who are still actively working in the cave. Since most of the cave lies within the Llangattock NNR it seems likely that it will be eventually absorbed into the reserve fully and administered by the cave management committee at some future date (see Appendix 2).

Most other caves have free access but it is usually a good idea to ask permission from the farmer first. The Cambrian Caving Council (formed 1969) has not recently published a handbook. The 1969 one is now out of date and out of print. The CCC is the only one of the four regional caving councils which specifically *does not* get involved in access arrangements on behalf of member clubs.

North Wales

Caves in North Wales are few and even more scattered than those of South Wales. One of the two most important caves, Ogof Dydd Byraf, has had its entrance sealed by its landowner (a quarry company) following cavers' success in winning a public enquiry over an extension to the quarry in 1973. For any further information on this area contact the North Wales Caving Club (see Appendix 2).

South Devon

Access to Bakers Pit Cave and nearby Reeds Cave is controlled by the Wm Pengelly Cave Studies Trust who have their field headquarters nearby. Kent's Cavern, Torquay, is the largest and possibly best-known cave in the area. It is also a show cave. For further information on South Devon caves contact the Wm Pengelly Cave Studies Association or the Plymouth Caving Group (see Appendix 2).

Derbyshire

Access in Derbyshire is mostly a straightforward matter of calling on the farmer and perhaps paying a small fee. This is the position at Giants Hole, where there is a slightly variable closed season for lambing. The other popular caves of this area are similar: Oxlow Caverns, P8, Gautries Hole and the Perryfoot Swallets – call at either Peakshill Farm or Perryfoot Farm.

Peak Cavern is in the ownership of the Duchy of Lancaster and an indemnity chit access arrangement has been arranged by the British Cave Research Association. Strictly this is for members of BCRA and member clubs, but in practice so long as there is a member present access can be arranged. It is, however, allowed only during the closed season for the show cave – October to April (see Appendix 2).

Knotlow Caverns and Hillocks Mine are kept bolted for the safety of children but not locked; a suitable spanner is all that is required.

Access to caves in Lathkill Dale (within the NNR) is controlled by the Derbyshire Caving Association. An annual permit is issued along with membership, which is open to caving clubs and individuals. Clubs from other areas may also obtain a permit from the DCA (see Appendix 2). Similarly with Waterways Swallet near Swinscoe, in the ownership of the Okeover Estates, an indemnity chit permit system is operated through the DCA. With the discovery of new caves or where it appears that an access problem is likely to arise it makes good sense to bring this to the notice of the relevant regional caving council – except, as mentioned, in Wales.

17 Accidents to Cavers

DR JOHN FRANKLAND

Most people who have never explored caves have a conviction that speleology is a sport appropriate for a psychopath with a deathwish. This prejudice is likely to be formed by emotive reporting by the media after well-publicised rescues. The concept has also been accepted by many life-assurance companies who 'load' policies sought by cavers. It does not, however, deter those who organise outdoor pursuits for the young from including caving in their curriculum; consequently increasing numbers of young people, some perhaps under pressures to participate, are being taken underground.

The specialised techniques and intricacies of cave rescue are beyond the scope of this chapter apart from a mention of principles and new developments. In the UK all caving areas have a locally organised rescue service. These have their own equipment and are ready to turn out at any time – perhaps the Cave Rescue Organisation's most unsociable request came at fifteen minutes to midnight on New Year's Eve! They have more experience than any others worldwide and are the pioneers of new concepts and technical innovations. This expertise is the result of the heavy and concentrated numbers of cavers participating in Britain. The CRO, based at Clapham in Yorkshire, is the oldest-established team in the world as well as the most experienced, with over 300 rescues completed. Its influence has spread worldwide.

Most team workloads have increased over the last thirty years but there exists no accurate data about those participating in caving and therefore at risk over this period. That the number of cavers has gone up is beyond dispute, and the increase in those at risk is perhaps larger than the increase in rescue incidents. It seems that caving is becoming safer. Few would disagree that modern equipment is less likely to fail than that used in early postwar years. The wetsuit and fibre-pile

suit conserve body heat better than earlier clothing, and deterioration in caver performance through heat loss is less likely. Also, the development of centres where formal caving instruction is given by the British Association of Caving Instructors must have helped many novices form safer habits (for address see Appendix 2).

British cavers lack a detailed publication similar to the American Caving Accidents series published by the National Speleological Society (USA), which gives an anecdotal description of likely causes and circumstances of incidents and the rescue methods used. The British Cave Research Association's *Manual of Caving Techniques* (Cullingford 1969) covers rescue but is not comprehensive, and there have been exciting developments since it was published. The lessons learnt from rescues are publicised by the local teams in their own reports, via the caving press and through periodical reports from the British Cave Rescue Council, which also acts as the representative body for cave rescue, with other roles including liaising with statutory authorities, exchanging information and supporting member teams (for address see Appendix 2).

The Risk

It is difficult to assess the normal risk to cavers. Standing (1973) published a review of cave rescue incidents in Britain over thirty-seven years, and concluded that 80 per cent of incidents involved novices. This figure remains the only data on this factor as most accident reports now lack information on the experience of those rescued.

If it is assumed that 15,000 people are regular cave explorers (a caving magazine calculated caving-club membership at 14,000 about five years ago), and if each member ventures underground just a modest ten times a year, then for

INCIDENTS/YEAR

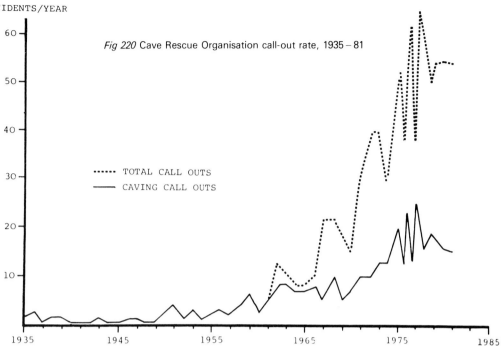

Fig 220 Cave Rescue Organisation call-out rate, 1935 – 81

····· TOTAL CALL OUTS
—— CAVING CALL OUTS

150,000 caving trips during 1980, the fourteen British cave rescue teams, in forty-one incidents, assisted ninety-two cavers, three of whom were killed. This gives a risk of needing rescue assistance of one in 1,630 every time a caver goes underground – once every 163 years in a caving career! Less than half of those assisted by rescue teams have any injury or need for medical care so the risk of injury to cavers falls to less than one in 300 years' participation. This is less than the risk of any British subject being injured in a road accident and makes the loading of insurance premiums for cavers appear extremely unfair.

Dr Ian Adams, a consultant at St James's Hospital, Leeds, specialising in sports medicine, has calculated that the risk of injury to an English First Division professional footballer is one in thirteen each time he plays. Thus a caver can venture underground in the knowledge that, with a statistical chance of injury every 3,000 trips, he is 230 times less likely to be injured than a First Division footballer.

Two of the three deaths in 1980 were those of cave divers; cave diving has an undoubtably higher risk than above-water caving. Twelve British cave divers have died since 1949, eight of these in the last decade and three in the last eighteen months. In Florida more than 200 lives have been lost (Halliday 1974), many being open-water divers tempted by vast submerged caves and not realising the special skills this environment demands. Safety techniques have improved but the numbers involved, their ambitions and their determination have grown. Those who courageously choose to dive face a different degree of hazard from explorers of air-filled caves.

The Philosophy of Rescue

The role of cave rescue teams is to help those cavers who cannot cope due to injury or other circumstances which can vary from being frightened to being dead. Some teams have been diverted from their original purpose of providing a self-help service for the community of cavers into becoming public service teams providing local help in situations beyond the resources of two ambulance men with a stretcher. Mountain and crag rescue present some problems similar to caves and the expertise and equipment of cavers are generally appropriate. Beyond this the demands for help are legion, varying from the bizarre to the ridiculous. The CRO now averages over fifty call-outs per year, up to two-thirds of which do

BCRC 1980 Incident Report

	Cave Rescue Organisation	Derbyshire CRO	Devon CRO	Gloucestershire CRO	Irish CRO	Mendip CRO	Midlands CRO	North Wales CRO	Scottish CRO	South East CRO	South Wales CRO	Swaledale FRO	Upper Wharfdale FRA	West Mercia URT	TOTALS
CAVE	15	5	–	(1)	1	9(1)	(2)	–	–	–	8	–	1(1)	–	39
Persons assisted	41	11	–	(1)	1	10(1)	(4)	–	–	–	26	–	1(3)	–	90
Fatalities	1	–	–	–	–	1	–	–	–	–	–	–	–	–	2
CAVE DIVING	2	–	–	–	–	–	–	–	–	–	–	–	(1)	–	2
Persons assisted	2	–	–	–	–	–	–	–	–	–	–	–	(1)	–	2
Fatalities	2	–	–	–	–	–	–	–	–	–	–	–	(1)	–	2
DISUSED MINE	1	1	–	–	–	2	1	2	–	–	–	–	1(1)	1	9
Persons assisted	3	–	–	–	–	6	2	2	–	–	–	–	(3)	1	14
Fatalities	–	–	–	–	–	–	–	1*	–	–	–	–	–	–	1*
OTHER INCIDENTS	26	4	–	–	–	–	(1)	–	–	–	–	2	2	–	34
Persons assisted	35	1	–	–	–	–	(1)	–	–	–	–	2	4	–	42
Fatalities	4	–	–	–	–	–	–	–	–	–	–	–	–	–	4
ANIMAL RESCUES	11	1	–	–	–	–	–	1	–	–	1	–	3	1	18

Notes:
1 * This person has not been found and is presumed dead.
2 The figures in brackets indicate incidents where a team has assisted another cave rescue team. These figures are not included in the totals.
3 'Persons assisted' means that a team has gone to the assistance of this number of persons, whether injured or not.
4 The number of fatalities is included in the number of persons assisted.
5 The 'other incidents' include fell/moorland rescues/searches, climbing incidents, searches for missing persons and recovery of objects. Teams in the North of England carry out these duties as part of their normal rescue work.
6 The 18 recorded animal rescues involved 29 animals.
7 Standby calls have not been recorded.

not involve cavers. The largest single source of incidents is a popular tourist waterfall walk; up to four deaths per year have occurred there more than once.

How much of this non-caving involvement is acceptable is decided individually by team members. The extended workload involves extra demands on resources, finances and time. Administration and fund-raising are not small tasks for a busy team. Increasing workloads encourage team spirit in some and deter others, particularly when hopelessly equipped. Sunday strollers, suicide attempts and farm animals are also rescued. Animal rescue can be an excellent public relations exercise with farmers and land-owners, without whose permission caves cannot be explored. This brings in more money by way of donations from the public than does the saving of human life.

When cavers are in trouble the aim is to get them out fast, comfortably and alive. There are two extreme philosophies: in France a rescue team at Grenoble felt that all medical resources should be available to the caver injured under-ground, including major surgery. To demon-strate the feasibility of this a large medical team including anaesthetists, surgeons, nurses and large amounts of equipment were transported down a cave. A dog was the subject of the demonstration and a splenectomy was success-fully carried out. The surgery was uneventful, the dog surviving a near-fatal strangulation during evacuation on a stretcher designed for humans! The Grenoble team have argued that major surgery is now practicable underground.

The other extreme of thought was summed up by a legendary postwar British caver who stated that all cavers should wear earrings so that if they were injured underground they could be nailed to a plank of wood and thus dragged out of the cave! Many experienced rescuers argue that this commonsense approach has much to commend it.

In America on one occasion a casualty's elec-trocardiograph was transmitted from the accident site to the surface by telephone cable and then by radio to hospital, where a cardio-logist was able to report that it was normal – hardly surprising, as the problem was a broken leg. British cave rescue has not felt the need for this refined telemetry.

Speedy evacuation must have the highest priority even with medical support under-ground. Accurate and comprehensive diagnosis is often not feasible or reliable where the environment makes it inadvisable to undress the casualty adequately. The fastest possible removal to daylight and perhaps hospital is very much in the casualty's interest both as regards more definitive treatment of his injuries (as diagnosed or undetected) and to best help his morale.

Rescue Incidents

A study of statistics from all British areas shows a consistency in the overall causes of rescue call-outs and in the reasons for injury or death. What remains unique is the variety of problems presented to the rescue teams – after a dozen rescues in the same cave system new problems can arise with each further incident.

Accurate, comprehensive data from the four-teen British cave rescue teams has not always been available in past years. Several authors have sought such information and published reviews (Leitch 1962, Standing 1973, Lloyd 1976, Frankland 1976, Forder 1981). The BCRC has collated accurate data for 1980 which represents a typical recent year, apart from the deaths of two cave divers. (*See table opposite*).

An overall pattern has emerged over several decades as to likely causes of call-out, reasons for injury and death and likely injuries and problems encountered. Local factors such as the amount and predictability of rainfall, the size and frequency of vertical drops, the stability of the limestone and even the accessibility of the cave entrances must affect the accident risk and type, but not enough regional data exists to quantify these variables.

Experience is a major factor in safety, as is borne out by Standing's data and more recently by the high number of call-outs involving novices. In 1977 out of thirteen cave rescue call-outs by the CRO, eight were to university, college or school parties.

In a series of 300 call-outs by the Yorkshire CRO the following reasons have initiated the request for help (other published data from the UK gives the same order of probability and almost the same percentage breakdown):

	per cent
Flooding preventing or hindering exit (no injuries)	23
Fractures to cavers after injury	19
Technical help needed but no medical problems present	18
Other injuries or exposure in caves	17
Cavers overdue – no assistance needed	13
Fatal accidents (including cave divers)	10
	100

Thus there is a 10 per cent chance of dealing with a fatality on a rescue team call-out or, as the optimist would see it, a 90 per cent chance of everyone involved surviving.

The flooding threat is inevitable in the British climate – some respect for the weather and appropriate choice of clothing should minimise the risk. On 15 November 1975, the CRO had six such call-outs. In one of these two cavers had to be brought out in diving gear by the team's divers. In many rescues the re-rigging of pitches allows exit, but in many more the victims have an uncomfortable time 'sitting it out' until the flood waters subside and they can be contacted.

About 46 per cent of call-outs involve injury or death to cavers. The 300 CRO incidents show the same pattern as data from other regions. Of the 138 call-outs in this category, the injury or death was caused as follows:

	Number	per cent
Falls	84	61
Rock falls	21	15
Drowning	16	12
Bad air	3	2
Others	14	10
	138	100

Thus the vertical sections of caves are predictably the most dangerous despite the safety techniques that should prevent accidents. Not enough clear data exists to allow the precise reasons for cavers falling to be quantified, but falls from a ladder whilst not protected by a life-line are by far the most common. Rock falls cause around 4 per cent of rescue teams' total call-outs (Forder 1981), but 15 per cent of the injuries or deaths sustained – their gravity is appreciable.

In the early 1970s the new method of vertical caving using single-rope techniques (SRT) appeared on the British caving scene. Many took to it avidly. Perhaps enthusiasm exceeded technical skills in the early days. In 1974 the first fatality resulted when an inappropriate rope broke while being used for the 360ft descent of Gaping Gill in heavy water conditions. Many feared more such accidents, which thankfully have not been as frequent as anticipated.

Since the 1974 fatality, just 6.5 per cent of cave rescues in the Yorkshire Dales (where the biggest series of vertical caves is found) have involved SRT in some aspect. This series – eight incidents out of 123 call-outs – has sadly included a further fatality where a girl abseiled on a rope found hanging down a pitch which was not belayed.

Further details of the CRO SRT incident series since 1974 are:

1 Polypropylene rope broke – fall – fatal.
2 Abseiling caver lost control – fractured ankle.
3 Stuck on rope – no injuries.
4 Rope jammed – ascent prevented – no injuries.
5 Abseiling belay failure – bruising, no fractures.
6 Abseiled down – could not climb out – no injuries.
7 Abseil rope gave way – not belayed – fatal fall.
8 Stuck on ascent – inadequate equipment – mild exposure.

Fatalities

Deaths from hypothermia, or more likely the exhaustion-exposure syndrome, in non-injured cavers are less likely now than a generation ago despite there being more cavers at risk. In the Yorkshire Dales there have been three such deaths: in 1946 (Grange Rigg), 1951 (Penyghent Pot) and 1969 (Meregill). None of these victims had a wetsuit (introduced into caving in the early 1960s) or fibre-pile clothing (first used in the mid-1970s). Lloyd (1964) has described two Mendip hypothermia deaths occurring in one and one-and-a-half hours after the onset of signs of hypothermia, despite help from a rescue team. The problem of heat loss remains, but is less threatening to those injured in modern caving garb, and rescue teams have more available in the way of efficient insulation and airway rewarming (Frankland 1972, 1981).

Until 1967 British caving had not known the tragedy of multiple deaths, but in that year six very experienced men were drowned when a flash-flood submerged Mossdale Caverns. In 1976 three deaths occurred in Langstroth Pot amongst six cavers free-diving a sump and meeting bad air in an air bell, not previously recognised as a likely hazard. At Cote Gill Pot in 1979 two cavers died of carbon-monoxide poisoning descending the system before the fumes from their generously applied home-made explosives had cleared. All rescue personnel going underground needed respirators for this, so far unique, set of circumstances.

In 1979 two cavers were washed away and drowned by flood waters in Ogof Ffynnon Ddu in South Wales.

Four incidents do not, let us hope, make a trend. In Mossdale the flood risk is known to be beyond that of almost all other British caves. In the second and third incidents lessons have been learned which should prevent a repetition. In the Welsh incident only, where rising water in a main streamway in a well-used system was to blame, is there a hazard which will be regularly but unpredictably repeated. Even here extra safety measures have resulted. Water level indicators have been placed at key points in the stream passage, and a recent flash-flood resulted in the cavers merely sitting it out on a ledge until the water level was reduced.

The only comprehensive data on fatal accidents is from the CRO, who have been involved with thirty-six underground fatalities since 1936. One of these was a non-caver taking a probably suicidal leap down Alum Pot. These fatalities can be broken down as shown below.

Drowning is the biggest single cause of death although perhaps appearing disproportionately high because of the increased risk attached to cave diving and the multiple deaths from the Mossdale tragedy. If these two factors are considered separately only two other cavers were drowned over forty-five years – one in Marble Steps in 1963 and one in Rowten Pot in 1939 following a fall.

Injuries

From the Yorkshire CRO's figures from 1935 to December 1981 fifty-five incidents (or 19 per cent) of call-outs have been due to cavers sustaining broken bones underground. The breakdown of these injuries, with fatalities excluded, is:

Fractures of tibia and/or fibula	13
Fractures of spine	12 (including one permanent paraplegic)
Fractures of femur	9
Fractures of ankle	9
Fractures of pelvis	8
Fractures of arm	7
Fractures of rib	6
Fractures of skull	5
Fractures of wrist	4
Other fractures	5
	78 fractures in 55 victims

This list represents likely injuries in a 'fall from a height', from which the vast majority were sustained. Dislocations were not included but may be as incapacitating and may demand equally careful handling by the rescue team.

Hypothermia or the more likely 'exposure-exhaustion syndrome' is difficult to quantify. Some degree of heat loss is likely in all injured cavers immobilised awaiting rescue. The supply of adequate insulation to allow spontaneous rewarming is now a routine procedure.

In some falls, lack of strength or co-

Reason	Number	per cent	Comments
Drowning	13	36	Six deaths in one incident (17 per cent) and five cave divers drowned (14 per cent).
Falls	10	28	Including one non-caver.
Bad air	6	17	Three deaths in one air bell. Two deaths from explosive fumes.
Rock fall	4	11	
Exposure	3	8	Last death 1969.
	36	100	

ordination due to exposure-exhaustion is a likely factor. A proportion of these cavers suffered their injuries through lack of protection, as the use of a lifeline during climbing would have prevented their fall. The non-injured exposed caver who has to be carried may present as challenging a rescue as one with broken bones and may be as much at risk from deterioration.

Self-help

Cavers in England and Wales are luckier than most others in having an adequate number of experienced and equipped rescuers close to hand. The spearhead team will generally be underground within an hour of call-out. In North America, teams may have to be flown a thousand miles to initiate a difficult rescue. Despite the availability of British rescuers the caving community should not neglect the concept of self-rescue which a few would claim is a dying art. In the far reaches of a difficult cave – unless the injuries are gross – even if a rescue team's help is being sought, improvised first-aid and early evacuation will give the casualty his best chance of survival.

Some have claimed that many incidents where a rescue team is now summoned would have been dealt with safely by a group of experienced and determined club cavers of an earlier generation. It has been said that some rescue call-outs amount to little more than 'nurse-maiding'. Many anecdotal incidents support this view, eg where a team (from an educational institution) realised when they reached a Dales pub that they had detackled a pitch and left a member underground. They called out the rescue team and went home.

Many weary or frightened cavers are just walked or talked out and exit unharmed, sheepish and tired. They do have the benefit of experienced support, strong pulls where necessary, nourishment and an undoubted boost to morale. Denied this, perhaps a proportion would deteriorate and not cope, with possible serious consequences. So it is perhaps prudent for teams to regard the 'sorry-for-themselves' or frightened cavers as genuine casualties who could soon be in a vulnerable state without help and encouragement. If a caver has been feckless, the rescue team controller might reasonably offer some admonition or words of warning.

Expedition Rescue

For expedition caving, self-help may be all that is available. In new territory with unknown hazards, the uncertainty of the flood risk, the likelihood of unstable rock in a new system and the need for long, tiring trips, where pressure to extend exploration could cause a compromise on safety margins, are all factors which could increase the accident risk. Perhaps the experience of those involved and the knowledge that only the expedition's resources are to hand have contributed to the remarkably good safety record of British expeditions.

With dozens of trips leaving each year to worldwide locations few serious accidents seem to have occurred. The 1970s saw three British deaths in northern Spain, one to a cave diver, one owing to an SRT rope failure and the third to a caver who fell while unprotected. A grave injury also occurred to a caver in New Guinea, but hardly any other life-threatening trauma is known to the writer. Accurate data on the risks is again not available as the number exposed cannot be calculated. Again it seems unlikely to be of a magnitude warranting loading life-insurance cover. Those who cave on expeditions can face them with an equanimity not available to the high-altitude Himalayan climber who faces a one-in-ten death risk on each expedition.

Equipment Developments and Trends

Experienced, well-equipped and quickly responding teams have meant that many incidents are dealt with quickly and casualties are brought to the surface more rapidly, and with less deterioration, than several decades ago. Most teams now have medical help available underground if required. This usually means little more than good first-aid. The presence of a doctor should help the victim's morale and ensure that adequate pain relief is available.

The neoprene exposure-bag was designed for sump rescue by divers in the 1960s but it became apparent that it was of enormous value as an insulating bag in normal rescue. Since about 1970 this has been its routine role (Frankland 1975). Made of thick neoprene with a water-resistant fastener, and enclosing the head, it is an effective preventer of heat loss for

minimal bulk. This equipment has probably saved more lives than any other technical innovation. Some models have the arms enclosed, but as most conscious cavers with injuries sparing the arms and shoulders prefer to be evacuated with the arms free for self-protection, a bag including sleeves but still covering the hands will allow the arms to be strapped out of the stretcher if appropriate. These sleeves can be turned inside-out if necessary to give a full cocoon.

Fibre-pile sleeping bags have been used occasionally. They are more efficient insulators than neoprene on laboratory testing even after a full immersion (Keighly 1980), but can absorb an appreciable weight of water and thus increase handling problems. A recent development is the use of a Flectron blanket for insulation. Made from thousands of fine strips of space-blanket sewn together to give a conventional sleeping-bag thickness, it is an efficient

heat insulator. It has a greater capacity than neoprene for gaining weight due to water absorption, but this should drain quickly. More experience with this material and more comparative data with neoprene are needed.

An American military invention is the 'Thermal Sarong'. This is a sleeping bag lined with thin tubing through which ethylene glycol, heated by a butane burner, is circulated. The concept sounds good for heating up cold cavers underground but the price (around $2,000) has so far precluded its use in British rescue. The Braemar Mountain Rescue team in Scotland is currently testing it. The American militia also use chemical heat-packs to apply to

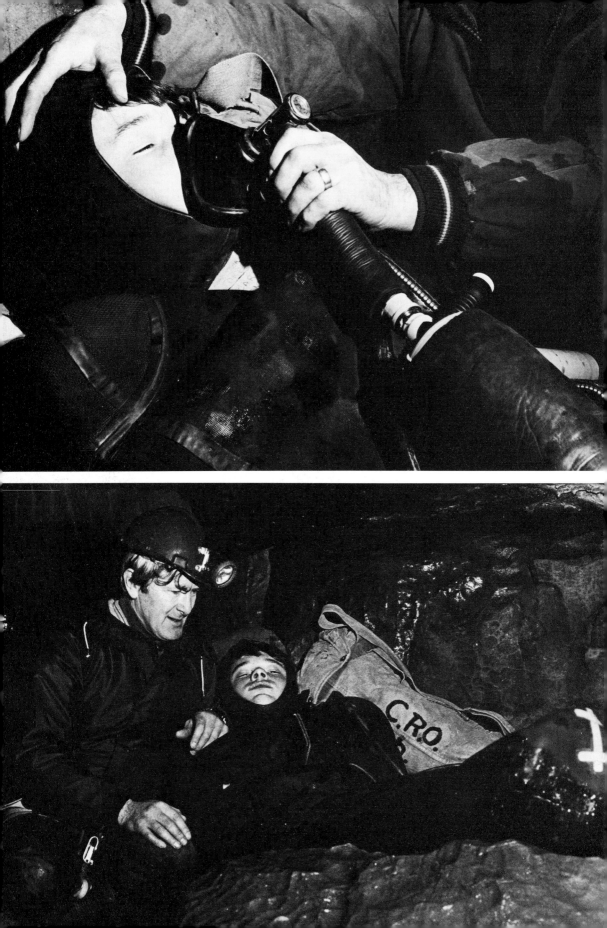

(*opposite top*) The Little Dragon
airway rewarmer

(*right*) Industrial safety harness.
Invaluable for lifting victims where
there is insufficient space for a
stretcher. Hauls from the
shoulders — useful for the weary
and non-seriously injured

(*left*) A neoprene exposure bag:
possibly the biggest lifesaver of all

The Neil Robertson stretcher — still widely used

The Heye's splint is most useful for cave rescue

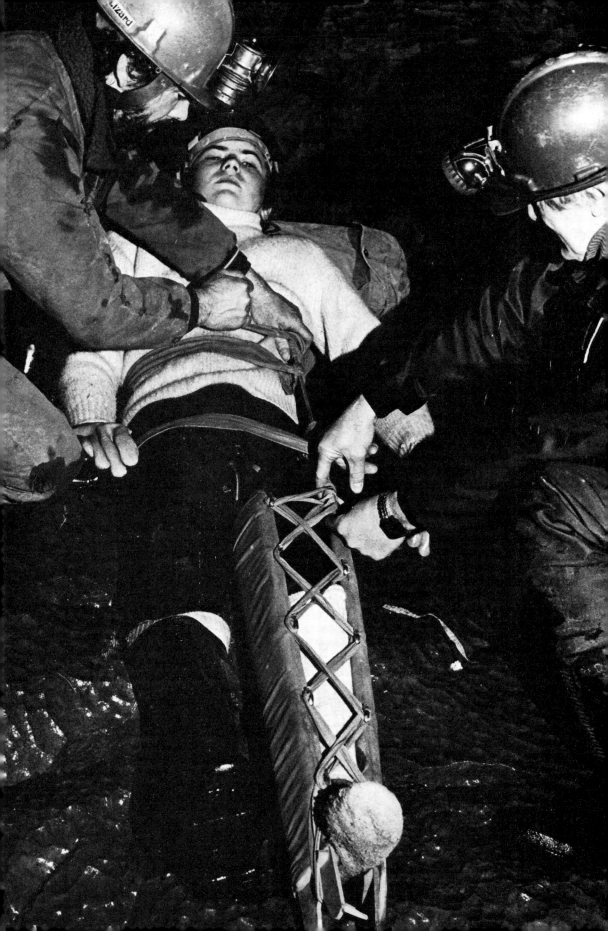

An adjustable neck splint: all unconscious patients should have one

the trunk of hypothermia victims. Apart from minute equivalents designed to rewarm the hands of skiers these are not yet available in the UK, but they offer an exciting development for on-site treatment.

The Norwegian Defence Research Establishment have developed a compact portable fan-heater based on charcoal combustion after electrical ignition. For a weight of about 1kg this unit has an output of 200 watts delivered as hot air directed into the victim's sleeping bag for eight to ten hours. Its use awaits evaluation; it sounds unlikely to be practical during cave evacuation, but could be of enormous value on the surface after rescue or for a period of stabilisation before rescue (Nordil et al 1976).

Airway rewarming as an on-site treatment for hypothermia was first described by Lloyd (1972), and in 1974 the Yorkshire CRO was the first team in the world to use this technique in the field (Lloyd and Frankland 1974). Warmed air or oxygen at around 50°C and with 100 per cent humidity is supplied for the victim to breathe. The heat supplied is of the order of only 5kJ/m²/hr, but the technique also prevents the normal respiratory heat loss of around 35kJ/m²/hr, which is the largest source of heat loss in those with profound skin cooling. The 'Reviva' was produced commercially in 1975 for on-site rescue use and a more compact

An expanding stemple — another useful rescue aid

version, the 'Little Dragon', came out in 1980; this will fit inside a standard ammunition box and is easily transportable. Its main and very valuable use has been with the non-critically cooled cavers who derive immense subjective benefit from breathing warm moist air. Those chilled by delay underground have often improved after using this equipment so that they are able to climb out of the system more easily and more safely. It is an adjunct to and never a substitute for adequate insulation.

In recent years an industrial safety-harness which fits around the whole trunk and has a thin nylon cover to minimise snagging has been widely used. Even if stretcher evacuation is planned, placing the casualty in such a harness before placing him in an exposure bag and stretcher will allow its later use in any tight sections of cave where the stretcher cannot be passed through. Unlike most climbing harnesses it gives a vertical hang. For the exhausted and those with below-knee injuries it provides an efficient, safe means of help.

For leg splintage the Heye's splint provides minimal bulk and very efficient immobilisation. Unfortunately the manufacture of these splints has been discontinued. The Derbyshire CRO has manufactured an efficient alternative. Poly-urethane-foam splintage was described as appropriate for cave rescue in 1972 but has only once been used on a casualty (Frankland *et al* 1972). Recently synthetic plastic casts have been found to be practical for difficult rescues and they have a promising future (Stone 1981).

Perhaps the most significant technical advance has been in the perfection of efficient 'through-the-rock' radio systems which penetrate 200m of solid limestone, making rapid and efficient surface-to-underground incident communications instantly available. A source of enormous support to those working underground, the Molephone is now available at around £1,000. None who have worked with this superb equipment would deny that it is money well spent for rescue teams. For addresses of suppliers of rescue equipment see Appendix 2.

The Rescue System

A request for assistance should be made in every case through the local police. Rescue is the statutory responsibility of the police force, and volunteer teams are called in at the request of police authorities whose only alternative tactic would be the impractical one of sending their uniformed officers underground. Only when the request is channelled through police hands does a Home Office policy giving insurance cover to rescuers become operative. Rescue teams have excellent relations with their local police forces and the co-operation is mutually advantageous. For details of British rescue services see Appendix 1.

18 Cave Biology

GRAHAM PROUDLOVE

Cave biology has four main aspects: the studies of animals; plants; organic materials in sediments (which provide the basic food supply for many organisms) and environmental variables such as temperature, humidity and substrate type (which influence the distribution and abundance of organisms). Brief details of methods are given here; the references contain further information for the seriously interested caver.

Animals

Basic collecting requirements are specimen tubes, preservative (4 per cent formalin or 40 per cent alcohol) and some means of picking up small animals. An effective technique is to place a licked paintbrush delicately onto the animal (it should stick to the brush), then transfer it to a tube. A pooter (aspirator) can be used to suck up small animals (Driver 1963, page 96). Mud and silt banks are good collecting sites, rich in inwashed nutrients; walls, calcite slopes and the surfaces of small pools should also be examined, as should the threshold or twilight zone at the entrance. Bat guano is usually rich in animals but few of them are true cave-dwellers. Mites and springtails are often found on the surface of silt and can be removed using floatation techniques (Driver 1963, page 96). By digging into the mud and silt earthworms can often be found. Pitfall traps with preservative in them (eg yoghurt cartons) are helpful in the collection of very mobile animals, which will wander into them, but to prevent overtrapping they must be frequently checked. It is important to search slowly and carefully.

Tea strainers and wide-mouthed pipettes are useful in the collection of animals from water. Plankton nets can be suspended in waterfalls to catch animals carried by the stream, and fish traps anchored in lakes to catch fishes. The undersides of stones should be examined, but you must replace them in the original position.

It is vital for identification that the animals are properly preserved (Hazelton and Glennie 1962, page 355). To prevent misidentification all specimens should be sent to the Biological Recorder of the British Cave Research Association who will forward them to the relevant expert (see Appendix 2). A notebook recording details of collection locality, habitats and substrate type should be kept and these details sent with the specimens.

Experimental studies within caves require detailed planning. Many ecological aspects can be examined without elaborate equipment (eg estimation of population size); however, this may be needed for other work (eg detailed comparisons of habitats).

The collection and study of bats is difficult and should not be attempted without proper equipment and training; Hooper (1976) should be consulted.

Further information on methods can be found in Hazelton and Glennie (1962, pp 349–57), Driver (1963) and Vandel (1965, pp 33–54).

Plants

Large plants such as sprouting seeds and the larger fungi can be put into plastic bags or jars and identified from standard botanical texts. The study of the more abundant and important plant life – the bacteria, actinomycetes and microscopic fungi – is difficult. They must be collected onto sterile agar plates and then cultured in a laboratory before identification is possible; Mason-Williams and Benson-Evans (1958, pp12–19, 39–41), Mason-Williams (1967, pp140–1) and Cubbon (1976, pp443–7) provide information on techniques and apparatus.

Sediments

Samples of muds, silts and sands can be collected into screw-top jars or polythene bags, labelled with their location in the cave and any other relevant details and transferred to the laboratory for examination. It is important for statistical accuracy to take enough material so that replicate analyses can be run.

Total moisture content should be determined first. The sediment must be weighed, then heated in an oven at 100°C for some time, and then reweighed (this should show a decrease in weight). Further heating will drive off more water and heating and weighing should be continued until the same weight has been obtained twice in succession showing that all of the water has been expelled.

Then:

$$\text{total moisture content (per cent)} = \frac{\text{initial weight−final weight}}{\text{initial weight}} \times 100$$

This is an important influence on the distribution of burrowing organisms like earthworms.

The next constituent to determine is total organic matter content. This can be done by two methods. In *dry oxidation* the sediments (which have had their water expelled as above) are heated at 450°C to burn off the organic matter and leave behind the mineral elements. The sediment should be weighed and then the same procedure of heating and weighing as described above should be followed. This method should be used only for coarse sediments since very fine ones may retain some water after the initial heating to 100°C, only to release it on heating at 450°C. This would lead to an erroneously high figure for organic matter content. *Wet oxidation* (using an oxidising agent such as chromic acid) is much more suitable for fine sediments. Details are given by Jackson

(1962, pp205–26). Total organic matter (per cent) is given by the same formula as that for moisture above.

Other constituents that can be measured are total organic nitrogen, protein, humic acids and carotenoid pigments. Particle size and sediment structure may also influence the distribution of organisms. Delay and Aminot (1975, pp499–504) and Jackson (1962) give details of methods for sediments.

Environmental Variables

In air the most important variables are temperature, humidity, wind strength and direction, and substrate type. Temperature is measured with a thermometer or a maximum/minimum thermometer if variation is expected over time. The easiest way of measuring humidity is with a wet and dry bulb whirling hygrometer. Wind strength and direction measurements require comparatively sophisticated equipment, details of which can be found in Unwin (1980). Substrates vary and methods for their examination and description are given in Murphy (1962, pp319–22). In the threshold zone light intensity is an important factor and can be measured with a camera light-meter, although more sophisticated devices are also available (Unwin 1980).

In water the most important variables are current velocity, substrate type, pH and chemical composition, with the first two being the most important. In most cave streams and lakes oxygen concentration will be very high, and not a limiting factor. Velocity is measureable simply with a floating object, a stopwatch, and a tape measure.

Substrate type should be noted. Methods for pH measurement and chemical analysis are given by Mackereth, Heron and Talling (1978).

19 Cave Geology

DR TREVOR D. FORD

Since caves are enclosed in limestones, and indeed owe their existence to them, the walls of any cave and the features thereon provide clues as to why the cave is there in the first place. Broadly, geological studies can fall into three categories: the rocks themselves, the geomorphological features eroded into them and the sediments within the cave.

Limestone Geology

For the first category, having surveyed the cave, try plotting onto the survey the positions of the beds of limestone: are they thick or thin? Can unusual limestone lithologies be recognised? Are they horizontal, gently inclined or steeply dipping? Does the cave follow the bedding or cross it? Are joints or faults present, and how do they influence the form of the cave system? Many cave passages follow the dip of the beds for long distances, but meandering as they do so; at first sight this meandering may be random, but a close look may reveal a controlling joint system. The vertical features within caves often follow major joints, or even faults if some displacement of beds can be detected. An apparently irregular winding cave may in fact be 'contouring' round folds barely detectable by other means. Alternations of horizontal passages with vertical pitches may be due to selective erosion of beds favourable to solution, separated by massive jointed limestones. The trend of such features may lead to the discovery of further extensions of the cave or may help to link it with its resurgences.

Geomorphology

The morphological features of cave walls are essential clues to working out the origin of particular passages and thus the history of development of a cave. Observe whether pass-

ages are phreatic tubes or vadose canyons; is there a sequence of tube development followed by incision of the canyons? Early tubes may be abandoned high in the roof above a canyon and thus may be overlooked by the explorer. Later flooding of a system may lead to renewed phreatic solution etching into the walls of a canyon. A study of junctions of passages may lead to applications of the theory of mischungs-corrosion, whereby two small passages may join to give an unexpectedly large one due to renewed solutional attack. The upward development of roof pockets may be due to rejuvenated solutional attack in joints. Plot out all the features on a survey and you will have gone a long way to understanding the evolution of the cave.

Sediments and Speleothems

Sediments in a cave supply evidence as to its history of running streams. A study of the distribution of sand and mud is important, for they are clues to the velocity of former streams or of the occasional flood flow today. As a current's velocity decreases so sand, silt and mud will be deposited downstream. Eddies in the stream passage may deposit sand or gravel to block a side passage completely, and its presence may be unsuspected until a study of sediments is carried out. Sediments may indicate that there were once other inputs into the cave system from unsuspected old entrances. The distribution of sediments in relation to morphological features may suggest the relative significance or duration of phreatic or vadose phases. Speleothems are really no more than chemically deposited sediments in caves. The many forms of stalactites are the responses to small variations in physico-chemical conditions. These may reflect former climatic changes, soil

cover, vegetation or changes in percolation routes. More importantly, an alternation from inwashed sands, etc, to stalagmite and back may reflect an oscillation of climatic conditions and, when studied in relation to morphological features and surface geology, may lead to the disentanglement of a cave's history in relation to ice-age climatic changes. The fossil content of sediments may provide relative age determinations, while a sophisticated analysis of uranium and thorium can sometimes give the absolute age of the speleothem and thus a minimum age for the cave being drained.

Observing the geological features outlined above means moving through a cave slowly. The features must be plotted onto the survey and discussed with caving colleagues. It is worth being accurate, so take a rough copy of the survey with you (one that you do not mind getting wet) and plot your observations as you go. Do not try to rely on memory. A notebook is often useful, or photograph the significant features and do not forget to have a scale in the photograph.

Geology is not a difficult subject when applied to caves. You do not have to be an erudite scientist; in fact many cavers pick up sufficient geology to turn their hobby into their profession; that is how I became a professional geologist!

20 Cave Archaeology

DR J.D. WILCOCK

Modern archaeology is not the dry-as-dust anti-quarian study beloved of Victorian gentlemen. It is rather a bridge subject, linking the arts and sciences. Archaeology is the study of man through his material remains and traces. It is thus a study of things left behind by man; not just manufactured items (artefacts), but also 'mentefacts': ideas, techniques, mathematics and science; and 'sociofacts': social behaviour, language, religion, politics, living conditions and even attitudes to sex.

Modern archaeologists have brought most sciences into their service. Resistivity meters and magnetic field detectors (proton gradio-meters) are used to detect archaeological remains below ground; systematic excavation, recording and drawing techniques are used at the excavation; conservation techniques are used to preserve the finds; biology, physics and chemistry to study the finds in detail to derive the ancient techniques of manufacture, the origins of raw materials, trade routes and the ancient environment; radio-carbon to date finds; and the computer to record, retrieve, compare, draw and publish the items.

What Has All This to Do with Caves?

Caves were the first shelters used by man, and in them he buried his dead and left remains of his industry. Cave mouths are the most interest-ing areas, with their remains of fires, bones from food animals and small tools such as flint implements, bone needles and spindle whorls. In France, Spain and North Africa cave paint-ings are found, though not in Britain. Even if man is not present, animals trapped or living in caves left their bones, and some of these, such as hippopotamus, form a fruitful study for palaeontologists. Cavers should be careful in their digs not to disturb archaeological or palaeontological sediments, particularly near the cave mouth.

Is Cave Archaeology a Valid Study?

Most archaeologists would say 'No'. Rather it is the practice to divide the approximately 3 million years that man has been around into periods, many of which have been given long Latin names. The Stone Age, when stone was used to make tools, is divided into the palaeolithic (Old Stone Age), the mesolithic (Middle Stone Age, when there were many fishing and shore-dwelling cultures) and the neolithic (New Stone Age, when agriculture, domestication of animals, the wheel, pottery, textiles and transport were developed). Next it was discovered how to smelt a mixture of copper and tin ores, to make the metallic tools and weapons of the Bronze Age. Finally iron was discovered to make much more durable tools, leading to the Iron Age, the Industrial Revolution, the discovery of electricity and the atomic/space age. All these are valid parts of archaeology; the timescale is from the first toolmaker right up to the present.

A typical cave deposit might have stone tools of the earliest palaeolithic hunters; microliths, bone spears and bone needles of the mesolithic fishers; pottery, cereal grains and spindle whorls of the neolithic farmers; beakers and bronze tools of the Bronze Age; perhaps even Roman coins, brooches and Samian ware from Romano-British refugees. These would probably receive description as specialist arte-facts from various periods, and the cave origin may be regarded as less important.

This is not to say that no archaeologist has turned his attention to caves; Dean Buckland, Boyd Dawkins and William Pengelly are historic figures of note, and more recently Wilfred Jackson and E. K. Tratman spring to mind. Industrial archaeology is also studied in those caves which have been mined for lead, by the various mining research societies.

The British Cave Research Association is a

An example of non-conservation: before and after. The entrance to the famous archaeological site Victoria Cave in 1870, *(left)* compared with the huge aperture (9m by 12m) left by the British Association team *(right)* in 1970. The original opening is just visible behind the stone wall above and to the left of the diggers, also seen as the top left hand corner of the second photograph. All archaeological excavation is destruction, but the lack of scientific method of these precursors of modern archaeologists may be judged from the statement that on the first day, 21 March 1870, three men 'excavated this day 3ft 6inches right and 4ft 6inches left on the datum and 8ft forward to a depth of 4ft' (a total of 7.2³m). Modern cavers digging to gain access to a new cave should note that most of the significant finds are discovered in the entrance deposits

member of the Council for British Archaeology, the co-ordinating body for all archaeological societies in Britain. BCRA has recorded archaeological cave finds where these have been published. One of the problems of research arises here; all archaeologists are individualists and some regard information as power, the source of their authority. Any suggestion that these records might be made available for computerised information-retrieval falls on stony ground. However, it is intended to persevere with records of cave finds, and much has been obtained from past publications as a foundation.

Caves Scheduled as Ancient Monuments

The following lists appear to have come into being as a result of local workers being active in some areas and not in others, rather than from any rational nationwide approach. Of particular concern are some important omissions: Paviland Cave, W. Glamorgan; Ogof-yr-Esgyrn, Powys. Perhaps the time is due for a review of these lists, carried out in a similar manner to the Geological Conservation Review recently completed by the Nature Conservancy Council.

ENGLAND   **Map ref**

Cumbria

23	Kirkhead Cave, Lower Allithwaite	SD 391756

Derbyshire

73	Creswell Crags, Mother Grundy's Parlour, Whitwell	SK 534744
69	Creswell Crags, Pinhole Cave, Elmton	SK 532741
152	Harboro Cave, Brassington	SK 243552
76	Hassett Cave, Upper Langwith, Scarcliffe	SK 519696
237	Robin Hood's Cave, Whitwell	SK 534742

Devon

602	Ashole Cavern, Brixham, Torquay	SX 938567
201	Kent's Cavern, Torquay	SX 935641
603	The Old Grotto, Dyer's Wood, Torbryan	SX 817674

Hereford and Worcester
143 King Arthur's Cave, Whitchurch   SO 545156

Hertfordshire
7 The Cave, Royston   TL 360408

Lancashire
13 Castle Hill, Halton with Aughton SD 499648
84 Dog Holes Cave, Warton Crag,
        Warton   SD 483731

Merseyside
2 Castle Hill, Newton le Willows   SJ 596961

North Yorkshire
296 Douky Bottom Cave, near
        Kilnsey, Hawkswick   SD 951688
324 Jubilee Cave, Langcliffe Scar,
        Langcliffe   SD 838655
330 Kinsey Cave, Giggleswick Scar,
        Giggleswick   SD 804656
290 Victoria Cave, Langcliffe Scar,
        Langcliffe   SD 839649

Nottinghamshire
42 Boat House Cave, Creswell Crags,
        Holbeck   SK 537742
157 Caves at Drury Hill, Nottingham SK 574395
181 Caves under Nos 3–7 Middle
        Pavement, Nottingham   SK 574397
161 Church Hole Cave, Holbeck   SK 534741
155 Rock cut houses N. of Castle
        Boulevard, Nottingham   SK 564393

Staffordshire
35 Elderbush Cave, Wetton   SK 099549

Shropshire
61 Caratacus' Cave, Church Stretton SO 478953
132 Kynaston's Cave, Great Ness   SJ 385193

WALES
Clwyd
Bontnewydd   SJ 01527102
Cae Gwyn   SJ 08527244
Cefn   SJ 02007054
Ffynnon Beuno   SJ 086724
Gop NW Cave   SJ 08658010
Gop Shelter   SJ 08658010
Lynx Cave   SJ 180600
Rhos Ddigre No 3 Cave   SJ 187533

Gwent
St Peter's Cave   ST 539927

Gwynedd
Ogof Arian   SH 485882
Ogof Tan-y-Bryn   SH 800810

West Glamorgan
Cathole   SS 538900
Longhole   SS 452851
Three Chimneys   SS 406929
Tooth Cave   SS 531909

SCOTLAND
Cunninghame
Ardeer Recreation Club (subterranean
        passage and cave)   NS 271419
King's Cave, Torbeg, Blackwaterfoot   NR 884309

Dumfries and Galloway
Mull Farm, St Medan's Chapel and
        Cave, Wigtown   NX 143316
St Ninian's Cave (Guardianship
        Monument), Whithorn   NX 421359

Fife
Wemyss Caves, Kirkaldy   NT 347973
                        NT 349969

Grampian
Sculptor's Cave, Covesea, Moray   NJ 175707

Highland
Creag nam Uamh, Sutherland   NC 268170

Lothian
Hawthornden Castle and Caves,
        Roslin, Midlothian   NT 286636

Strathclyde
Eilean Mor, St Cormac's Cave, Argyll
        and Bute   NR 666753
Keil Cave, Argyll and Bute   NR 671077
St Ciaran's Cave, Achinhoan
        Headland, Argyll and Bute   NR 765170

NORTHERN IRELAND
Co. Antrim
Dunluce Castle (sea-cut cave under the
        basalt promontory on which the castle
        stands; State Care Site)   C 904413

Co. Fermanagh
Aghanaglack townland (cave adapted for
        use as early Christian period
        souterrain; scheduled)   H 108436
Lettered Cave, Knockmore townland
        (cave with rock scribings; scheduled)   H 088505

Appendix 1: BCRC Cave Rescue Services and call-out list

Cave Rescue Services

Police-force Area	*Cave-rescue Service Provided By*
Avon and Somerset	Mendip Rescue Organisation
Bedfordshire	Derbyshire Cave Rescue Organisation
Cambridgeshire	Derbyshire Cave Rescue Organisation
Cheshire	Derbyshire Cave Rescue Organisation
	North Wales Cave Rescue Organisation
Cleveland	Swaledale Fell Rescue Organisation
Cumbria	Cave Rescue Organisation
Derbyshire	Derbyshire Cave Rescue Organisation
Devon and Cornwall	Devon Cave Rescue Organisation
Dorset	Mendip Rescue Organisation
Durham	Cave Rescue Organisation
	Swaledale Fell Rescue Organisation
Dyfed-Powys	South Wales Cave Rescue Organisation
Essex	South East Cave Rescue Organisation
Gloucestershire	Gloucestershire Cave Rescue Group
Greater Manchester	Cave Rescue Organisation
	Derbyshire Cave Rescue Organisation
Gwent	South Wales Cave Rescue Organisation
Hampshire	South East Cave Rescue Organisation
Hertfordshire	South East Cave Rescue Organisation
Humberside	Swaledale Fell Rescue Organisation
	Upper Wharfedale Fell Rescue Association
Kent	South East Cave Rescue Organisation
Lancashire	Cave Rescue Organisation
Leicestershire	Derbyshire Cave Rescue Organisation
Lincolnshire	Derbyshire Cave Rescue Organisation
Merseyside	North Wales Cave Rescue Organisation
Metropolitan	South East Cave Rescue Organisation
Norfolk	Derbyshire Cave Rescue Organisation
Northampton	Derbyshire Cave Rescue Organisation
Northumbria	Cave Rescue Organisation
North Wales	North Wales Cave Rescue Organisation
North Yorkshire	Cave Rescue Organisation
	Upper Wharfedale Fell Rescue Association
	Swaledale Fell Rescue Organisation
Nottinghamshire	Derbyshire Cave Rescue Organisation
South Wales	South Wales Cave Rescue Organisation

Police-force Area	Cave Rescue Service Provided By
South Yorkshire	Derbyshire Cave Rescue Organisation
Staffordshire	Derbyshire Cave Rescue Organisation
	Midlands Cave Rescue Organisation
	West Mercia Underground Rescue Team
Suffolk	South East Cave Rescue Organisation
Surrey	South East Cave Rescue Organisation
Sussex	South East Cave Rescue Organisation
Thames Valley	Gloucestershire Cave Rescue Group
	Midlands Cave Rescue Organisation
	South East Cave Rescue Organisation
Warwickshire	Derbyshire Cave Rescue Organisation
	Midlands Cave Rescue Organisation
West Mercia	West Mercia Underground Rescue Team
West Midlands	Midlands Cave Rescue Organisation
West Yorkshire	Cave Rescue Organisation
	Upper Wharfedale Fell Rescue Association
Wiltshire	Mendip Rescue Organisation
	Gloucestershire Cave Rescue Group
Scottish Police Forces	Scottish Cave Rescue Organisation
Northern Ireland	Irish Cave Rescue Organisation
Republic of Ireland	Irish Cave Rescue Organisation

Notes

1 Cave and disused-mine rescues mainly occur in certain police-force areas. Occasionally an underground rescue occurs in a police-force area which has not met this problem before. The British Cave Rescue Council has therefore allocated cave rescue services to cover all police-force areas.

2 If police forces require assistance from the cave-rescue services, they are requested to contact the named cave-rescue service in accordance with the call-out list.

3 When more than one cave-rescue organisation covers one police-force area, contact should be made with the nearest cave-rescue organisation to the incident.

Call-out List

Cave Rescue Organisation: 12 controllers, 160 members, 2 MRC posts, 2 Land-Rovers, 3 trailers, comprehensive rescue equipment, radios, depot at Clapham.
  Call-out: N. Yorkshire Police, Settle. Tel: Settle (07292) 2542/2543

Derbyshire Cave Rescue Organisation: 10 wardens, 140 members (6 teams), 2 MRC posts, considerable amount of equipment, radios.
  Call-out: Derbyshire Constabulary HQ. Tel: Ripley (0773) 43551

Devon Cave Rescue Organisation: 7 wardens, 50 members, 2 MRC posts, small amount of equipment (generally club based).
  Call-out: Devon and Cornwall Constabulary HQ. Tel: Exeter (0392) 52101

Gloucestershire Cave Rescue Group: 12 wardens, 80 members, 1 MRC post, 1 trailer, fair amount of equipment.
  Call-out: Gloucestershire Constabulary HQ. Tel: Cheltenham (0242) 21321

Irish Cave Rescue Organisation: members drawn from the cavers in N. Ireland and the Republic, equipment store at Enniskillen (basic equipment), some equipment in the Republic.
  Call-out: Royal Ulster Constabulary HQ. Tel: Belfast (0232) 650222
  Or: Garda Siochana, Dublin. Tel: Dublin 01-771156

Mendip Rescue Organisation: 20 wardens, 100 members, 2 MRC posts, good amount of equipment, radios.
  Call-out: Avon and Somerset Constabulary, Yeovil. Tel: Yeovil (0935) 5291

Midlands Cave Rescue Organisation: 5 wardens, 40 members, club equipment, acts mainly as back-up team to other CROs.
  Call-out: West Midlands Police HQ. Tel: Birmingham (021) 236-5000

North Wales Cave Rescue Organisation: 8 wardens, 20 members, 1 MRC post, fair amount of equipment.
  Call-out: North Wales Police HQ. Tel: Colwyn Bay (0492) 57171

Scottish Cave Rescue Organisation: members drawn mainly from the Grampian Speleological Group, some equipment kept at Edinburgh, Elphin, Sutherland (GSG hut), Inchnadamph (Assynt MR post), Glencoe MRP.
  Call-out: Lothian and Borders Police HQ. Tel: Edinburgh (031) 311-3131

South East Cave Rescue Organisation: no information available on members, club equipment used.
  Call-out: Metropolitan Police HQ. Tel: London (01) 230-1212

South Wales Cave Rescue Organisation: 11 wardens, 90 members, 1 MRC post, 2 other rescue posts, 1 Land-Rover, 1 trailer, considerable amount of equipment.
  Call-out: Dyfed-Powys Police HQ. Tel: Carmarthen (0267) 6444
  Or: South Wales Constabulary HQ. Tel: Bridgend (0656) 55555

Swaledale Fell Rescue Organisation: 40 members, 1 MRC post, 1 Land-Rover, fair amount of equipment (being increased), radios.
  Call-out: North Yorkshire Police, Richmond. Tel: Richmond (0748) 3055

Upper Wharfedale Fell Rescue Association: 80 members, 1 MRC post, 2 Land-Rovers, 2 trailers, comprehensive rescue equipment, radios, depot at Grassington.
  Call-out: North Yorkshire Police, Grassington. Tel: Grassington (0756) 75222
  Or: North Yorkshire Police, Skipton. Tel: Skipton (0756) 3377

West Mercia Underground Rescue Team: 4 wardens, 15 members, clubhouse depot and small amount of equipment, all based on Shropshire Caving and Mining Club.
  Call-out: West Mercia Constabulary HQ. Tel: Worcester (0905) 27188

Appendix 2: Addresses

Equipment Shops and Suppliers (Chapters 1–5)

The Bivouac, 56 North Parade, Matlock Bath, Derbyshire

Cave and Crag, Walker Barn, Church Street, Settle, N. Yorks

Caving Supplies, 19 London Road, Buxton, Derbyshire

Field & Trek (Equipment) Ltd, 23–25 Kings Road, Brentwood, Essex CM14 4ER

Inglesport, The Square, Ingleton, Via Carnforth, LA6 3EB

Lyon Ladders, Rise Hill Mill, Dent, Sedbergh, Cumbria

Magic Mountain, 93 Castleton Road, Hope, Via Sheffield

Mole Products, 41 Cliffe Street, Keighley, W. Yorks

Don Morrison Ltd, 343 London Road, Sheffield S2 4NG

Don Morrison Ltd, 43 Harrington Street, Liverpool L2 6PR

Quip-U for Leisure Ltd, 38 Stokes Croft, Bristol BS1 3PY

Redmayne & Todd, Carrington Street, Nottingham

Rocksport, The Bus Station, Wells, Somerset

Jo Royle, 6 Market Place, Buxton, Derbyshire

Up and Under, 148 Ninian Park Road, Cardiff CF1 8JG

Venturgear, 30 Cricklade Road, Swindon, Wilts

Watersports & Outdoor Centre, Chapel Street, Settle, N. Yorks

Whernside Caving Shop, Dent, Sedbergh, Cumbria

YHA Sales & Services:
131 Woodville Road, Catheys, Cardiff
164 Deansgate, Manchester M3 3FE
35 Cannon Street, Birmingham B2 5EE
14 Southampton Street, London WC2E 7HY

Cave Diving (Chapter 6)

Cave Diving Group, Hon Sec Mr M. Bishop, Bishop's Cottage, Priddy, Wells, Somerset

Abandoned Mine Workings (Chapter 7)

BCRA Mining Recorder, Mr P. B. Smith, 21 Lees Hall Road, Sheffield S8 9JH

National Association of Mining History Organisations, Hon Sec Mr M. Gill, 38 Main Street, Sutton-in-Craven, Keighley, W. Yorks BD20 7HD

Water Tracing (Chapter 8)

BCRA Hydrological Recorder, Dr J. D. Wilcock, 22 Kingsley Close, Stafford ST17 9BT

Instructed Caving (Chapter 9)

British Association of Caving Instructors, Hon Sec c/o The Sports Council, Coronet House, Queen Street, Leeds LS1 2TW

National Caving Association, Training Officer, Mr M. K. Lyon, Whernside Cave and Fell Centre, Dent, Sedbergh, Cumbria

Communications (Chapter 12)

University of Lancaster Engineering Services, Bailrigg, Lancaster. Tel: 0524 65201 ext. 4473

Expedition Planning and Organisation (Chapter 13)

British Caving Expeditions Equipment Store, c/o Mr A. Eavis, Tidesreach, Redcliff Road, Hessle, N. Humberside

BCRA, Foreign Secretary, Mr J. R. Middleton, 2 Broad Elms Close, Sheffield S11 9ST

BCRA Insurance Officer, Mr G. Wells, 39 Linden Road, Redland, Bristol BS6 7RN

Ghar Parau Foundation (and Sports Council grant applications), Hon Sec Mr D. M.

Judson, Rowlands House, Summerseat, Bury BL9 5NF

Mount Everest Foundation, c/o The Alpine Club, 74 South Audley Street, London W1

Royal Geographical Society, 1 Kensington Gore, London SW7 2AR

Winston Churchill Memorial Trust, 15 Queensgate Terrace, London SW7 5PR

World Expeditionary Association (WEXAS), 45 Brompton Road, London SW3

Cave Conservation (Chapter 15)

BCRA Conservation Officer, Mr D. M. Judson, Rowlands House, Summerseat, Bury BL9 5NF

Cambrian Caving Council Conservation Officer, Mr W. Gascoine, 18 Groveside Villas, Pontnewynydd, Pontypool, Gwent NP4 6SZ

CNCC Conservation Officer, Mr A. Hall, 342 The Green, Eccleston, Chorley, Lancs

CSCC Conservation Officer, Mr G. Price, 31 Waterford Park, Radstock, Bath BA3 3TS

Department of the Environment (Ancient Monuments Inspectorate), 2 Marsham Street, London SW1

Department of the Environment for N. Ireland (Conservation Branch), Stormont, Belfast BT4 3SS

Department of the Environment for N. Ireland (Historic Monuments and Buildings Branch), 66 Balmoral Avenue, Belfast BT9 6NY

Derbyshire Caving Association Conservation Officer, Mr P. T. Mellors, Fairview, Station Road, Edingley, Newark, Notts NG22 9BX

National Caving Association Conservation Officer (see CSCC above)

Nature Conservancy Council, Geology and Physiography Section, Foxhold House, Thornford Road, Crookham Common, Newbury, Berks RG15 8EL

Scottish Development Department (Ancient Monuments), 3–11 Melville Street, Edinburgh EH3 7QD

Welsh Office (Ancient Monuments Branch), Dinerth Road, Colwyn Bay, Clwyd LL28 4W

Access to Caves (Chapter 16)

Agen Allwedd Permit Secretary, Mr A. S. Nutt, 12 The Crescent, Cwmbran, Gwent NP44 7JG

Charterhouse Caving Committee, Hon Sec Mr T. Large, 53 Portway, Wells, Somerset

North Wales (NWCC), Mr G. Bryan, 64 Park Avenue, Mynydd Isa, Mold, Clwyd

Ogof Craig a Ffynnon, Mr J. Hill, 11 York Avenue, Ebbw Vale, Gwent

Ogof Ffynnon Ddu Permit Secretary, Miss D. Samuel, 4 Brent Court, Church Lane, Hanwell, London W7 3BZ

Peak Cavern, Dr J. Beck, Glebe Cottage, The Hillock, Eyam, via Sheffield

Plymouth Caving Group, Mr R. Cawthorne, 22 Devonport Road, Stoke, Plymouth PL3 4DH

Regional Caving Councils and NCA:

Council of Northern Caving Clubs, c/o The Sports Council, Byrom House, Quay Street, Manchester M3

Council of Southern Caving Clubs, Hon Sec Mr A. Butcher, 14 Little Parks, Holt, Trowbridge, Wilts

Derbyshire Caving Association, Hon Sec c/o The Sports Council, 26 Musters Road, W. Bridgford, Nottingham

National Caving Association, PO Box 363, Geography Dept, The University, Birmingham B15 1TT

Accidents to Cavers (Chapter 17)

British Cave Rescue Council, Hon Sec Mr B. Boardman, 8 Yealand Avenue, Giggleswick, Settle, N. Yorks BD24 0AY

Rescue Equipment Suppliers

Flectron Blanket: available from J. C. Jones, CUIC, University College, PO Box 78, Cardiff

Industrial safety harness: made by R. F. O. Mills Equipment Ltd, 88 Cotteshall Lane, Godalming, Surrey GU7 1LH

Little Dragon: made by M. F. Mitchell, Capplerigg, Kentmere, Kendal, Cumbria

Molephone: available from R. Mackin, Engineering Dept, The University, Lancaster

Reviva: made by Peter Bell Engineering, The Slack, Ambleside, Cumbria

Thermal sarong: manufactured as Warm-rite by Energy Systems Corp, 1 Pine Street, Nashua, New Hampshire, 03060 USA

*Cave Biology, Geology and Archaeology
(Chapters 18–20)*

BCRA Archaeological Recorder, Dr J. D. Wilcock, 22 Kingsley Close, Stafford ST17 9BT

BCRA Biological Recorder, Mr M. C. Day, 118 Whitmore Road, Harrow, HA1 4AQ

Council for British Archaeology, 112 Kennington Road, London SE11 6RE

General

British Cave Research Association, Hon Sec Mr R. G. Willis, Basement Flat, 6 Worcester Terrace, Clifton, Bristol BS8 3JW

Cambrian Caving Council, Hon Sec Mr F. Baguley, 15 Elm Grove, Gadlys, Aberdare, Mid Glamorgan CF44 8DN

Wm Pengelly Cave Studies Trust, Buckfastleigh, Devon

Appendix 3: Caving Organisations

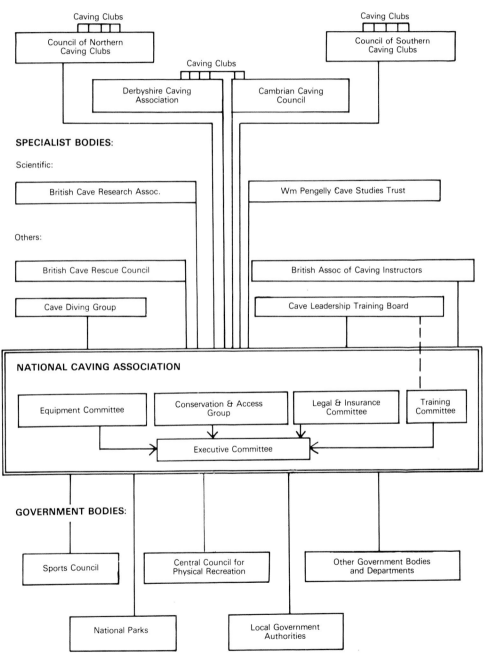

REGIONAL CAVING COUNCILS:

Caving Clubs

Council of Northern Caving Clubs

Caving Clubs

Council of Southern Caving Clubs

Caving Clubs

Derbyshire Caving Association

Cambrian Caving Council

SPECIALIST BODIES:

Scientific:

British Cave Research Assoc.

Wm Pengelly Cave Studies Trust

Others:

British Cave Rescue Council

British Assoc of Caving Instructors

Cave Diving Group

Cave Leadership Training Board

NATIONAL CAVING ASSOCIATION

Equipment Committee

Conservation & Access Group

Legal & Insurance Committee

Training Committee

Executive Committee

GOVERNMENT BODIES:

Sports Council

Central Council for Physical Recreation

Other Government Bodies and Departments

National Parks

Local Government Authorities

Bibliography

Baguley, F. S. and Brandon, D. P., 'Ladders' in Cullingford, C. H. D. (ed), *Manual of Caving Techniques* (Routledge & Kegan Paul, 1969)

Balcombe, F. W., 'Cave diving' in Cullingford, C. H. D. (ed), *British Caving: an introduction to speleology* (Routledge & Kegan Paul, 2nd edn 1962)

Bird, R. H., *Yesterday's Golcondas: notable British metal mines* (Moorland Publishing, 1977)

Bogli, A., *Karst Hydrology and Physical Speleology* (New York, Springer-Verlag, 1980)

Boon, J. M., 'Cave diving on air', *Cave Diving Technical Review*, 1 (1966)

Brindle, D., 'Digging for cave systems', in J. Craven PC 2 (3) (1957), pp184–6

British Standards, CP2003: 1959, *Earthworks British Sub-Aqua Club Manual* (incl. decompression tables)

Brown, M. C. and Ford, D. C., 'Quantitative traces methods for investigation of karst hydraulic systems', *Trans CRG GB* 13, 1 (1971), pp37–51

Carter, W. L. and Dwerryhouse, A. R., 'The underground waters of NW Yorkshire', *Proc Yorkshire Geol Soc* part 1: 14 (1905), pp1– 18; part 2: 15 (1905), pp248–92

Childs, J. J., 'The strength of bolt belays', *Trans BCRA* 3, 2 (1976), pp100–9

Christopher, N. S. J. (ed), *Cambrian Caving Council Handbook* (1969)

Churcher, R. A. and Lloyd, O. C., 'British cave diving accidents', *Proc Univ Bristol Speleol Soc* 15, 3 (1980), pp161–82

Cousins, P., 'Calibration of cave survey instruments', *Trans BCRA*, 5, 2 (1978), pp85–9

Cousteau, J. Y., *The Silent World* (Hamish Hamilton, 1953)

Cowlishaw, M., 'The characteristics and use of lead-acid cap lamps', *Trans BCRA*, 1, 4 (1974), pp199–214

Cubbon, B. D. 'Cave flora' in Ford, T. D. and Cullingford, C. H. D. (eds), *The Science of Speleology* (Academic Press, 1976), Chapter 11

Cullingford, C. H. D. (ed), *Manual of Caving Techniques* (Routledge & Kegan Paul, 1969)

——. *British Caving: an introduction to speleology* (Routledge & Kegan Paul, 1953, 2nd edn 1962)

Davis, J. S. 'The design of scaling poles', *Trans BCRA*, 7(4) (1980), pp200–4, and 9(3) (1982), pp195–9

Davis, Sir R. H. *Deep Diving and Submarine Operations* (De Montfort Press, 1961)

De Lavour, G. *Caves and Cave Diving* (Robert Hale, 1956)

Delay, B. and Aminot, A. 'Données sur la nature chimique de la matière organique présente dans les sédiments souterrains' *Ann Speleol* 30 (1975), pp495–512

Dibben, N. 'Cave surveying programs', *Trans BCRA* 6 (3) (1979), pp131–2

Dressler and Minvielle, La Spéléo (Editions Denoel, Paris, 1979)

Drew, D. P. 'Cave diving', in Cullingford, C. H. D. (ed), *Manual of Caving Techniques* (Routledge & Kegan Paul, 1969a)

——. 'Water tracing', *J. Brit Speleol Ass* 6 (1969b), pp96–110

——. 'Limestone solution within the East Mendip area, Somerset', *Trans CRG GB* 12 (1970) pp259–70

——. and Smith, D. I. *Techniques for the Tracing of Subterranean Drainage*, Brit Geomorphol Research Group technical bulletin 2 (1969)

Driver, D. B. 'Some simple techniques and apparatus for the collecting and preservation of animals from cave habitats', *Trans CRG GB* 6 (1963) pp91–101

Dugan, J. L. *Man Explores the Sea* (Hamish Hamilton, 1956)

Dunster, J. A. 'Karabiners', *Trans BCRA* 3 (1) (1976), pp43–7

Eavis, A. J. 'The rope in SRT caving', *Trans BCRA* 1 (4) (1974), pp181–98

Ellis, B. M. *Surveying Caves* (BCRA, 1976)

Farr, M. *The Darkness Beckons* (Diadem, 1980)

Ford, T. D. *et al. Lead Mining in the Peak District* (Peak Park Planning Board, 1970)

——. and Cullingford, C. H. D. (eds) *The Science of Speleology* (Academic Press, 1976)

Forder, J. 'The causes of caving accidents', *Trans BCRA* (1981)

Frankland, J. C. 'Hypothermia for cavers', *Trans BCRA* (1981)

——. *Hypothermia and its Relevance to Cave Rescue*, Brit Ass Caving Instructors bulletin 7 (1972), pp1–7

——. (1975), 'Medical aspects of cave rescue', *Trans BCRA* 2 (2) (1975), pp53–63

——. (1978), 'Medical aspects of cave rescue', *Handbook of Cave Rescue Operations*, Nat Speleol Soc (USA) (1978), pp86–96

——. *et al.* 'Polyurethane foam splintage – a new technique', *The Practitioner* 209 (1972), pp831–4

Geological Survey, *Mineral Resources of Great Britain* (many volumes covering most mining areas of Britain)

Gregory, K. and Walling, D. *Drainage Basin Form and Process* (Edward Arnold, 1973)

Halliday, W. *American Caves and Caving* (Harper & Row, 1973)

Harvey, P. I. W. *Scaling Equipment*, CRG publication 11 (1962), pp47–59

Hazleton, M. and Glennie, E. A. 'Cave fauna and flora', in Cullingford, C. H. D. (ed), *British Caving: an introduction to speleology*, (Routledge & Kegan Paul, 1962)

Hiscock, P. 'Resistivity survey over Stoke Lane slocker', *Trans BCRA* 3 (2) (1976), pp110–11

Hooper, J. H. D. 'Bats in caves', in Ford, T. D. and Cullingford, C. H. D. (eds), *The Science of Speleology* (Academic Press, 1976)

Hoseley, R. J. *Cave Surveying and Mapping* (Crown Press, 1971)

Jackson, M. L. *Soil Chemical Analysis* (Constable, 1962)

Keighly, J. H. 'A comparison of mountain rescue bags', *Clothing Research J* 8 (1980) pp46–56

Leitch, D. E. *Some Cave Accident Statistics*, CRG publication 7 (1962)

Lewis, I. and Stace, P. *Cave Diving in Australia* (Lewis, 1980)

Lloyd, E. L. I. *et al.* 'Accidental hypothermia – an apparatus for central rewarming as a first aid measure', *Scot Med J* 17 (1972), pp83–91

——. and Frankland, J. C. 'Accidental hypothermia – central rewarming in the field', *Brit Med J* iv (1974), p717

Lloyd, O. C. 'Cavers dying of cold', *Brit Med Chirurgical J* 79 (1964), p261

——. *A Cave Diver's Training Manual*, CDG technical review 2 (1975)

——. 'Cave rescue', *Med J of the South West* 11 (280) (1976), pp37–49

Mackereth, F. J. H., Heron, J. and Talling, J. F. *Water Analysis: some revised methods for limnologists*, Freshwater Biol Ass scientific publication 36 (1978)

Marbach and Rocourt *Techniques de la Spéléologie Alpine* (F.38680, Choranche, Vercor, 1978)

Mason-Williams, M. A. 'Ecological methods in caves', *Trans CRG GB* 9, (1967), pp140–1

——. and Benson-Evans, K. 'A preliminary investigation into the bacterial and botanical flora of caves in South Wales', CRG publication 8 (1958)

Meredith, M. *Vertical Caving* (Lyon Ladders, 1980)

Montgomery, N. *Single Rope Techniques*, Sydney Speleol Soc, PO Box 198, Broadway, NSW 2007, Australia (1977)

Mount, T. *Safe Cave Diving*, Nat Ass for Cave Diving, USA (1973)

Murphy, P. W. *Progress in Soil Zoology* (Butterworth, 1962)

Myers, J. O. 'Cave location by resistivity measurements . . .', *Trans BCRA* 2 (4) (1975), pp167–72

Nobel Division of ICI advisory publications: *Blasting Explosives and Accessories; 'Cordtex' Detonating Fuse and Detonating Relays; Electric Shotfiring; Explosives – Safe Practice and Storage; The Initiation of Explosives* – available from ICI Nobel Division, Stevenston, Ayrshire (licence holders only)

Nordil, B. *et al. Fan Heater Based on Charcoal Combustion*, Norwegian Defence Research Establishment interim report VM 44 (1976)

Price, G. (ed) *Handbook and Access Guide* (Council of Southern Caving Clubs, 1980–1)

Reckert, N. 'Pitch rigging for SRT', *Trans BCRA* 5 (1) (1978) pp55–60

Riddick, T. M. 'Dowsing – an unorthodox method of locating underground water supplies or an interesting facet of the human mind', *Proc American Philosoph Soc* 96 (1952), pp526–34

Robey, J. 'Exploring old mines', in Cullingford, C. H. D. (ed), *Manual of Caving Techniques* (Routledge & Kegan Paul, 1969)

Seddon, P. 'Bolt belays for SRT', *Caves and Caving* 12 (1981), pp20–5

Smart, P. L. and Laidlaw, I. 'An evaluation of some fluorescent dyes for water tracing', *Water Resources Research* 13 (1977), pp15–33

Smith, B. J. (ed) *Northern Caving* (Council of Northern Caving Clubs, 1979)

Smith, D. I., Atkinson, T. C. and Drew, D. P. 'The hydrology of terrains', in Ford, T. D. and Cullingford, C. H. D. (eds), *The Science of Speleology* (Academic Press, 1976)

Standing, I. J. 'Cave rescue incidents in Britain 1935–1972', *Cave Science* 50 (1976), pp13–20

Stone, A. 'The use of alternative casting material underground', *Trans BCRA* (1981)

Sweeting, M. M. *Karst Landforms* (Macmillan, (1972)

Tailliez, P. *et al. The Complete Manual of Cave Diving* (Putnam, 1957)

Terrell, M. *The Principles of Diving* (Stanley Paul, 1965)

Todd, D. K. *Groundwater Hydrology*, (Wiley, 2nd edn 1980)

Unwin, D. M. *Microclimate Measurements for Ecologists* (Academic Press, 1980)

Vandel, A. *Biospeleology: the biology of cavernicolous animals* (Pergamon Press, 1965)

Wagner, G. 'Der Karst als Musterbeispiel der Verkarstung', *Natw Monatschr Dtsch Naturkdever*, 62 (1954), pp193–212

Ward, R. *Principles of Hydrology* (McGraw-Hill, 2nd edn 1975)

Williams, R. M. and M. A. M. 'Hazards of using explosives', *Trans BCRA* 2 (2) (1975), pp89–92

Wilmut, J. (ed). *Access to Caves* (National Caving Association, 1975)

Young, I. 'The programmable pocket calculator in cave surveying', *Trans BCRA* 5 (3) (1978), pp153–8

Zohdy, A. A. 'Application of surface geophysics to ground-water investigations', *US Geol Survey Techniques of Water-Resource Investigations* D1 (2) (1974)

Acknowledgements

This book has been written by members of the British Cave Research Association and edited by David Judson – its Conservation Officer. All views expressed are those of the individual authors and/or the editor and do not necessarily reflect the official policies of the Association. The overall aim has been to present a review of caving practice and equipment in use in the early 1980s. Broadly it is intended to replace C. H. D. Cullingford's *Manual of Caving Techniques* (1969) although in many respects a wider field of activities is now covered.

The chapters dealing with surveying and photography should be read as resumés of separate BCRA publications on these subjects by the same authors, (*Surveying Caves*, 1976, and *Photographing Caves* – in press). The very short chapters on biology, geology and archaeology have been included purely as introductory items. BCRA is planning to publish separate volumes on these subjects at future dates.

I would like to thank all the chapter authors for their various contributions, and in particular David Elliot for his major contribution of Chapters 2, 3 and 4. Thanks are due to Juan Corrin (editor *Caves & Caving*) for his careful reading through of all chapters, helpful comments, and assistance with captions for line drawings, and to Richard Lawson for the (many) initial pen-and-ink drawings for Chapters 2, 3 and 4.

I would like to thank Dr G. P. Black, of the Nature Conservancy Council, for his very considerable advice and assistance given to me in the compiling of Chapter 15, Pauline Fenton for assistance with Chapter 18, and also various officers of the four regional caving councils for their assistance with Chapter 16. Finally I would like to thank Mrs I. Tutt for the typing of the final manuscript.

David Judson

Index